EQUIPPING THE SAINTS TO DO THE
MINISTRY OF THE CHURCH

Transformed
into His Image

Hidden Steps on the
Journey to Christlikeness

For Those Who Want to Press on Toward the
Mark of the High Calling in Christ Jesus

BY A SERVANT OF JESUS CHRIST

David Foster

Published by MASTERING LIFE MINISTRIES
P.O. Box 351149, Jacksonville, FL 32235

Cover design and book typeset by Nancy Humphreys, Atlanta, Georgia

Cover photo: Copyright © 2002 MMI, Roger Miller, Photographer
Cover photo was taken in the Chapel of the Naval Academy in Annapolis, Maryland

ISBN 0-9645000-5-1

Back cover photo: Copyright © 2001, Oscar Sosa, Photographer

Questions, comments or invitations for speaking engagements:

    MASTERING LIFE MINISTRIES
    P.O. Box 351149
    Jacksonville, FL 32235
    904-220-7474 (phone or fax)
    Internet: http://www.MasteringLife.org

Printed in the United States of America

Table of Contents

Failure to Pursue and Embrace Humility.

Failure to Nurture the Marriage with God.

PART TWO - THE CORRECTIVE VISION

The Four Voices of God.

Religious Development.

Spiritual Development.

PART THREE - WALKING IT OUT PRACTICALLY

Preparing the Ground for Battle.

The War.

The Secret Weapon of Darkness.

Dying to Self—The Old Man/New Man Battle.

Taming Wild Horses Means Aiming for the Right Target.

Letting God Do It For You.

Strategic Warfare Tips.

A Working Model for Responding to Temptation.

The assumption that I can find healing without entering into a loving and dependent relationship with God through Jesus Christ.

The assumption that I have to achieve healing through my own will, power, and effort.

The assuming of a time-frame and a particular order for seeing results.

The Evidence for a True Relationship with God.

The Process of Healing Described.

So, What Does it Look Like to Be Healed?

PART FOUR - WHEN GOD INVITES YOU TO MINISTER TO OTHERS

Failure to make an across-the-board commitment to holiness.

Failure to believe in and act upon God's power to deliver and keep us.

Failure to undergo a transformation of the will through a belief in and embracing of God's unconditional love.

Failure to see healing as a process with a purpose.

Failure to develop an intimate relationship with God the Father.

Failure to humble ourselves in absolute dependence on God.

Failure to learn and practice spiritual warfare.

To Everyone who

Hungers

and Thirsts

after Righteousness.

You Will Be Filled!

Introduction

Wearied from the journey and anxious for some rest, I pushed open the door of my hotel room. As if beckoned, my eye immediately zeroed in on two neatly stacked magazines next to the bed. I recognized one from many years of having been steeped in bondage to hard core pornography. Ignoring the question of how they had gotten into a newly rented room, I began to wonder what they contained. It had been fifteen years since I had looked at such magazines. Surely pornography had gotten much worse over the years. Perhaps I should take a peek just to more accurately know what I was preaching against, I thought. Just one glance to refire the knowledge and righteous indignation in my lectures against sexual sin. After all, I was free now. I had been faithful to the Lord for fifteen years and was fast becoming a well-known figure for teaching people how to stay free from life-dominating bondages like sexual sin and brokenness. Surely just a glance would not hurt.

As I began to pry open the pages, the Holy Spirit said, "David, Satan is trying to take you out!" Immediately, the spell of deception broke, and I realized my folly.

Angrily throwing the magazines into the trash can and stomping them down to the bottom with my foot, I heard the Holy Spirit literally shout in my spirit, "I will crush him under My feet!!!" The voice seemed to reverberate throughout the entire universe.

The Lord had prophesied to me, telling me not only of His victory on my behalf in that hotel room, but of His plan for this age, and I have been sharing it ever since.

Despite the choices that men are making in this world, God has called the entire world to holiness, and He has made available both plan and provision for anyone who desires to sacrifice their life toward that end.

First, God has made provision to forgive our sins by dying on the Cross, suffering the penalty for sin on behalf of anyone who will come to Him for cleansing and salvation.

Second, He has reconnected the lines of communication between man and Himself by giving those who will receive Him a new birth through Jesus Christ. Third, He has made Himself available to fight our battle with sin for us. If we believe, if we turn to Him with sincerity, if we yield to His power working through us to defeat temptation when it comes, He will destroy its power for us. Fourth, He has beckoned us to intimacy with Him, for it is in that ongoing relationship of intimacy where our fire for holiness continues to be kindled. In other words, for those who give themselves to Him fully, the very power of His presence fuels a holy flame so that their ardor for Him and His holy ways burns clear and strong.

Of course, as long as we remain in this fallen world, with God's glory hidden from our eyes, the feast of the world parading before us minute by minute, and the battle between the old and new natures allowed to continue as a mechanism to test our faith and desire, we will sin (1 John 1:8). But with the sin comes God's mercy and grace (1 John 1:9). For those of us who sincerely desire to walk in God's ways, He has made a way to restore us to the path of holiness whenever we fail.

Our culture—even our Christian culture—has forgotten or lost hope in God's call and provision for holiness. In some misguided effort to build self-esteem, we have ceased to preach holiness. We no longer cast the vision of the high calling in Christ Jesus. We have adopted the syndrome of the perfectionist who attempts only what he can perfectly achieve. Because we glorify each other and reward pride, even believers have lowered their expectations to the level that can reasonably be achieved by proud men.

We must once again embrace humility, so that our failure to perfectly achieve holiness doesn't become the impetus for failing to preach holiness. We must awaken to our true state in life—one of being weak and dependent upon God. We must, in fact, glory in our weakness so that the power of God can all the more pour forth through us (2 Corinthians 12:9-10).

God only pours His power into men and women who acknowledge their weakness and who depend upon Him completely. He resists the proud, but gives grace to the humble (1 Peter 5:5).

This book has been written as a course correction for those who are on the journey to Christlikeness and those who are in the ministry of "spiritual formation."

The cardinal error in modern catechesis is that we have been telling people to be pure without teaching them how to be intimate with God. We have made holiness a rational proposition unsupported by the means for practical empowerment. We have laid down the gauntlet of law without preparing the ground where the will, the affections, and the emotions are engaged. It's been all head and no heart. This is no different than telling someone to play tennis without providing tennis balls, a racquet, and a court.

For too long, the church has been teaching people a performance-based religion, saddling them with a weight that fallen men cannot carry. We have demanded a level of performance that man cannot achieve without God. We have failed to lead people into an intimate relationship with Him where they can receive the passion and desire for holiness, where they can learn how to yield to God's Spirit and be kept from falling (Jude 24), and where their faith to believe in the love, grace, favor, goodness, and awesome power of God can be continuously replenished.

There have been plenty of books (Christian and secular) that have examined the details of the process of healing man's soul. Few, however, describe or focus on the superstructure upon which healing must come if it is to be permanently transforming. I hope that this book will help rectify that error.

In Pedro Calderon de la Barca's short play, "Life is a Dream," he says that to live is only to dream; that even our dreams are dreams. He suggests that everyone in the world only dreams that his life is real and that one day we are going to wake up from our dream to find our real life. Reality, he suggests, is only what is eternal. Therefore, we should live rightly; we should live for God. In other words, life is like a play, and we awake from it to our real life, which is the reality of God.

In similar fashion, the world is living in a trance, a state of reality that is not real, seeing things as being important that really aren't. That dream world includes their attempts to heal man's broken condition, individually and corporately. It is often the blind leading the blind.

Let us then look at the deeper things of God. Let us discover together His plan and provision for holiness. Let us be transformed by the discovery that God's desire is to live in such a state of unconditional love and union with us that the only earthly tradition that comes close to describing it is holy matrimony.

God's promises for victory over the flesh are not empty. They are, however, conditional. Even as evil abounds, God is pouring out His Spirit in unprecedented measure in this age to crush Satan under our feet. But that provision is being made available only to those who value the blood that was spilled to release such power on behalf of man. God will fight our battles with sin for us, but only as we engage Him from a heart motivated by love, only as we desire for Him to do so with everything that is within us, only as we commit to holiness in every area of our lives. We are all called to be saints. If we will but yield our lives entirely into His care, He will jealously guard us, and when we fail Him, He will forgive and cleanse us and set us back on the path to holiness. There is no power in Hell that can resist His passion for our holiness once it is properly engaged.

As we grow in Christlikeness, the focus of life will shift from ourselves to God and what will bring Him glory. It is at this point in life when God begins to share His ministry with us—where He allows us to participate in His redemptive acts by ministering to one another. The final chapters of this book will examine elements of that dimension of the call for both professional and lay minister.

Come with me now and learn how to be transformed into His image, from glory to glory. Come with me, and learn the practical lessons of being holy as He is holy.

Part One:

The Problems

1

The Purpose of Life

I know the plans I have for you . . .
plans to prosper you . . . to give you a hope and a future.
(Jeremiah 29:11)

Many of us have lost the vision of who God saved us to be. Our cultural environment has become so toxic to a Kingdom perspective that many Christians are ignorant of their true high calling. According to George Barna's research:

- Most first-time decisions for Christ do not last beyond eight weeks.
- Most new believers never move from decision to conversion.
- Almost half the adults in this country are functionally illiterate and so cannot receive much of the teaching of the church.
- Because of the influence of media, people today have a six- to eight-minute attention span.
- Linear thinking has been replaced with mosaic thinking: People are synthesizing their own faith from pieces of numerous religions.
- They fashion a personal faith that revolves around themselves rather than God.
- God is consulted solely for their utility and benefit.[1]

The church's greatest fault, says Barna, is in not applying what it believes in compelling ways, and in failing to address the fears and anxieties of the people.[2] His solution is:

- a rekindling of our passion for God,
- a rethinking of our strategies to reach the world,
- and the recapturing of an urgency to do so.[3]

There is a problem inside so-called "believing" churches as well.

- Twenty percent of all churchgoers attend multiple churches on a rotating basis.
- The really committed ones give only two blocks of their time to church per week (down from four, 20 years ago).
- We see religion as a commodity that we consume, rather than one in which we invest ourselves. (e.g., "Oh, I loved the worship today," or "That sermon didn't move me.")
- We see religion as a source to draw on rather than one in which we must also invest.[4]

Postmodern attitudes predominate more and more, such as:

- moral relativity
- political correctness
- live for the moment mentality
- time is money
- avoid commitment
- maintain independence and individuality at all costs
- trust feelings to guide you
- pursue love and acceptance from others with abandon
- develop competence only in areas of interest to you
- immediate gratification rules
- have fun
- stay in control of your life at all costs
- Christian values (e.g., commitment, sacrifice) appear to be limiting, unrealistic; relative to one's personal opinion; and outdated.[5]

Barna writes:

> ...the culture encourages us to treat God as an equity partner focused on our personal development.[6]
>
> ... In short, the spirituality of most Americans is Christian in name only. We desire experience more than knowledge. We prefer choices to absolutes. We embrace preferences rather than truths. We seek comfort rather than growth. Faith must come on our terms or we reject it. We have enthroned ourselves as the final arbiters of righteousness, the ultimate rulers of our own experience and destiny. We are the Pharisees of the new millennium.[7]

Barna says that the only hope now is to restore the Church and all in it to spiritual wholeness. We must ruthlessly root out the ways we limit or deceive ourselves from seeing things the way they truly are.[8]

I believe that another huge phenomenal shift that has taken place in our culture over the last few generations is the replacement of real relationships with "holodeck relationships" (a "holodeck" is a Star Trek engineering feat where false realities are created by computers through holographic images to satisfy the fantasies of the individual). These contrived and controlled "holodecks" serve to protect us from the possibility of rejection, humiliation, failure, or abandonment by real people. They serve to make our world safe and predictable and they eventually become more real than reality itself to the person they serve. How real depends on how fervently the person needs for them to be real. It's the power of faith being used for evil.

One common modern holodeck is the media, which creates an unending supply of unrealistic media-worlds that present caricatures of reality according to our fantasies, prejudices or the brainwashing goals of those who control its production. This has produced what I call "media mind" (where an image is more real to you than an actual person) and "media think" (where the so-called facts and assumptions of media words and images are unconsciously assumed to be accurate reflections of reality). Most people fall into these traps—even those who believe they are intelligent or sophisticated enough to prevent themselves from becoming victims —because the emotional buttons pushed in us by media images and stories cause our brains to disconnect from most of their critical defenses. We are taken along on a carpet ride of feeling and emotion simply because it feels better than reality and because we are naive to the real dangers presented by the carpetbaggers on whose carpets we ride. That is why advertising works and why advertisers spend billions of dollars on media.

People today trust and find reality in media images more than in real people. Let me provide an example. Have you ever had a good seat at a concert, yet, still watched the big screens rather than looking at the live person onstage? Somehow the image on the screen was more real, more intimate, more desirable. Believe it or not, we are so thoroughly saturated with media images these days that video and film images are more real, more compelling than actual people. If you don't believe me, try giving a twenty minute lecture, followed by a twenty minute film on the same topic and then ask the audience which they found more motivating, and which they found more memorable.

The use of media implies relevance to many minds. It creates an aura of legitimacy for the message. In addition, the media safely replaces our need for social interaction. I can have friendships and love affairs with the media people and avoid all the risk of real people. (A related phenomenon is the growing world of pornography and cybersex that often replaces a spouse as the "partner of choice" in meeting personal sexual need).

Another common holodeck in today's world is the relationship between a psychologist and a client.

Psychologists have become necessary in our culture because of the lack of interpersonal connectedness today. Studies have shown that the counsel of a friend can be just as healing as that of a psychotherapist, yet we continue to opt for the "paid friendship" that a therapist provides.

Why?

- Because the world of the paid friendship is safely controlled.

- The chances of embarrassment, rejection and humiliation are mini-mized. None of one's friends and associates need know that you have a weakness or vulnerability.

- There is a belief that the chances of getting bad advice are also being mini-mized, but owing to the moral and philosophical corruption found in the therapeutic world today, in many cases, this is not true at all.

- And when it is all over, the only commitment required is the dollar.

Have you noticed that it's only when the power goes out or during some disaster that we seem to ever meet and interact with our neighbors? Yet when the power is restored, we retreat back to our image-filled enclaves. Holodeck relationships are safer because they are controlled. They can be terminated if one becomes bored. No responsibility and no commitment is required. They are perfect for the self-centered post-modern man.

Only the impact of authentic love, unconditional and servant-like, can break through such defenses.

So, again I submit: we have lost the vision of who God saved us to be and what He wants us to do while still on this earth. With smoke and mirrors, the world has diverted our attention and seduced us into compromising our purpose. We have given in to our fallen desires and forsaken the real purpose of God for our life. No wonder our methods of ministry are so ineffective. Our first task must be to rouse ourselves back to our high call-ing in Christ and to sharpen our focus once again. What is that focus?

- to be holy, as He is holy
- to love Christ above all things[9]
- to love our neighbor as ourself
- to take up our cross and follow Him
- to be conformed to His image
- to be reflectors of His glory
- to be ambassadors of His Kingdom
- to be magnets that draw the world to come to Christ for salvation

We've got to wake up and break free from the deceptive images project-ed by this world system. We have to take an honest look at our penchant to compromise and then reason our way out of it at those times when it's easier to feed the flesh than to deny it.

Avoiding failure has sometimes become the controlling watchword, rather than becoming of no reputation. Perfectionism is often a dominating power in many of our lives—a perfectionism that doesn't want to attempt something that cannot be perfectly achieved.[10]

Let God do it for you. Let God live His righteousness through you (Galatians 2:20).

Even our spiritual lives bear examination. Often, they are actually focused on self. In various subtle and clever ways, we use our time with God only to try to get Him to do our bidding. A good litmus test is to ask yourself: Who is the focus of my spirituality? Me or God?

Being motivated is a big part of maintaining our vision of becoming who God saved us to be. The greatest single motivator is Christ's love displayed on the Cross. One night, I was complaining to God about why He allowed innocent people to be harmed, and He replied, "What you really want to know is how could I love them and allow them to be harmed." "Now that you mention it, yes, that is what I want to know," I answered. He said to me, "Look at the Cross. I proved My love there, and when the Cross becomes enough for you, then you will have the peace and the understanding that you are seeking."

Grace is another powerful motivator. With grace, God writes the law on our hearts, meaning, He makes it our own interior wish to keep the law rather than some outside rule imposing itself on us.

One night, I was sinning and God spoke to me, saying, "David, if you will turn to Me now, I will love you, forgive you, and embrace you." I thought it crazy that God would even be in the room while I was sinning, much less offering to embrace me, so I rejected the thought and continued on with my sin. The second I finished my sin, the Lord spoke the same words to me: "David, if you will turn to Me now, I will love you, forgive you, and embrace you." Then, I knew it was the Lord. I remember thinking, "God, I just rejected your offer of love for a pathetic little sin, just like I've done ten thousand times before, and you still want to love and embrace me? If that is what you are really like, then I *want* to follow you!" Inside, something profound had changed. I went from being motivated to follow God because I was *supposed* to, to following Him because I *wanted* to. My interior motivation had been entirely overturned by grace. As it says in the Book of Titus, with grace, He teaches us to say "No" to ungodliness and makes us "eager to do what is good" (Titus 2:11-14). This matter is of such importance that we will take a much closer look at it later in the book.

"Being forgiven much" is a part of what properly motivates us (Luke 7:47). All of us have been forgiven much. Some realize it more clearly than others, that's all.

So choose life! Deny your darkened, selfish, fleshly nature. Choose to love God more. Choose to sacrifice short term pleasure for long-term happiness with God.

How do you start?

Holiness can only be birthed from intimacy with God. It is not an achievement, but rather the fruit of intimacy with God. It is given life only as we share ourselves deeply and fully with our divine spouse. Choose to make intimacy with God the top priority of your life—to love Him more than you do the things of the world.

A Jewish boy named Keith Green was lit afire by God, though he died just a few years after finding Christ. Saved out of the hippie culture of the 60's and early 70's, his book, *No Compromise*, became an anthem of love and praise for Jesus Christ. Just before he was saved, he wrote these words in his diary:

> Oh, I feel the calling so strong tonight, to join the holy army and fight the numbness in the world toward God. Even the very belief in the existence of God is a battle. But when I truly believe in God, and I have to fight the insidious evils around me, and more horrifying, right inside of me, I find myself feeling beaten and hearing the satanic words, "Give up. You're too human. Only the saints, priests, monks and nuns are clean enough from the world and its forms to reach the Lord and be chosen for His holy service." [Praying] Please God, in Christ's name and teachings, I want to be chosen to be with You—on Your side only —no possibilities of any other master or side or path or pseudo-life or pseudo-god. I want to die for You, God, and be reborn a whole disciple, living, emulating and shining Your will, Your teachings, and bearing fruit everyday to everyone. The devil hates me more every day, the more I get closer to You, but he's losing his grip. Praise God! Your light is the only thing I want to see and the only thing I want to reflect.[11]

Later, after giving his heart to Christ, Keith wrote the words to this song:

> You're the Sun, You're the starlight, You're a wave upon the sea.
> You're the glory of the sunrise, as it sets the morning free.
> You're my hope for the future, it's Your love that covers me.
> And if I have my choice, I'll spend my life, watching You watching me.
>
> When You came, I was weary, and I thought You couldn't see,
> but You saw right through my masquerade, right to that secret place in me.
> Then Your love held me gently, whispering "Everything's alright",
> I was born again, into Your love, born again into Your life.
> Jesus, sometimes my mind grows cloudy, and it's all so hard to see,
> that there's a life I'm meant to live for You, sometimes I live for me.
>
> When You came, I was weary, and I thought You couldn't see, but You saw right through my masquerade, right to that secret place in me.
> Then Your love held me gently, whispering "Everything's alright",
> I was born again, into Your love, born again into Your life.[12]

Let us each ask God, and keep asking, until He grants us such a vision of His love.

2

Love Is Not Love:
What does it really mean to love?

One major area where we have gotten off track is in the proper defining and practice of love.[1] In our world, love is not love.[2] It is favor or affection granted to one who has pleased you, or served you well. It is a feeling, a romantic notion, and in many quarters, it is defined by sexual pleasure. Since "love is from God" and God Himself is *defined* as love,[3] it makes sense that the world does not know or practice real love. In fact, even for a believer, our actions will only be from love when God Himself is being released through us in what we are doing.[4]

Loving Humbly

Let's take a look, then, at two arenas where love is often not love. One area is the response of the church to the homosexual. Too often, we are judgmental in ways that do not reflect knowledge or wisdom, but rather ignorance, prejudice, and fear.

The first thing that love demands is that we repent for the unkind, unchristian, and unloving ways in which Christians have, in the past, responded to those who struggle with homosexual confusion. We have condemned them in our hearts. We have reacted with revulsion and fear. We have considered ourselves better than they. Many of us have simply turned away and offered no help at all. We have sinned as great a sin against them as they may have sinned against God (provided they have responded to their homosexual inclinations in ways that make them culpable before God).

Every scientific attempt to prove that people are born homosexual has failed. But what is also true is that most people with homosexual neurosis never consciously choose to be homosexual. In fact, many (perhaps even most) spend endless years begging God to take it away. It is a condition of arrested emotional development primarily caused by circumstances outside of the control of the person and against which most children and adolescents who develop it have little defense.

It is true that, at some point, many become co-conspirators in the development of their condition—through "sins of response," e.g., judging; condemning; dishonoring; seeking identity, completion, and fulfillment in the creature rather than the Creator; welcoming unholy fantasies; or acting out immorally. However, the original orientation is mostly the fault of others who are beyond the control of the individual, as in the case where sexual abuse creates fear and confusion over one's identity, or when someone fails to emotionally bond with their same-sex parent figure.

Like the person with an inclination to alcohol abuse, they can either respond in rebellion against God through "sin tantrums" and self-medication, or they can embrace the trial of their condition as an opportunity to grow in the knowledge of their absolute dependence on God and, eventually, find healing and transformation in Him. It is the call of the Church to show them the way that the Father has provided through His Son, Jesus Christ. We must do this with unconditional love and with wisdom and knowledge.

Until the Church reforms, how can we ever expect society to reform? Today, we elect pedophiles to Congress, we sell their books and frequent the stores that stock them; we make bishops, priests, and pastors of men and women known to live immoral lives; and we endow seminaries and colleges that teach their students not to believe the Word of God.

On the other hand, when fellow believers waver and fall, we shoot them and bury their memory rather than lead them to repentance through grace and love; we teach and we model salvation by works, performance righteousness, and the dishonest posturing of sinless perfection.

I do not believe that the so-called "gay church" would exist today if it weren't for these and other sins that we, the Church, have committed. And so, our first task is to repent, crying from the heart:

> "God, I am sorry for the ways I have failed to communicate your grace and love to others. I am sorry for the times when I have judged homosexuals and others as though they were lower forms of life, as though their hearts were darker than mine, as though I was better than they. And I pledge this day, Lord, to respond in love and in grace, to be a reflection of Jesus' heart to those who are fallen and lost, for I know that it is by grace that we come to Christ; it is grace that teaches us to say 'No' to ungodliness (Titus 2:11), and it is the love that pours itself out on a cross that brings people to repentance."

Loving a Community in Crisis

Love demands that we respond to their plight. But like the alcoholic of fifty years ago, we have turned our backs on a population that is destroying itself. Now, however, as with today's alcoholic, we must love them enough to risk igniting their ire and losing their approval through acts of tough love and attempts at heroic rescue.[5]

The gay community lives with a death wish wrought from interior self-hatred. Their lives are ballads of self-destruction. Examine the statistics! From the way they've lobbied to prevent the reporting of sexual partners with AIDS to the way they continue to engage in behaviors known to cause death, this self-contempt exhibits itself throughout their ranks.

In 1998, CNN's *Impact* aired a story citing some frightening but telling statistics. They noted that in a CDC[6] study conducted in six US cities over a six month period, forty percent of gay men (15-22 yrs.) were still engaging in the most high-risk, unsafe type of sexual behavior known—unprotected anal intercourse.

Despite years of "safe-sex" messages and millions of condoms distributed throughout their communities, they continue to defy expert medical advice in order to engage in this particular form of sexual behavior.

The same CNN study showed that one in four gay men (18-29 yrs.) in South Beach (Miami) tested positive for HIV.

Also cited was a recent study conducted by the South Beach Health Survey (a gay study), showing that forty-seven percent (almost half) of young gay men had had high-risk, unprotected sex over the past year. It's like lemmings going over a cliff!

In his brilliant book, *Homosexuality & the Politics of Truth*, Dr. Jeffrey Satinover, (a former Fellow in Psychiatry and Child Psychiatry at Yale University and past president of the Carl Jung Foundation, with degrees from MIT, the University of Texas and Harvard University), cites even more frightening statistics. Quoting from *Clinical Psychiatry News*, October 1994, he writes:

> The American Psychiatric Association Press reports that "30 percent of all 20-year-old gay men will be HIV positive or dead of AIDS by the time they are age 30" because they are resuming "unsafe sex" anyway.[7]
>
> . . . medical literature still speaks of homosexuality as the major risk-factor for AIDS, . . . [because] gay male anal intercourse and promiscuity created the American reservoir for HIV . . . and continues to preserve it.[8]
>
> . . . In 1963 the New York Academy of Medicine . . . reported that: "homosexuality is indeed an illness. The homosexual is an emotionally disturbed individual who has not acquired the normal capacity to develop satisfying heterosexual relations. . . .
>
> . . . some homosexuals have gone beyond the plane of defensiveness and now argue that deviancy is a 'desirable, noble, preferable way of life.'"[9]
>
> Just ten years later—with no significant new scientific evidence—the homosexual activists' argument became the new standard within psychiatry. For in 1973 the American Psychiatric Association voted to strike homosexuality from the officially approved list of psychiatric illnesses. How did this occur? Normally a scientific consensus is reached over the course of many years, resulting from the accumulated weight of many properly designed studies. . . The APA vote to normalize homosexuality was driven by politics, not science. . . .[10]

In 1970 the leadership of a homosexual faction within the APA planned a "systematic effort to disrupt the annual meetings of the American Psychiatric Association. . . ."[11]

. . . Eric Pollard formerly belonged to the prominent homosexual organization ACT-UP and founded its Washington, D.C. chapter. In an interview with *The Washington Blade*, a major homosexual newspaper, he stated that he and other group members learned to apply "subversive tactics, drawn largely from the voluminous *Mein Kampf*, which some of us studied as a working model."[12]

In the 1971 APA conference, gay activists threatened and carried out further disorder and disruptions, including breaking into one meeting, grabbing the microphone and turning it over to an outside activist.

When the APA Committee on Nomenclature met in 1973:

The outcome had already been arranged behind closed doors. No new data was introduced, and objectors were given only fifteen minutes to present a rebuttal that summarized seventy years of psychiatric and psychoanalytic opinion.[13]

Next, members of the National Gay Task Force purchased the APA membership mailing list and sent out a letter urging them to sustain the decision, without indicating that it was coming from a gay activist group, making it look as though APA psychiatrists had written and sent the letter. Only one-third of the 30,000 APA membership actually voted to sustain the decision, surely based in part, on the letter that had seemed to have come from the APA board.

In 1975, the American Psychological Association (the professional psychology guild that is three times larger than the APA) voted to follow suit.

In 1978, the journal *Medical Aspects of Human Sexuality* did a survey of APA members that showed that "69 percent of psychiatrists disagreed with the vote and still considered homosexuality a disorder."[14]

Satinover then quotes Ronald Bayer, (then a Fellow at Hastings Institute in New York), who commented:

The result was not a conclusion based upon an approximation of the scientific truth as dictated by reason, but was instead an action demanded by the ideological temper of the times.[15]

In 1994, a gay APA committee chairman prompted the Board of Trustees of the APA to alter the code of ethics to make it:

a violation of professional conduct for a psychiatrist to help a homosexual patient become heterosexual, *even at the patient's request*. This is in spite of the fact that one of the association's own professional standards holds that psychiatrists need to accept a patient's own goals in treatment so as to "foster maximum self-determination on the part of clients."[16]

Fortunately, this first attempt was defeated in the APA Assembly (its legislative body). But it won't be the last attempt.

The chairman of the APA Gay and Lesbian Task Force made it clear that the activists had in their sights not only psychiatrists . . . , but eventually psychologists, social workers, and even pastoral counselors and ministers.[17]

Gay activists have made similar attempts at political pressure within the National Association of Social Workers.

Of the three major mental health guilds, the NASW is farthest along in the attempt to politicize clinical questions regarding homosexuality. All of these changes in the definition and classification of homosexuality have occurred in a scientific vacuum. . . .

. . . (Gay activists) seek to create the impression that *science* has settled these questions, but it most certainly has not. Instead, the changes that have occurred in both public and professional opinion have resulted from politics, pressure, and public relations.[18]

Unfortunately, gay activist manipulation of the professional psychological societies isn't the only problem. Simple health among homosexuals has become an unmitigated disaster. In a 1998 newspaper report, for example, it was reported that gonorrhea cases among gay men was skyrocketing:

Cases of gonorrhea among homosexual men have more than doubled at some U.S. clinics, suggesting that safe sex is not being taken as seriously now that the AIDS epidemic is slowing, the government said yesterday. . . .

. . . Homosexual men accounted for 8.7% of all gonorrhea cases in clinics in 26 U.S. cities in 1996, up from 5% three years earlier, the CDC said.[19]

Considering that only 2-3% of the population is gay, that is a very telling statistic. In a 2000 newspaper report, an even more dire revelation:

New HIV infections in San Francisco increased sharply in 1999, primarily because of increases in sexually risky behavior, the San Francisco Department of Public Health said Friday. . . .

. . . "This should sound a warning bell for the rest of the country," said Dr. Thomas Coates of the AIDS Research Institute at UC San Francisco. "We see in San Francisco what is going to happen next in the epidemic (elsewhere)." . . .

. . . That rise has also been accompanied by sharp increases in other sexually transmitted diseases . . . rectal gonorrhea . . . for example, . . .

. . . The proportion of gay men who say they have unprotected anal sex with more than one partner grew from 23% in 1994 to 43% in 1999. The proportion who said they always used a condom, meanwhile, dropped from 70% to 54% during the same period.

The data indicate a clear regression toward unsafe behavior . . . And by keeping HIV-positive men alive, the [AIDS] drugs enlarged the pool of people who could transmit the disease.[20]

Satinover tries to put it in perspective for us:

What would you think if a relative, friend, or colleague had a condition that is routinely, even if not always, associated with the following problems: . . .

- A significantly decreased likelihood of establishing or preserving a successful marriage
- A twenty-five to thirty-year decrease in life expectancy
- Chronic, potentially fatal, liver disease - infectious hepatitis, which increases the risk of liver cancer
- Inevitably fatal immune disease including associated cancers
- Frequently fatal rectal cancer
- Multiple bowel and other infectious diseases
- A much higher than usual incidence of suicide
- A very low likelihood that its adverse effects can be eliminated unless the condition itself is
- An at least 50 percent likelihood of being eliminated through lengthy, often costly, and very time-consuming treatment in an otherwise unselected group of sufferers (although a very high success rate, in some instances nearing 100 percent, for groups of highly motivated, carefully selected individuals)[21]

Epidemiologists estimate that 30 percent of all twenty-year-old homosexual males will be HIV-positive or dead of AIDS by the time they are thirty.[22]

And just when you thought the news couldn't get any worse, another report about the serious brokenness that pervades the gay culture says:

> In his new book, *Sexual Ecology*, gay activist Gabriel Rotello gives a startling fact you should know about. Young gay men entering into homosexual behavior today have a 50% chance of being infected by the AIDS virus by the time they are 55 years old. . . . Rotello quotes a study by Donald R. Hoover . . .[23]

A telling indicator of the death wish that dominates the gay community is the fact that the suicide rate among gays (especially gay teens) is extremely high and going higher. The gay activist community would have us believe that these teenagers are committing suicide in record numbers because society disapproves of their behavior. However, societal approval of homosexuality has gone way up in the last 40 years, so if societal disapproval were the cause, the suicide rate among gays would be going down, not up. Ironically, the reason young gays are killing themselves in record numbers is because the gay community itself is telling them that they are fixed in their orientation and there is no hope for change. They have robbed these confused youths of hope. The response of many a young gay is, "I would rather not live at all than to have to live such an unnatural, painful and immoral life!"

Several studies have even shown that the age at death for gays (not even factoring in AIDS deaths) is eight to twenty years younger than for other men.[24] The numbers of gay victims (per capita) of venereal disease, AIDS, hepatitis, suicide, incontinence, etc., make nihilistic heterosexual

Americans look like Puritans in comparison.

And one other shocking evidence of gay self-hatred according to several articles in *Mission: America*:

- Domestic violence among lesbian couples is the highest ever found in studies of various groups, higher than male to female violence;
- 47% of lesbian couples studied had experienced violent episodes (in sociologist Claire Renzetti's 1992 book, *Violent Betrayal: Partner Abuse in Lesbian Relationships*);
- a 1996 study by the National Coalition of Anti-Violence Programs found that violence occurs in 25-33% of all same-sex relationships—a much much higher rate than among heterosexual couples.[25]

What is really going on, and what we are being told, are two very different things. The Bible teaches us that as sin, homosexual behavior is destructive to the bodies and souls of those who practice it (1 Corinthians 6:18; James 4:1; 1 Peter 2:11). I cannot even say in public what I know from my own experience to be the sexual perversions common to homosexuals. The public is being shown a sanitized, "family-friendly" and grossly inaccurate picture of homosexual relationships that has been ingeniously calculated to undermine our resistance to the promotion and propagation of their lifestyle. According to gay activist, Marshall Kirk, in "Waging Peace," his detailed strategy for changing the way America thinks, depicting such a lopsided view of homosexuals is part of the strategy of winning over straight America:

> Mr. and Mrs. Public must be given no extra excuses to say "they are not like us." To this end, the persons featured in the public campaign should be decent and upright, *appealing and admirable by straight standards*, (italics mine), completely unexceptionable in appearance—in a word, they should be indistinguishable from the straights we would like to reach.[26]

Kirk refers to using "R-type, straight gays" as public spokesmen rather than "Q-type," (queer), meaning they should only use gays who do not reflect the reality of typical gay appearance and behavior but rather those who look as much like straights as possible. In short, they are engaged in a publicity campaign of deceptive image control so as to present unreal images of a gay America that will not threaten straights.

Kirk suggests a six-part plan to change the way America thinks. First, "desensitize" the American public by using a "large-scale media campaign" that talks about homosexuality so much that people become tired of it and are rendered non-resistant. He calls the media "a gateway into the private world of straights, through which a Trojan horse might be passed."[27]

He suggests:

> When conservative churches condemn gays . . . we can use talk to muddy the moral waters. . . we can undermine [their] moral authority . . . by portraying

them as antiquated backwaters, badly out of step with the times and with the latest findings of psychology. . .

Portray gays as victims . . . in need of protection so that straights will be inclined by reflex to assume the role of protector . . . we must forego the temptation to strut our "gay pride" publicly whenever it conflicts with the Gay Victim image. . .

. . . the mainstream should be told that gays are *victims of fate,* . . .

. . . the gay community . . . must manipulate the powers of the weak, including the play for sympathy. . . .

. . . portray gays as *victims of society.* . . .

. . . Our campaign should not demand direct support for homo*sexual* practices, but should instead take *anti-discrimination* as its theme. . . .

Make gays look good. In order to make a Gay Victim sympathetic to straights you have to portray him as Everyman. . . , the campaign should paint gays as *superior* pillars of society. . .

. . . a skillful and clever media campaign . . .

. . . Make the victimizers look bad. . . , we intend to make the anti-gays look so nasty that average Americans will want to dissociate themselves from such types.

The public should be shown images of ranting homophobes whose secondary traits and beliefs disgust middle America. . . include: the Ku Klux Klan . . . ; bigoted southern ministers drooling with hysterical hatred to a degree that looks both comical and deranged; menacing punks, thugs, and convicts . . . ; a tour of Nazi concentrations camps where homosexuals were tortured and gassed.

A campaign to vilify the victimizers . . . with all of America watching.[28]

Some gay activists even pose as spokesmen for the Church on such shows as *Nightline* and *Larry King Live.* Andrew Sullivan is notorious for publicly claiming support from the Roman Catholic church for his homosexuality. However, the actual position of the Roman Catholic Church is very different from what he portrays.

In a Letter to the Bishops on the "Pastoral Care of Homosexual Persons," Joseph Cardinal Ratzinger, who is the prefect in charge of official Roman Catholic doctrinal statements, wrote:

homosexual actions. . . (are) deprived of their essential and indispensable finality, . . . "intrinsically disordered," and able in no case to be approved of. . .

. . . Although the particular inclination of the homosexual person is not a sin, it is a more or less strong tendency ordered toward an intrinsic moral evil; and thus the inclination itself must be seen as an objective disorder. . . .

. . . , there is . . . a clear consistency within the Scriptures themselves on the moral issue of homosexual behavior. The Church's doctrine regarding this issue is thus based, not on isolated phrases for facile theological argument, but on the solid foundation of a constant Biblical testimony. . .

. . . A person engaging in homosexual behavior therefore acts immorally

. . . when they engage in homosexual activity they confirm within themselves a disordered sexual inclination which is essentially self-indulgent. . . .

. . . The Church's ministers must ensure that homosexual persons in their care will not be misled by [a] point of view, so profoundly opposed to the teaching of the Church. . . there are many who seek to create confusion regarding the Church's position, and then to use that confusion to their own advantage. . . . One tactic used is to protest that any and all criticism of or reservations about homosexual people, their activity and lifestyle, are simply diverse forms of unjust discrimination. . . .

. . . The Church . . . is really concerned about the many who are not represented by the pro-homosexual movement and about those who may have been tempted to believe its deceitful propaganda. . . .

. . . this Congregation wishes to ask the Bishops to be especially cautious of any programs which may seek to pressure the Church to change her teaching, even while claiming not to do so. A careful examination of their public statements and the activities they promote reveals a studied ambiguity by which they attempt to mislead the pastors and the faithful. . . .

. . . departure from the Church's teaching, or silence about it, in an effort to provide pastoral care is neither caring nor pastoral. Only what is true can ultimately be pastoral. The neglect of the Church's position prevents homosexual men and women from receiving the care they need and deserve. . . .

. . . His Holiness, Pope John Paul II, approved this Letter, adopted in an ordinary session of the Congregation for the Doctrine of the Faith, and ordered it to be published.[29]

Scientific studies related to the development of homosexual orientation is another area where gay activists have purposely deceived the public. Former gay leader Bobby Jones, prior to his death from AIDS, went on Christian talk shows, revealing the back room strategies of gay activism, one of which was to simply lie to the public about the statistics and science of homosexuality. The theory—if you say something often enough, people will just believe it. If we would only take the time to actually read the studies, or even just the expert response to the studies, we would see that there is no scientific basis for asserting the normalcy of homosexual behavior or orientation.[30]

Finally, there is one more significant sign of the profound brokenness that can come from homosexual neurosis—the high incidence of pedophilia and pederasty. Some of the factors that help create sexual identity confusion are the same ones that can, in certain people, also create a psychosexual obsession with children, or more often, teenagers. Childhood sexual abuse is the primary causal factor, although it can be other traumas that create a fixation or an obsessive need to be close to children or teens. While most homosexually oriented people do not have this added disorder, due to these shared factors, a much higher percentage will develop such an obsession than is found among heterosexuals. Even some in the "ex-gay" community would like to ignore this fact because there is already enough fear and hatred of gays in the church without providing more ammunition for the fire. However, hiding the truth never brings healing. Those who do have this problem need help.[31]

So you see, at every level, the homosexual condition cries out for healing. It cries out for compassion, understanding and a willingness to sacrifice ourselves as tools for that healing. In the gay community, and in our culture at large, love is not love. In other words, it is not loving to encourage, promote, bless, or ignore a condition caused by such profoundly arrested emotional development. It is not loving to tell people who are dying in record numbers, with record levels of disease, alcoholism, domestic violence, and suicide to be warmed and go about their way. Such a posture borders on the contempt of the disinterested and uncaring.

Would it not be unthinkable to sit idly by while an alcoholic friend drinks himself to death when there is help available that could save his life? It is just as unconscionable to ignore the plight of the homosexual friend when there are hundreds of Christian organizations that exist specifically to lead the person who struggles with homosexual neurosis into the healing power of Jesus Christ[32] and hundreds more professional therapists whose therapeutic techniques for healing the homosexual struggler have proven even more successful than those for the alcoholic.[33]

The loving thing to do is to offer the healing power of Jesus Christ —healing not only for their emotional brokenness, but for their soul as well.

Does the parable of the "Good Samaritan" teach us to pass by on the other side when we encounter such self-destruction, or does it tell us to sacrifice our own comfort for the good of those who are torn and conflicted? To love them is not to pass by on the other side. To love them is to risk their anger, their rejection, and even their sometimes ruthless tactics of personal destruction against those who dare cry out, "The emperor has no clothes!" We must do this for the homosexual, and we must do this for every broken person Christ sends our way.

Will you love as Christ loved? Will you give your life's blood to those who may try to crucify you? Or will you leave it to the next guy, or the church expert, or into the hands of those who hate and revile them?

One of the full-page ads that the gay community ran in *USA Today* and other newspapers in the summer of 1998 stated: "All leading medical experts agree . . . gay people are just as likely to be healthy and happy as the rest of us."

The denial is profound. Let's love them enough to tell them the truth.

* * * *

By examining the beliefs and behaviors misnamed "love" both inside and outside of the gay community, hopefully, we have begun to see more clearly just how faulty are the contemporary notions of love. Moderns consider "love" to be a feeling, a romantic idea, sexual pleasure, or something one possesses as long as one's partner meets one's needs. They have taken minor elements of how love may be expressed and made it the whole—precisely what one might expect from a generation epitomized by arrested emotional development. They know very little of the Biblical definition of love, which is epitomized instead by self-donating sacrifice and commitment.

This is a critical area that must be corrected if we are to grow in Christlikeness. Why? Because God is love, and if we are to be transformed into His image, we must learn what love is, how to express it, and how to be infused with it by the indwelling Savior.

Correcting faulty definitions of core virtues doesn't stop there, however. Just as we must be brave enough to tell the culture (and ourselves) Who and what true love is, so must we be willing to teach the full-orbed picture of what the Christian life entails. Too often, people are persuaded to come to Christ in response to the unbalanced and inaccurate representation of Christianity that they see and hear from modern pitch men who present only the "health, wealth, and blessing" side of things. Many modern Christian leaders fail to help them understand the silence of God in times of trial.

They fail to tell them about the wilderness periods, the dark nights of the soul, when God seems to have disappeared altogether. This is a major flaw in modern Christian apologetics and evangelism that results in new believers falling away in massive numbers. Let us examine then the "dark matter" of the Christian life, when our claims of love and fidelity to the One who died for us are challenged—where God seeks to render them more whole, complete, and real.

3

The Dark Night
of the Soul

C otton candy Christianity. It pervades western ideas about life. It subverts sound healing and transformation to Christlikeness.

In adopting a "Madison Avenue" approach to evangelizing people, we've compromised the truth so as to only show the good side of what is a far more complex reality. In order to "close the deal," we've sometimes told the half truth, and nothing but the half truth, to the detriment of those we were trying to help. We've apologized for God's judgments and refused to acknowledge His wrath against unrighteousness. We've minimized the gravity of sin and modeled compromise and half-heartedness in the way we live our lives before a lost and dying culture. Not wanting to be rejected in our witness, we've revealed only the easy side of living for Christ.

When things don't show themselves as rosy as we've painted them to be, an already jaded public concludes that it was just another bogus bill of goods that money-grubbing shysters tried to pass off on them once again.

We never told them about dying to self, about taking up one's cross daily, about forsaking the things of this world. We told them they could have it all. We implied that being a Christian was health, wealth, and happiness all the way to the bank and to heaven.

Even in telling them about the intimate relationship with God that is offered through Christ, we have often failed to describe the complete picture of what such a relationship requires. We've failed to tell them of the wilderness periods, when all evidence of God's love and acceptance seems to vanish. We've conveniently forgotten to appraise them of the cost and of the schemes of the enemy designed to lead them astray during times of trial and temptation.

. . . It's What You Didn't Say

One of the most common ways that Christian leaders miscommunicate the reality of walking with Christ is in the way they sometimes tell their stories. After years of serving the Lord, they regale audiences with descriptions of dreams, visions, and life-changing revelations from God and wittingly or unwittingly give the impression that God talks to them all the time, that He regularly provides immediate answers to their questions and visions to show them the way out of the various predicaments of their lives. What these teachers often fail to tell their audience is that they are telescoping many years of stories into their talk or their book and that there was, in fact, plenty of "dead air" between their great and grand stories of supernatural blessing and deliverance.

It's not that they intend to deceive their listeners. It's just that there isn't any information to communicate about the much lengthier and more numerous times when God doesn't tell them anything. So they tell the stories of when He did.

The problem is, the person in the audience listening to this litany of wondrous interventions by God is often thinking to him or herself, "Wow, God really is active in that person's life. He must have a special calling. He is surely loved more by God than I am. God doesn't answer right back when I ask Him questions. He hasn't shown me a vision or miraculously rescued me from such disasters. That sort of divine intervention must be for saints, for priests, for people who have been given a greater fervor for God than I have."

When we aren't honest about all the waiting and crying and praying that we did in between our marvelous stories of God's supernatural actions on our behalf, our stories of great revelations from God can actually serve to deepen the self-doubt and ensconce the mediocre life of someone who is listening.

Some speakers make matters worse by exaggerating their stories, creating expectations for things that will never come to pass, and consequent discouragement for the one who goes after them. Wrong as it is, many believers compare themselves with one another and measure how much God loves them based on whether their experiences with God approximate those of others.

Another incorrect belief that many of us unconsciously hold is that greater revelations from God mean a greater call on someone's life or that He loves such people in greater measure than He loves us. These ideas are just as untrue.

In fact, the Bible indicates that those who "do not see and yet believe" are more blessed (John 20:29). There are many reasons why God might give a supernatural revelation to one and not another. In my case, when I began pursuing the Lord, I was in a cult worshiping a guru. I was living a massively addicted and hedonistic life and therefore needed something quite dramatic to turn me around. The great revelation that God gave me at that point had nothing to do with a greater call or greater love for me—it simply had to do with what it was going to take to rescue me from my life of destruction.

The Bible teaches that those who are given more light are held to a higher level of responsibility. People who have learned more of the things of God so as to be able to teach others, will be given a stricter judgment (James 3:1). Jesus taught that we will be judged according to the light we have received (John 9:41; 15:22-24). And Paul indicated that because of the surpassing revelations that he received, he was required to suffer a "thorn in the flesh" so that he would stay humble (2 Corinthians 12:1-9).

I could go on at length listing the reasons why one person might hear or see more from God through supernatural revelation than another, but let me simply give one illustration of how unexpected the reasons can be. One night, I was wrapped up in worship and asked the Lord to show me His glory. I figured, even though I wasn't Moses, it wouldn't hurt to ask. In response, the Lord said to me, "David, isn't this the most beautiful time of intimacy that we are having right now?" "Yes it is," I replied. Then He said, "If I showed you My glory, it would ruin the sublime peace and beauty of this moment because you would be dropped to the floor as a dead man at the sight of it." I began to weep over the exacting care and concern that had kept Him from such a revelation and realized anew that whatever His response might be to my cries for revelation, it would always be perfectly designed to bless me, even if it was silence.

The Divine Therapy of Dark Nights

No one ever warned me about the dark night of the soul—no pastor, no seminary professor, no TV teacher or preacher, no Christian book or tape— no one! It has been an area of serious denial in modern western Christianity to avoid the mention of this aspect of the Christian life.

I'll never forget the day the spiritual music died for me. I was certain that I had failed God. It happened after a particularly sweet and powerful period of intimacy and revelation in God. Without any warning or apparent reason, the delicious and unexcelled consolations of being in God's presence gradually began to fade away. Finally, they just stopped and I was left with silence from God.[1]

The problem was, I had no paradigm for a growth in Christ that had periods where the sense of His favor and His presence would seem to diminish or vanish altogether. I knew that if I were to go out and willfully enter into sin, there would be a diminishment of a sense of intimate relationship with Him, but as long as I remained faithful, seeking first the Kingdom of God and His righteousness (Matthew 6:33), it should only get better in terms of the interior life, so I thought.

And so, I was left with questions. "Why have you left me God? What have I done wrong? Am I not living up to your expectations? Have you raised the bar?" (Notice the performance orientation in this).

As Gregory of Nyssa said (referring to future rewards):

. . . disregarding all those things for which we hope and which have been reserved by promise, *we regard falling from God's friendship as the only thing dreadful* [my italics], and we consider becoming God's friend the only thing worthy of honor and desire. This, as I have said, is the perfection of life.[2]

I believed that my worst nightmare—that of falling from God's friendship—had come true, and I was utterly devastated. Imagine how Jesus must have felt when God turned His face away from Him on the Cross when He became sin (2 Corinthians 5:21; Habakkuk 1:13)!

I knew that the common western prescription for this malaise was to read the Bible more and pray more, but in my anger and confusion, I drew different conclusions. I decided that the problem lay with modern evangelical devotional expectations—that they were derived not from scriptural teaching, but rather from modern-day Pharisees who liked to parade their righteous devotional life before men in order to receive praise from them (which is no doubt true in some cases). In my place of hurting, I chose to believe that "performance-oriented" control freaks in the church had made up rules that God never intended to impose on His children.

It is important to understand that this is also the thinking of many people in the church, who are gun shy of controlling ecclesiastical structures and individuals. Many of them do not maintain a regular devotional life because they look upon "super-spiritual types" as having dreamed up devotional systems in order to put their spirituality on display; to justify their existence or calling; to get money from them; to control them; or maybe to get the extra wherewithal that "super-spiritual" types need in order to operate within their abnormal "super-spiritual" calling. And so they think to themselves: "If I'm not called to be the next Moses, why spend all that time preparing myself for something that just ain't going to happen! God's got me installing windshields in cars at the Saturn factory, and that's all I'm ever going to do, and that's all He's ever going to expect of me." Similar thoughts went through my mind as well.

Finally, in the silence one evening, God spoke clearly to me that He was teaching me to believe in His love, acceptance and protection without the spiritual feelings that had previously been my assurance of those things.

So I made a conscious decision to embrace that lesson, and having learned it, expected that God would return to the intimate exchange of feeling and emotion that had previously been such a dear consolation to me.

It did not come.

That's when I got angry at God and my true heart surfaced. "Why are you playing such games with me God?" I railed. "Do you get your kicks from holding back such a priceless thing as intimacy from me to tease me? It makes me feel like a dumb ass who continually falls for the carrot on a stick trick. It makes me feel so controlled, so dependent, so much like the creature that, well, I guess I am." It was an anger born from the realization that I was not the God of the universe and that I could not command answers or action from God as though I were. It was the unveiling of yet another level of pride. (Needless to say, when you're angry with God, your progress in sanctification tends to slow down just a wee bit).

I also felt betrayed. I had consented to embrace the lesson, and in being so humbled felt deserving of a prize that was never delivered. Great subterranean systems of wrong thinking and misbelief surfaced.

So I stewed for many more months.

God then sent Joyce Meyer, who gave a televised teaching on her own experience in this regard. She said that she had had that same expectation—that the experiential rewards of intimacy with God, once achieved, would never diminish as long as one remained faithful. But God removed those warm spiritual fuzzies as a means of growing her up into a mature woman—one who believes, even though she cannot see (or feel) the reality of God's presence and His promise. God taught her through her wilderness period of dry, unfruitful personal intimacy with Him, to believe in His faithfulness and His love even though all evidence was vanished. He taught her to see through a glass even more darkly, to be even more blessed in believing more, even as the seeing became less.

"But," I then protested, "how can I worship when there is no response? How can I pray or read Scripture when there is no evidence of Your presence or that You even care?"

Along came the writings of St. John of the Cross, a 16th century monk who wrote *The Dark Night of the Soul* while in prison, about how God works on the soul through sorrow and darkness. St. John taught me that it was a self-focus that had elicited my devotional protest. Without consciously understanding why, I had been refusing to remain in the discipline of devotion until such time as God complied with my unspoken demand that He participate in ways that were felt and rewarding.[3]

St. John of the Cross described me well when he wrote:

> The "dark night" is when those persons lose all the pleasure that they once experienced in their devotional life. This happens because God wants to purify them and move them on to greater heights. . .
>
> . . . But there will come a time when God will bid them to grow deeper. He will remove the previous consolation from the soul in order to teach it virtue and prevent it from developing vice. . .
>
> . . . They will beg God to take away their imperfections, but they do this only because they want to find inner peace and not for God's sake. They do not realize that if God were to take away their imperfections from them, they would probably become prouder and more presumptuous still. . .
>
> . . . Many . . . beginners will also begin to have spiritual *greed*, the second capital sin. They will become discontented with what God gives them because they do not experience the consolation they think they deserve. . . Their hearts grow attached to the feelings they get from their devotional life. They focus on the affect, and not on the substance of devotion. . . But those who are on the

right path will set their eyes on God and not on these outward things nor on their inner experiences. They will enter the dark night of the soul and find all of these things removed. They will have all the pleasure taken away so that the soul may be purified. For a soul will never grow until it is able to let go of the tight grasp it has on God. . . .

. . . When the soul begins to enjoy the benefits of the spiritual life and then has them taken away, it becomes angry and embittered. This is the sin of spiritual *wrath*, the fourth capital sin, . . .

. . . Their problem is that they lack the patience that waits for whatever God would give them and when God chooses to give them. They must learn spiritual meekness which will come about in the dark night. . . .

The fifth sin is spiritual *gluttony*. Many souls become addicted to the spiritual sweetness of the devotional life and strive to obtain more and more of it. . . . They will often try to subdue their flesh with great acts of submission . . . working on their own will, and thus, grow in vice rather than in virtue. . . . They do these things not for God but for themselves, and for this reason they will soon grow weary in them. . . . The problem is this: when they have received no pleasure for their devotions, they think they have not accomplished anything. This is a grave error, and it judges God unfairly. For the truth is that the feelings we receive from our devotional life are the least of its benefits. The invisible and unfelt grace of God is much greater, and it is beyond our comprehension. . . .

. . . Spiritual sloth happens when the pleasure is removed from the spiritual life. Such souls become weary with spiritual exercises because they do not yield any consolation, and thus, they abandon them. They become angry because they are called to do that which does not fit their needs. They begin to lose interest in God for they measure God by themselves and not themselves by God. . . . Let it suffice to say, then, that God perceives the imperfections within us, and because of His love for us, urges us to grow up. His love is not content to leave us in our weakness, and for this reason He takes us into a dark night. He weans us from all of the pleasures by giving us dry times and inward darkness. In doing so, He is able to take away all these vices and create virtues within us. Through the dark night, pride becomes humility, greed becomes simplicity, wrath becomes contentment, luxury becomes peace, gluttony becomes moderation, envy becomes joy, and sloth becomes strength. No soul will ever grow deep in the spiritual life unless God works passively in that soul by means of the dark night.[4]

And so, I realized that the arrested devotional life that I had been experiencing had been partially related to a world-view that viewed self as the focus of intimacy with God. Thus, without tangible affirmation from God that He was participating in our relationship, I adopted the tragic figure of an abandoned one, freezing in place and stamping my feet in protest. I did not go out and sin in protest, because in my sophisticated sinfulness, I wanted God to be the guilty party in this crisis![5]

Though even modern-day writers like Thomas Merton had warned: "We should not . . . judge the value of our meditation by 'how we feel,' "

I was much too blinded by immaturity and emotion to heed what he wrote.[6]

God is never closer than when He seems the most absent. We must believe that. We must move forward in serving Him, in declaring His praise, in telling our stories of His love and grace whether we receive immediate tangible reward or not. Why? Because He is worthy.

As we share the Christian faith with others, and as we lead them along the path of healing, we must tell them the whole story. We must provide a complete and accurate picture of what Christ has done, what He asks of us, and the consequences for our choices.

Keep telling your story. Tell it with words, with actions, and by your example. Remember He who is for you. Remember He who is with you, never to leave you nor forsake you. Remember the chain of authority in which you stand. Remember who your Father is. Stay in His presence. Let Him fight your battles for you.

Dark night or party time, decide now that you are going to teach and stand firm in the truth. Feast or famine, hell or high water, Jesus Christ remains the way, the truth and the life. He is all that matters. His calling, His life, His healing power, His riches in glory, His love and grace are yours now and forevermore!

As the Apostle Peter said:

> You are a chosen people, a royal priesthood, a holy nation, a people belonging to God, that you may declare the praises of Him who called you out of darkness into His wonderful light (1 Peter 2:9).

* * * *

Perhaps the reason that so many of us become spiritually disabled by the "dark nights" or "wilderness periods" of life is that we are unknowingly infected with "performance orientation." In my experience, "performance orientation" stands out as the single most debilitating challenge to the flow of Christian life and growth among modern believers. It is pervasive and insidious simply because it has been exalted as normal and right in our culture. In fact, it is rewarded as a virtue. Let us examine, then, its dangers and its antidote, so that we may serve our Lord more perfectly.

4

𝕷𝖎𝖛𝖎𝖓𝖌 𝕭𝖞 𝕲𝖗𝖆𝖈𝖊 𝕽𝖆𝖙𝖍𝖊𝖗 𝕿𝖍𝖆𝖓 𝕻𝖊𝖗𝖋𝖔𝖗𝖒𝖆𝖓𝖈𝖊 𝕺𝖗𝖎𝖊𝖓𝖙𝖆𝖙𝖎𝖔𝖓

The Problem Described

If there is one primary, gigantic problem with the way people think and operate, other than sin, it is performance orientation. Everyone has this problem to one degree or another, because it is native to human culture. It is regarded as a virtuous way of living that fits very nicely into the good ole American work ethic. From day one, we are programmed to operate in it: by the awarding of good grades for performing in school, plaques and trophies for excellent performance in athletics, raises and promotions for performing at work, etc. It is an integral part of the way things work in this world. It's everywhere, in everything! And to a certain extent, it is indeed helpful in motivating us to do our best.

The perversion, however, is that man carries that performance mode into his love relationships—trying to earn the love of God and his fellow man. So ensconced is this way of thinking that this "love that is not love" is now thoroughly, albeit unwittingly, confused with and tied to performance. No one is seriously trying to correct the matter, either.[1]

What's the matter with performing for God? The first problem is that we we will fail. Any attempt by man to meet God's standards of perfection is doomed to failure, simply because we are not perfect. Therefore, it can never work. That's a pretty good reason!

"There is no one righteous," the Bible says, "not even one; there is no one who understands,... no one who does good, not even one" (Romans 3:10b-12).

So if I try to prove myself worthy before God by being a good and faithful servant, I will eventually demonstrate just the opposite of what I'm trying to prove, and will end up feeling condemned. And that's the trap that performance orientation gets a person into. It is a snare designed by Satan himself to keep us so filled with feelings of defeat and condemnation that we will not go to God for fear of His wrath or because we don't want to face the disappointed look that we think will be in His eyes.

Romans 7:18 says: "I know that nothing good lives in me, that is, in my sinful nature. For I have the desire to do what is good, but I cannot carry it out."

Jesus said in John 15:5c: "apart from Me, you can do nothing." Nothing? Talk about being doomed to failure! Fortunately, Jesus added the "apart from Me" clause, which hints at a way to overcome the disaster of our fallen condition. He has devised a way whereby our efforts, when united with His, will produce results. For He says in Matthew 19:26: "With man this is impossible, but with God all things are possible." In fact, He likes to lead us into impossible situations so that we will all the more quickly learn the necessity of partnering with Him in our day to day lives.

A second problem with performing for God's love is that it creates a form of religion that Jesus rejects—a worldly version of loving and serving God. Since the world has been given over by God to foolishness (1 Corinthians 1:18-31), this is a significant problem—one that the world itself, in its foolishness, is blind to.

Christian evangelist Mario Murillo has given the best definition of this kind of religion that I have ever heard. He said, "Religion is a picture of God painted by the devil." It's the way the world does things. And the world's value system is corrupt. In fact, the way the world does things is antithetical to everything about Christ and God and the Kingdom of God. It's totally opposed to it. It's anti-Christ. According to Dudley Hall, performing for God is a problem of "hardening of the oughteries," i.e., "I oughta do this, I oughta do that." However, it wasn't service for which we were created, which is what a performance oriented person thinks. It was for fellowship with Him. Hall writes:

> You don't have to prove you are somebody by what you do. God alone gives you your identity and that's settled, regardless of what you do. . . Your worthiness is not dependent upon how well you perform.[2]

Rick Joyner has also written a tremendous book that addresses the fundamental choice that man faces between living a life of independence from God (the performer's route) and living a life out of a relationship with God (provided by grace). He writes:

> Satan did not tempt Eve with the fruit of the Tree of Knowledge just because of the Lord's prohibition. He tempted her with it because the source of his power was rooted in that tree. Furthermore, the Lord did not implement this restriction just to test Adam and Eve; He prohibited the eating of its fruit because He knew it was poison. When He instructed Adam not to eat from the Tree of Knowledge, He did not say "If you eat from that tree I'm going to kill you" but "On the day that you eat from it you will die." It was not *just* man's disobedience that brought death to the world; it was the fruit from this tree.
>
> The Tree of Knowledge of Good and Evil is a powerful Biblical model of the Law. As the Apostle Paul declared: "The power of sin is the law" (1 Corinthians 15:56). This is because it is through the Law that we derive our knowledge of good and evil. . . . The knowledge of good and evil kills us by distracting us from the One

who is the source of life: the Tree of Life—Jesus. The Tree of Knowledge causes us to focus our attention upon ourselves. Sin is empowered by the law; not just because the evil is revealed, but the good as well. It drives us either to corruption or self-righteousness, both of which lead to death.[3]

Hall agrees, saying:

The real prisoners in life are those whose focus is on themselves. . . .

. . . Self-righteousness shows itself in a search for one's own identity apart from relationship. Identity is sought in performance, position, and success.[4]

In the world we're expected to earn our keep—to earn what we receive. In the world, nothing is free. And if something is offered "for free," we're suspicious of it, right? If I were to walk up to you and hand you a $100 bill, you'd be suspicious of me, wouldn't you? You'd want to know what my angle was—what I was after. You'd wait a bit to see if the other shoe was going to drop. In fact, it would be a most uncomfortable moment for you, because as much as you'd want the money, you'd want to avoid being played a fool.

Why would your mind automatically begin questioning my motives? *Because you didn't earn it.* There'd be no reason for me to give you a $100 bill. It would make no sense outside of there being some catch.

Let's look at it from another angle. Let's say we were best of friends, and you decided to express your love for me by fixing me a fancy dinner, with everything in it that I loved. You cooked and slaved all day to prepare the feast. With a heart bursting with love, you brought out the finest china and silver, and decorated the table with a homemade centerpiece. Then we ate this marvelous, sumptuous meal, and upon finishing, I stood up, handed you a $20 bill, said "Thanks," and walked out the door.

What would you think about that? You'd be hurt, wouldn't you? You'd be insulted. You didn't do that for my money. How dare I think that you did that for money! It would hurt you deeply. You were trying to express your unconditional love for me, and I responded by trying to pay you for it. To your way of thinking, I couldn't give you a $20 or even a $1,000 bill and earn what you had just done for me. That's what you'd be feeling in your heart.

While we might not take it to that extreme, it's very difficult for us to accept something that we didn't earn. When we're given things for free, we feel like we have to pay the person back, "return the favor," or in some way do something to even out the obligations in the relationship. We are so steeped in the performance mode that the reception of a free gift instantly makes us feel beholden to the giver.

A secondary issue is that we are so afraid of commitment that a free gift makes us feel as though an obligation of commitment or concomitant generosity has been thrust upon us, and we don't like that. It destroys our little fantasy world of autonomous control and independence.

In a similar fashion, when we're trying to earn God's love and acceptance by performing for Him, we are in a very real sense trying to pay Him back for the Cross. We're uncomfortable with the idea that we didn't do anything to earn God's forgiveness. And the more aware we are of how sinful we are, the more uncomfortable we get, because it causes us to realize all the more that we don't deserve what God is freely offering. Pride and selfishness are very much caught up in performance orientation.

Does not the Scripture say that "the message of the Cross is foolishness to those who are perishing" (1 Corinthians 1:18)?

Even some who initially accept Christ's free gift of salvation turn around and try to pay Him back with good works. In other words, their motivation for obeying and serving Him is not love so much as it is an attempt to return the favor or pay the debt that they feel they've incurred by accepting His offer of salvation.

Others launch off on a campaign to prove themselves worthy, out of fear that God's love is conditional and thus must be fed. In a sense, it's as if they're traveling back 2000 years to the Cross, walking up to Jesus and trying to slip Him a $20. Oh, how we must grieve the heart of God sometimes!

What we are doing when we try to perform for God's love is really no different than trying to slip Him a $20. We're trying to tip Him, really, for dying on the Cross for us. His love is priceless, so any amount, any service we would try to offer as a repayment is an insult and a grievous wound to His heart. I believe that it wounds the heart of God just as deeply as it would have wounded the heart of my friend if I had handed him or her a $20 for making that sumptuous meal for me. We don't realize how much we wound God's heart, yet He is so humble and so loving that He just takes it and continues to pour out His love on us.

So it is extremely important that we examine our hearts, with God's help, to see whether our so-called love and service for God is performance-based or love-based. We can never pay Him back for the blood of His Son. All such efforts are doomed to failure.

Another problem with performing for God's love is that it is tantamount to living by sight rather than by faith. It's unbelief. The assurance we need that He loves us will never come from any performance of righteousness on our part. It will only come as we gaze with the eyes of faith on the Cross, which is God's awesome demonstration of His love for mankind.

The world does things by sight and is thus caught in the unforgiving wheel of performance and reward—a system that has no provision for failure. The TV program on NBC aptly declares the world's opinion of those who fail: "You are the weakest link! Goodbye!"

God has asked us to be "certain of what we do not see" (Hebrews 11:1).

The world bases reality on what it feels, thinks, and experiences. But the Kingdom of God is very different. It calls on us to look through a glass darkly—to take obedient actions without knowing why or what the outcome will be, but only that the God who asks is trustworthy. True faith is demonstrated in action.

It is hard to believe in unlimited, unconditional, unpaid for, unsolicited love and forgiveness. It's just very difficult to believe in that. After all, if I were God, I wouldn't do it that way. If I were God and had created someone like me, I'd have snuffed him out of existence long ago. Since I'm prone to cast God in my image, that makes it truly inconceivable that He could still love me in the face of my ongoing failure to love Him. And my perfectionism only exacerbates the problem.

It's also difficult for many of us to believe that Jesus' death on the Cross cancels sin, so we tend to find ways to atone for it ourselves. We bathe in thoughts and feelings of condemnation as though we were in some way helping to balance the scales of justice. Refusing to take ourselves off the hook doesn't appear to be the affront to God that it really is since it plays so nicely into the world's version of religion. Oh, we'll confess our sins alright, but many of us will refuse to truly embrace the forgiveness that God offers.

Mike Bickle has often said that God "offends the mind to reveal the heart." It's such a true statement. Did Jesus really need to put mud on that man's eyes to heal his blindness (John 9:6-7)? Of course not. He had the power to raise people from the dead! He was offending the minds of those witnessing the event, so as to reveal what was in their heart.

Another time, Jesus told His followers that they had to eat His flesh and drink His blood, and the Bible says that many who were following Him left Him and never returned (John 6:48-66). Why did He say that? He lost half [*sic*] of His people! The passage explains it by noting: "Jesus had known from the beginning which of them did not believe" (v 64b). He was, it seems, getting rid of the hangers-on—pruning away those who weren't truly behind Him—offending the mind to reveal the heart.

God is concerned about what we *really* believe. He's not moved by empty words. He's not fooled by pretense and show. He responds to what is truly in the heart.[5] And if something untrue is going on in our heart, He will offend our mind so that we can see our self-deception and be challenged to change. That's what He's doing to the world with His offer of unconditional grace, with His dying on the Cross. He's offending the spirit of performance, independence, and self-righteousness with an offer built on grace, dependence, and His singular righteousness. And many hearts are turning away, never to return again, because the offer requires the surrender of pride and self-sufficiency.

Many of us live by faith in what the world tells us and shows us. Reality for us is what we've experienced, rather than what God says is true. We live and move according to the illusions of eye, ear, mind, and heart that have been concocted by the evil one to lead men astray from the path of eternal life. And so, by all appearances, evil is in control, triumphing over good, far more powerful than good. It seems as if God, if He really is all-powerful, doesn't really care about us. When we're living by what we see and by what we feel, we sometimes give in to such appearances and excuse ourselves from obedience to our imagined, absent Father. We take on the identity of "victim" so as to justify our decision to yield to worldliness and temptation.

The world teaches us that the purpose of life is realized through position, power, prestige, and material goods. This lie has found its way into the very heart of Christendom. The worship of power, position, prestige, and materialism is rampant in the Body of Christ. And the core of the problem is our performance orientation. We do not know how to live in humble response to grace.

About all of this, God says, "Do not conform any longer to the pattern of this world, but be transformed by the renewing of your mind" (Romans 12:2a). "May I never boast except in the Cross of our Lord Jesus Christ, through which the world has been crucified to me, and I to the world" (Galatians 6:14). "Do not love the world, or anything in the world [referring to the world's system]. If anyone loves the world, the love of the Father is not in him" (1 John 2:15).

The Bible also talks about "reckoning" ourselves dead to sin (Romans 6:11a) and considering ourselves "aliens and strangers in the world" (1 Peter 2:11a). In fact, in that same verse in Peter, a clear connection is made between considering ourselves aliens and strangers to the world and the ability to abstain from sinful desires. I have discovered that there are countless such oblique connections between God's commands and seemingly unrelated strongholds of sin.

One day when I was in prayer, the Lord asked me to stop all lying. I had been a masterful liar before giving my life to Christ and had already given up all but the little "lies of convenience" that we use from time to time—lies that make life smoother; such as when mom comes home from the beauty parlor and asks, "How do you like my hair?" and you just tell her it's wonderful, no matter how bad it looks—simple lies to make life easier and that avoid unnecessary offense. But God was very clear—I was to stop *all* lying. I was to be a man of truth.

So I made the commitment and, to my amazement, discovered that every time I came upon one of those uncomfortable situations where "lies of convenience" had been so helpful, God always gave me something really wise to say that was true, but that also protected the feelings of the other person.

But what surprised me even more was to see how directly connected my lying had been to a struggle that I had with sexual temptation. In order to maintain my immoral lifestyle, I had to hide my activities under a shroud of lies and secrecy. When God led me into a commitment to truth, the enabling foundation for that sin was removed, and I had to commit also to a life of sexual purity. When the lies went, so did the power of a firmly entrenched and seemingly unconnected stronghold of sin. Isn't God good![6]

In the same way, though a performance orientation seems so abstracted from and unconnected to the more pressing issues of sin, it is a key foundation for the strongholds of most sin. Why? Because performance orientation is a foundational departure from God's ways. It is a direct attack against the Cross, which is the power source for holiness. It is a gateway sin, or a key root of sin that feeds most of the sins that man commits. It is what generates the need or desire to sin, the justification for sin, the frustration that poisons our faith in the goodness and promises of God. It is that insidious! When the habit of performing for God's love and acceptance is eradicated, like knocking over the first in a line of dominoes, numerous other sins begin to falter as well. Their fuel source has been cut off and they begin to weaken and die.

One final observation about the error of performing for God's love: if you are performing for Him, you are not having an intimate relationship with Him. The two are diametrically opposed to each other and thus cannot go on at the same time. Putting it another way: if you are not abiding in the Vine and receiving His life-giving love and affirmation, you are probably striving to earn the same. If you are not experiencing His affirming, healing presence on a regular basis, you are probably walking in performance orientation. Why? To paraphrase Augustine, our hearts are restless until they find themselves in Him. If we can't find Him one way, we will try to win Him the other way.

The result of living that way is massive insecurity. Just look at the world. They're running here and running there, killing themselves with work, striving for this, trying to achieve that, experiencing this, encountering that, finding themselves, losing themselves, toning up, dialing down, going within, letting it all out, and self-helping themselves to death! They're trying to find peace by focusing on self, trying to find God by focusing on their own reason, and trying to find love by proving themselves worthy.

Some insist on performing for God because they are afraid of intimacy. The many good works that they do keep them sufficiently busy to create an excuse for not taking the time to develop an interior life with Him. A large portion of the American church is just so occupied. We are frantically running about serving God because deep inside we are afraid of getting too close to Him, afraid that He will reject us, and trying to waylay such a judgment by building up a war chest of worthiness through holy deeds. We refuse to believe that Christ has made a way through our unworthiness, so that we can feel safe and at peace in the arms of the Father.

Satan has a field day with such folk. He knows that the deepest desire of God's heart is to have an intimate relationship with His people, so he robs God of that pleasure by instilling this performance diversion in the thinking of His people. In fact, Satan will help get someone to the mission field if it will keep them so busy, so steeped in trying to earn God's favor, that they never really develop a love relationship with Him.

Many simply prefer the world to God. They are sufficiently talented and, thus, sufficiently rewarded by the world system for their admirable performance, and so God never seems necessary. The world provides them with the psychological highs that they need in order to feel affirmed, loved, and important. Over time, they devise sophisticated, psychological justifications for the hollow and temporary nature of the world's version of love and affirmation. Though it is sad that it is that way, they draw comfort by saying things to themselves like: "That's all there is after all, and I have been fortunate to have experienced more of life's blessings than most;" or "There is no God anyway, and I can't expect to have had better than what I've had;" or "Life is a matter of just making the best of it, and I'm satisfied that I've done just that."

Instead of sentiments like those that serve to mask their selfish choices in life, they should acknowledge their emptiness, take a running leap into the Father's arms, and exclaim, "Worthy or not, here I come!" In truth, that's exactly what God wants them to do.

How to Fix It

Although the possible causes and reasons for being performance oriented are plethoric, and the damage wrought by it is legion, the cure is singular. The cure is not a method or a model. It is the grace that comes through Jesus Christ (John 1:14,17). Let's take a look at the Scripture that lays it out most clearly—Titus 2:11-14:

> . . . the grace of God that brings salvation has appeared to all men. It teaches us to say "No" to ungodliness and worldly passions, and to live self-controlled, upright and godly lives in this present age, while we wait for the blessed hope— the glorious appearing of our great God and Savior, Jesus Christ, who gave Himself for us to redeem us from all wickedness and to purify for Himself a people that are His very own, eager to do what is good.

Verse 11 tells us that "grace has appeared to all men." It doesn't discriminate. It has appeared to all men, and it brought salvation. Grace saves, it forgives, and it is offered to everyone. So, if you consider yourself a special case outside of the grace of God—you're wrong. The grace of God does not discriminate. It reaches to the deepest, darkest places of the globe and rescues anyone who wants to be rescued.

Verse 12 tells us that grace "teaches us to say 'No' to ungodliness and worldly passions." How does being given the grace of forgiveness when I sin persuade me not to sin? I should think it would do just the opposite. In Romans 6:1-2a, Paul broached that very question. "What shall we say, then? Shall we go on sinning so that grace may increase?" The reply: "Megenoito" (one of the strongest words in the Greek)—i.e., "Never!" "God forbid" is another way of interpreting the word that he used.

Worldly logic might suggest that if I'm going to get forgiven every time

I sin, then why not just sin all the time? The person saying such a thing doesn't love God, doesn't know Him very well. And so, love for God is what makes the difference in how one might respond to grace.

Titus 3:4-5a reveals that "when the kindness and love of God our Savior appeared, He saved us, not because of the righteous things we had done, but because of His mercy." And so, grace teaches us to say "No" to ungodliness first of all by removing the burden to perform righteousness. In other words, I don't have to perform righteousness in order to be loved by God. That removes an incredible burden from my shoulders—a burden that I was incapable of carrying anyway.

I don't have to generate holiness in order for God to love or accept me. He has done that for me. God comes into my life and performs righteousness for me. It is Christ in me performing the righteousness, provided I yield to Him to do so—as one Scripture said, provided I "hunger and thirst for righteousness" (Matthew 5:6).

It is very clear in Scripture that the battles that God leads us into are ones that He intends to fight for us, if we will ask Him to do so. Look at the example of the battle of Jericho (Joshua 6) or the battle between David and Goliath (1 Samuel 17:47). Behind the simple actions that He asked His people to perform, God was fighting the battle for them. So the Scripture says, "the battle is the Lord's." Look also at Jehoshaphat's fight against Moab and Ammon, when God told him to put the praise and worship team in front of the army as they went out to fight (2 Chronicles 20:15). It seemed like a ridiculous order. All the better to demonstrate that the battle was the Lord's. God honored their obedience and destroyed the enemy for them.

Similarly, when I am faced with fighting a battle with temptation or some other trial and, knowing my weakness, I refuse to fight the battle myself and instead turn to God, saying, "Father, send Your power to destroy this temptation, to destroy this evil power for me," He honors my "declaration of dependence" and destroys the enemy for me as soon as its redemptive purpose is completed. That's the plan. That's how it's supposed to work. "I no longer live, but Christ lives in me" (Galatians 2:20a).

Once we are in Christ, God's love and acceptance of us will never again be based on our behavior. We have been made a member of Christ's body, so love and acceptance are guaranteed. God accepts us because we have united ourselves with His Son.

If you are trapped in performance thinking, that idea is likely to be most unwelcome. For you, the motivation to do good has been an assumed need to earn God's love and acceptance. If that reason is taken away, there is nothing left to motivate you to do good.

The fact remains: Your acceptance by God is based on Christ's work for you, not your own righteousness. That means that even if I went out tonight and committed adultery, God's love for me would not waiver. His acceptance of me would not change. I would certainly have to face consequences for my sinful actions, some of which might be quite serious. But God's love would not change because it is not, nor has it ever been, based on my performance. It has been based on the redemptive actions of His Son. This eliminates the power of condemnation, which is Satan's greatest trick, and it is why the Bible says categorically that there is "no condemnation for those who are in Christ Jesus" (Romans 8:1).

All you need to do after failing God is return back again to His arms for cleansing and forgiveness. Satan is trying to keep you from running back into God's arms by making you think that God doesn't like you anymore, that God doesn't approve of you anymore, that God wants you to go into a corner and think about what you've done before He'll consider your pleas for mercy. Satan is trying to give you this wrong image of God because he knows that if you return to the Father's loving arms, God's love and grace will persuade you even more to be faithful the next time you are tempted.

The Apostle Paul wrote: ". . . the grace of God . . . teaches us to say 'No' to ungodliness . . . to live . . . godly lives in this present age, . . . , eager to do what is good" (Titus 2:11-14). It is in being provided a safe haven from condemnation—the very arms of God—that we become persuaded to choose righteousness over evil. Grace works slowly, but it works powerfully to bring about that transformation of the heart, so that we develop a desire to obey God in response to His unconditional grace, love, and favor. The only defense against grace that Satan has are the lies that he tells us so that we won't believe in such love and grace. For if we believe that God loves us no matter what, and run to His arms even when we've failed Him, Satan has lost us. God's arms changes hearts.

The truth is, God is the father in the story of the prodigal son (Luke 15:11-32), who stands with loving arms outstretched, at the start, the middle, and the end of your sin and rebellion, saying: "Just come back to Me." And He'll stand there through ten thousand sins if He has to, saying the same thing: "Just come back to Me. I only want to embrace you."

One day, that grace will finally have its way in you. You'll realize that God is not someone you have to protect yourself from. He is not the adversary. His commandments are not designed to restrict or control you, but rather, to protect and guide you to the highest order of fulfillment possible. He is the only One who loves you perfectly and completely.

Grace takes longer to work than law. But grace is permanent. It doesn't just keep the behavior in tow. It transforms the heart, so that the person goes from following God because they're supposed to, to following God because they want to, fully and completely, from their heart. God does not create saplings. He creates oak trees, and oak trees take a while to grow. But when they grow, they are not so easily knocked down by hurricanes. That's the genius of God's way.

The ingenuity of God is how He uses what seems foolish—letting people get away with sin—to convince them not to sin. Grace is what God uses to transform the rebellion of our hearts, making us humbly obedient.

In the Book of Ezekiel (Ezekiel 36:24-27) and the Book of Jeremiah (Jeremiah 31:33), God said He was going to write His law on our hearts. What does that mean? It means that He is going to create in us a pure and natural desire to keep the law. And He uses grace to do it.

Yes, He knows that we will take advantage of His grace—we all will. But He knows that, in the long run, grace will have its effectual work in our hearts. Mercy will triumph over judgment (James 2:13).

Don't mistake this message as being one of "cheap grace," however. Christ paid a heavy price for grace. He died a horrible death for it. This is not cheap grace by any stretch of the imagination. This is very, very expensive and priceless grace.

Neither is it strewn about cavalierly by God. It is handed only to those who understand the value of it and who want it with all of their heart. If you want it with all of your heart, if you want your heart transformed supernaturally from the inside out so that the law becomes a delight to you, truly a delight to you, then this chapter was commissioned by the Lord for your sake. Receive His Son, Jesus, as your Lord and your Savior. Believe in His unconditional offer of pardon and grace for your sins, and begin the transformation this very day. Say to God, "Worthy or not, here I come!"

The Great Escape

For those of you who have already given your life to God but who now realize that you are seriously trapped in performance orientation, and want out, you may be wondering what you can do to extricate yourself from such a hellish bondage. Just a few thoughts.

Your first instinct will be to try to perform your way out, since that has been your natural *modus operandi*. Consequently, you must set a close watch on your mind and heart for any such approach. It's not that there aren't things that you should do. Rather, it is the interior motivation for doing them that becomes the linchpin. Ask the Holy Spirit to "red flag" any actions that spring from a "works righteousness" mode.

In truth, the Holy Spirit is really the One who will guide you in how to make the change. Simply and repeatedly go before Him and say, "God, this is what I want, and I will do whatever it takes to be conformed to Your image." Go before Him with persistence, fervor, and passion until He blesses you with the transformation you seek (cf. Gen 32:26).

Practice believing the great and precious promises of Scripture—not just intellectually, but from your heart. As it suggests in Romans 6:11, "Reckon yourself dead to sin and alive to Jesus Christ."[7] Consider as fact the statement in Galatians 2:20: "I have been crucified with Christ, and I no longer live, but Christ lives in me. The life I live in the body, I live by faith in the Son of God, who loved me and gave Himself for me."

Every time you catch yourself performing for God—trying to earn His favor—simply stop what you're doing and say, "Wait. I'm not going to do it this way. I am loved by God regardless of my behavior. I will love Him and serve Him for that reason and that reason alone!" You'll probably have to do this a thousand times a day for a while until it starts becoming a natural way of thinking.[8] This is not an easy turn-around. It takes significant time and attention. It takes complete dependence on God working in you to bring it about, but it is worth every second that you put into it.

The Bible suggests that we need to forcefully take the Kingdom of God (Luke 16:16), yet that we are to rejoice in our weakness so that the power of God may rest on us (2 Corinthians 12:9-10). So in a seeming paradox, we are to aggressively take ground for the Kingdom by resting in God's power to do it through us. This is very different from a straightforward "performance" model.

Consider again Rick Joyner's description of the two trees in the garden. The Tree of Life represents the choice of relationship with God, where we choose to be dependent on His wisdom and direction at all times, like Jesus was. Jesus never did anything until He heard it from the Father or saw the Father doing it.[9] That choice to live in total dependence on God's direction is the way of relationship and intimacy. The Tree of the Knowledge of Good and Evil that Adam and Eve ate from represents independence from God, self-effort, and self-righteousness. They chose to make their own way—to use their own wisdom.

We need to deliberately and habitually discipline ourselves to choose the right tree each time we are faced with an impulse to do the right thing. In short, we need to learn how to guard our heart and mind with God's peace, God's rest (Philippians 4:6-9). Where do you get that peace? It comes from being in His presence. We also need to deliberately and aggressively set our mind on things above and then put into practice what we hear from God. We know this, but need to be regularly exhorted and reminded to put it into practice on a daily basis.

Another important matter that needs to be addressed is how to live by faith rather than feelings. Our culture is steeped in the practice of living by feelings. It began to take hold as the predominant model for Americans in the 1960's when eastern philosophers began infiltrating institutions of higher learning with their amoral brand of mysticism at the same time that young people were throwing off the restraints of institutional and parental authority. "If it feels good, do it" was a common mantra of the time. We were taught to go with our feelings, that they accurately reflected a truth that was relative and equally valid to any other, and that to do otherwise was unhealthy, unnatural, and hypocritical.

Americans today have been raised with these relativistic assumptions and are no longer consciously aware of how entrenched this philosophy has become. Even Christians uncritically allow thoughts and feelings that emerge from their personal, subjective experience to overrule the fixed source of objective truth found in Scripture.

One day I was lecturing and a lady abruptly stood up and marched out of the room. I kept on teaching, but began pondering why she had left. Clearly, I had offended her, I thought, but I could not recall what it was that I could have said that would have sent her out the door. Then I thought to myself, "David, you are so insensitive, you don't even know what you said that was so insensitive. You are a menace! Get out of the pulpit before you destroy someone's life. You don't belong in the ministry." On and on I went with my self-remonstrations. Within thirty seconds I had talked myself out of the ministry. Five minutes later, the woman returned to her seat. She had gone to the bathroom.

Let's examine what had happened. When the lady abruptly left, my thoughts and feelings began interpreting the event to my heart and mind— and they were lying to me. I didn't even consider the fact that they might be lying to me. I simply believed them and responded to what they were telling me. At that point in my life, I had no mental framework for identifying and correcting thoughts and feelings that were misleading. Why didn't I have such a framework? Because the philosophy of this age—that personal thoughts and feelings are reliable sources of truth—was so ingrained in me that I was blithely unaware of the need for such a framework.

To combat this state of affairs, we need to immerse ourselves in the presence of God and allow Him to correct our thinking. We need to fix our thoughts and our eyes on Jesus (Hebrews 3:1; 12:2). We need to let the Word of Christ dwell in us richly (Colossians 3:16). We need to become partners in truth with God and partakers of truth from God. These practical and invaluable disciplines found in Scripture must become a lifestyle for us so that God can turn our thinking around.

Ann Ortland once wrote that it's the *look* to Jesus that saves you, but it's the *gaze* upon Jesus that sanctifies you.[10] *Keeping* your focus on Him as a practical, daily discipline is the key. It is *fixing* your eyes on Him as a permanent way of life that enables the sanctification process to work and right thinking and acting to emerge. This is the catalyst that enables, motivates, and empowers grace.

We need to meditate on the truth and discipline ourselves to turn to God in weakness and dependence at the first sign of temptation, confident in His power to handle the temptation for us. We need to enter into a *lifestyle* of worship, rather than only using it as a means to please our senses or to get what we want from God.[11]

Let me emphasize once again how very important this problem with performance orientation is. Our culture is steeped in the worship of self, with an attached "performance paradigm" by which we glorify certain selves over others. Entire magazines, television shows, and academic curriculums are based on this worship. It even underlies much of our religious expression. It is the only accepted form of public worship that is not restricted.

One consequence of this religious system is found in how self-centered man responds to the divine message. The message of "Repent!" is an affront![12] The idea of love and acceptance no matter what has been achieved is an insult to pride.

For those in our culture who have failed to function in the performance mode, (e.g., addicts, criminals, etc.), the message of "Repent!" only pours gasoline on the burning coals of their internalized self-hatred because they see success, favor, and being lovable only in terms of achieving standards that they know they can never meet. Without the knowledge of God's grace, they are simply driven deeper and deeper into self-hatred (a derivative form of self-centeredness).

One mistake that the modern church often makes is in delivering the "Repent!" part of Jesus' message without first laying down the grace message. We tell people how wretched they are, (a message that worked wonderfully in revivals of previous centuries), without discerning the times—without taking into account how that singular message will be taken by people who are steeped in worship and/or hatred of themselves.

Receiving and living from grace circumvents this system of roadblocks to faith that the evil one has erected. It deflects the requirements of performance and the penalties of failure onto the only One who can meet such requirements—the divine Son of God. It frees us from self-involvement so that we can live for higher reasons, and in doing so creates a conduit (the connection between Christ and His Church) through which God communicates His own Being, including His power to live a holy life, to those who will yield their lives to such an end.

God has called us to be ministers of this gospel. Considering the dynamics of this present world system, grace needs to be front and center in our lives and in our ministry. It is not enough to proclaim man a sinner. We must also offer him God's grace, so that when he falls, it will be into God's arms rather than condemnation. And as we have already seen, over the long-term, rather than causing him to want to sin even more, God's grace will actually persuade him to sin even less.

Dudley Hall says, "Becoming what you were meant to be is not something you can do on your own. It only happens as we live in relationship with the Father."[13]

As people whom God has called to minister to others, we must ask ourselves, "Do I understand and live in grace?" because we will never be able to communicate grace until we have learned to live from it ourselves.

Here's a test. When someone looks into your eyes and confesses a sin that seems utterly detestable or horrible to you, what is the look in your eyes that they see? Is it love and compassion? Is it complete acceptance of them as persons in spite of their grievous actions?

They must see the eyes of a person who fully believes that if it wasn't for the grace of God, they might have done the same thing. And when they see humility, when they see unconditional love and compassion in response to the confession of their deepest and darkest sin, they will be seeing Jesus, and their hearts will be won back to Him in that moment. And they will listen and receive ministry and find the transformation that they've been hoping for.[14]

> [It is] the grace of God that . . . teaches us to say "No" to ungodliness and worldly passions, and to live self-controlled, upright and godly lives in this present age, . . . eager to do what is good. (Titus 2:11-12, 14c)

*   *   *   *

There are many subtle ways, like the temptation to live under the law of performance, that Satan uses to derail Christians from bearing fruit that will last into eternity. Let's take a look at ten of his best schemes—rackets that are so devious that we usually engage in them without even being aware that we are operating at serious levels of sin. If we are prepared in advance for such tricks, we will be better able to overcome them, with God's help.

5

Satan's Greatest Hits

S atan is a mobster—a hit man—and he wants nothing more fervently than to rub you out. He's a murderer, a liar, a gangster, and he's got a contract out on your life. His final days as god of this world system are spent maniacally battling the angels of God for the souls of men. And if he can't have your soul, he'll settle for desecrating your call as an ambassador of the Kingdom of God.

As children of light, we have no business even dabbling in Satan's kingdom. We have no business sleeping with the enemy in compromise and sin. Everything he lures us with is a lie. It's darkness. It's cursed. Church of the living God, we've got to wake up and declare, "No more! My life of compromise is over. I am going to serve the Lord and walk in His ways and bring glory to His name with every breath that is in me! I am through playing games with evil. I am going to develop an intimate relationship with my Father in heaven and live in humble dependence on Him to keep me from falling and to walk in His ways. May God Almighty, this day, write across my forehead, 'Holy unto the Lord' and may it never be erased again!"

It is dangerous to focus on Satan too much. However, the Bible clearly teaches that we should be aware of the ways in which he operates. The Apostle Paul indicated in his second letter to the Corinthians (2 Corinthians 10b-11) that they were not to be unaware of Satan's schemes, so that the devil could not outwit them. Again, in Ephesians 6:11 Paul refers to "standing against the devil's schemes". That, of course, presumes one knows what his schemes are!

Satan's most effective devices, by far, are those that operate unseen in people's lives. They are subtle schemes, that take on the appearance of being natural, normal, unavoidable, and sometimes godly. They're effective because they are so integrated into the norms of our culture that they don't appear to be contrary to the ways of God. Consequently, we allow them to remain a part of our lives. Long term, these are the sins that provide a foundation for more obvious acts of rebellion.

Performance Orientation

Let's briefly look again at this very effective trick of the enemy—this time from the perspective of a satanic strategy that is designed to keep us enmeshed in efforts that lead to self-righteousness; efforts that also divert us from the plan of God to keep us holy through the power of His grace and His indwelling presence. Face it—due to our fallen condition, even if it were possible for us to commit a pure and holy act through our own efforts, we would become proud as a result of our achievement. Since Christ alone is going to receive all glory and honor and praise, it must necessarily be that in some ingenious divine plan, God desires to work His own righteous life through us and thus make what is impossible with man, possible with God. Human self-righteousness interferes with that plan.

Our entire culture is steeped in the pursuit of approval, worth, and value via performance. It is what motivates most of the great achievements of mankind, thereby deceiving us into honoring it and teaching it to our children. At a recent Renovarè conference, author Richard Foster said: "Even in the church, we preach grace but live in legalism and performance."

Performance orientation manifests itself at the level of motivations. So ask yourself, "What motivates me to obey God, to seek Him, to do good works?" If you respond with words like, "I'm supposed to", "I ought to", "I should", odds are you are living out of a sense of obligation toward God, a need to pay Him back for saving you, or out of a compulsion to buy His love or approval. Such tasks are doomed to fail. And what is worse, they call into question the sufficiency of Christ's sacrifice in obtaining forever the love and acceptance of God for those who have received His Son as Lord and Savior.

Grace puts things in an entirely different light. In grace, I serve, I obey, I do for God, purely and simply because I love Him and for no other reason. In grace, I operate from a place of already being approved, already being forgiven, past, present, and future. In that place, I follow Him because I *want to* rather than because I am *supposed to*.

Again, Titus 2:11-14 is the key text in this matter. Paul reminds us that *grace* is what teaches us to say "No" to ungodliness and worldly passions, and *grace* teaches us to live self-controlled, upright, and godly in this present age, eager to do what is good! When I understand that my acceptance by God is no longer dependent on my performance, and when I experience the continual application of God's love and grace in the midst of my periodic unfaithfulness, my stony heart of rebellion dissolves, and I begin following the Lord not out of obligation, but out of desire. His grace transforms my heart into one that is yielded and loving. In grace, the prophecies of Jeremiah 31:33 and Ezekiel 36:25-28 are fulfilled—God gives me a new heart, one with His law written into it. With this new heart, the love of God's law comes "factory installed", and I obey it out of natural desire.

When we truly believe that Christ has forever earned love and acceptance from the Father for us, when we accept and receive His continual
flow of forgiveness even for our most evil sins, then we find freedom and
peace in letting go of performance. We serve Him because our hearts have
been transformed by His awesome grace and love. It is then that one of
Satan's most clever schemes is thwarted.

Condemnation

Another of Satan's greatest "hits" is condemnation. This one is also insidious because it takes on an appearance of being normal, even righteous.
People who suffer from chronic feelings of low self-worth are suckers for it.
When they fail God, they try to atone for their sin by embracing condemnation, as if it were well deserved punishment sent from heaven. Satan
whispers into their minds thoughts like, "Failed God again! You call yourself a Christian! You're just a hypocrite, a failure, never going to do anything right. This thing is just too powerful for you. It's your cross to bear,"
and on and on and on. Being unaware of Satan's schemes, they mistakenly
embrace such thoughts as truthful revelations from their own mind and
heart.

What is the sin here? It is believing your thoughts and feelings and/or
the voice of the enemy when God has said something different. In Romans
8:1-2, God unambiguously proclaims that there is now *no condemnation* for
those who are in Christ Jesus. Are you going to believe your thoughts and
feelings, or are you going to believe God?

As I have previously noted, a deceptive philosophy was adopted in the
1960's by a generation of people, one that has since become invisibly
entrenched in the belief system of our entire culture. It suggests that truth
is found in what you feel and experience. It further suggests that to operate
contrary to one's thoughts and feelings is to be hypocritical, dishonest, or
unnatural. The problem with this philosophy is that it presumes that
thoughts and feelings are the source of truth, that they are accurate barom-
eters of reality—an idea which is patently false. Thoughts and feelings continually lie to us and mislead us. It may be a convenient philosophy for
those who choose to believe that they are God, or for those who choose to
live as if they were, but it is illogical and contrary to reality. God is the only
reliable source of truth. With our finite minds and limited experience, we
cannot know anything with certainty unless it has been revealed to us by
the One who is omniscient. That is why the Bible is so very important. It is
our ground of truth, sent from God. All thoughts and feelings are subject to
its revelation.

Satan's plot to get us to embrace condemnation, even when it contradicts
God's Word, is a long and winding road. He sets us up by first getting us
to repeatedly compromise in seemingly minor areas (gossiping, lying,

cheating, holding on to unresolved anger, etc). At this stage, he's tilling the ground, getting us to carelessly spend our spiritual currency on pottage and thereby forsake that intimate place in God from which the Lord keeps us from falling. Then Satan sends the big temptation—the one he knows carries a lot of emotional investment in how we perceive ourselves and our value to God. Having no ground left to stand on by that point, we become an easy victim. Then, after we succumb to the "big temptation," Satan persuades us to embrace feelings of guilt, shame, and condemnation. What he's really tempting us with is the sin of unbelief. If we take the bait, then hopelessness, frustration, and anger sets in, followed by more temptations and more falls.

Do you know what the greater sin is in this vicious cycle? It is believing the lie that God accepts us based on our performance, rather than on the finished work of Christ on our behalf, and the compounding of that sin by embracing the condemnation that God says is no longer ours to bear. In this two-stage plunge into unbelief, we have doubted the character and integrity of God and what He has said is true. That is the greater sin that fertilizes the womb from which more overt sinful acts are born.

Since it is a trap, reject such thoughts and feelings! Aggressively embrace the truth of who you are in Christ and the forgiveness you stand in through Him. Run back to God the moment you have sinned—not away from Him! The genius of Satan's trap is that it is designed to keep you from seeking intimate communion with God, out of fear of Him and from doubting His goodness and His word.

In his book, *Passion for Jesus*, (pp. 113, 114, 117 and 120), Mike Bickle comments:

> When the Lord's presence departs from us in our place of compromise . . . you and I must arise in obedience and faith and seek Him . . . He does not condemn us for our immaturity or accuse us of our failures. Instead, He calls things that are not as though they were, because He sees those things in seed form in our hearts (Romans 4:17). . . .
>
> . . . Even when we are weak, even when we fail, the Lord looks at the sincerity and devotion of our hearts and exclaims, "You are so beautiful to Me!" The knowledge that Jesus continues to enjoy us as we are maturing is a foundational truth that empowers us to mature. . . .
>
> . . . Even though your actions sometimes fall short of your intentions, the devout resolution of your heart overwhelms Him with affectionate emotion. He looks at you and yearns over you, longing to draw you into a more intimate relationship with Him. It is this revelation of Jesus' ravished heart for you that awakens your heart to fervency for Him, igniting your progression in holy passion. And it is His passionate love for you and your response of love and devotion for Him that act as a breastplate of love, guarding your heart with holy affections in times of temptation and in the difficult hours of life (1 Thessalonians 5:8).

Unforgiveness and the Judging of Hearts

When we have been unfairly treated, when we have been abused, slandered and defiled by others, and when we choose to work through these traumas apart from God's enablement, we often end up creating elaborate systems of justification for holding unforgiveness against those who have injured us. The greater the trauma, the more innocent we were when it was done, the more justified we feel in refusing to yield to God's desire that we forgive. Such responses to hurt begin in childhood, when we do not yet understand the power of grace nor see the ultimate justice of God in the eternal perspective of faith. And so, we try to create a sense of justice in a world that seems to have none by becoming judge and jury in our heart against those who have hurt us. These "sins of response" give Satan ground to bring even greater deception and bondage into our lives.

Sometimes, the judgments we make against people aren't based on actual harm done, but on *perceived* intent. In other words, we presume to know what was in their heart—what motivated them to say or do what they did. That gives birth to inner justification for condemning them in our heart and refusing to forgive them. As adults, we must come to grips with the fact that such condemning attitudes of the heart are rebellion against God—a way of choosing to live in a sea of self-pity and anger, rather than trusting that He is the proper judge for sin.

Satan's deceptions in this area are quite elaborate, and one of his most effective is in persuading us to believe (by planting thoughts in our mind) that forgiveness is something more than it really is.

- He would like for us to believe that forgiveness is tantamount to saying that what was done was okay. That's not what it means at all!

- He'd like us to believe that in forgiving, we are releasing the guilty party from the legal or divine consequences of their behavior. That's not at all what we are doing! We have no such authority.

- Satan would like us to believe that forgiveness is something we have to achieve on our own. Nonsense! Some things seem unforgivable, but if we will ask Him, God will enable us to forgive even those things.

- The evil one would like for us to believe that forgiveness is achieved merely by mouthing certain words so as to satisfy some legal standard. Although saying words can help us to embrace the meaning of them, the ability to forgive from the heart is something that must be sought and received from God.

- Satan would also like us to believe that forgiveness is dependent on the perpetrator's response. That is also untrue. It does not matter if the person who harmed you acknowledges or repents of their sin. If you truly forgive them from your heart, then you have accomplished God's will for you in the matter.

What then is forgiveness?

- It is taking yourself out of the judgment seat simply because it belongs to God alone. Imagine that future day when you will stand before God in heaven. Do you really think that you are going to be so presumptuous as to go sit in His throne? I don't think so! Then why sit in it now?

- Forgiveness is acknowledging that having accepted Christ's forgiveness for yourself, you have no right to withhold it from others. It is therefore an act of the will, not a servant of feelings.

- Forgiveness is also an act of God's grace poured out through your heart. It is a result of being transformed into His image, taking on His mind and heart, clothing yourself with Him.

- It is as much an opportunity to set yourself free as it is an opportunity to set the perpetrator free.

- Forgiveness is a removal of a significant part of Satan's ground that has allowed him to re-victimize you over and over again so as to emotionally destroy you and your relationship with God.

In his book, *Passion for Jesus*, Mike Bickle says:

An intimate relationship with Jesus can heal any wound of the human heart. How are the inner wounds of the heart healed? We have to give everything to God, including our bitterness, self-pity and desire for revenge. Our grief, anger, shame and pride—even our hopes, dreams and ambitions—must be laid on God's altar, along with our personal rights and the desire to run our own lives. Jesus Christ must become the focus of our hearts—not our tragedies, our past or all that might have been. Only Jesus can transform self-pity into praise or tears into triumph. A focus on intimacy with Jesus heals the inner wounds of the heart.

Idolatry

The siren song of idolatry is exquisitely effective today, not only because idolatry is in itself seductive, but also because man is ignorant of the many forms it takes. Most think of idolatry as being limited to prostrating oneself before a carved figure. The Bible gives a far broader picture, however. Take Ephesians 5:3-5 for example, where idolatry is said to include the sins of:

- sexual immorality
- greed
- foolish talk
- any kind of impurity
- obscenity
- coarse joking

When I commit one of these sins, (and I am certain there are others that are associated with idolatry), Satan deceives me into thinking them relatively unimportant. I do not confess my sin of idolatry because I do not see my sin as idolatry. Thus, I remain bound to the sin and blinded by an unrepentant heart.

What then is idolatry? It is putting one's hope of fulfillment in something other than God. It is giving one's heart, one's primary devotion to something other than Him. This can occur in a marital relationship when one spouse gives first place in their heart to the other spouse, rather than to God. Without ever saying or thinking it, they place their hope of fulfillment in their mate and relegate God to second or third place.

We must understand what idolatry is and ruthlessly eradicate it from our lives by asking the Holy Spirit to search our heart and reveal if there be any wicked way in us.

Trials in the Wilderness

We all must go through various trials in this life. They are necessary for producing perseverance, character, and hope. It is what Satan tries to do in the midst of those trials that is one of his greatest hits. He tempts our faith with our flesh.

Examining how he tempted our Lord reveals his most common tactics. When he tempted Jesus in the wilderness with all the kingdoms of the world, Satan was tempting Him with the idolatry of putting material things before God (and the sense of control that would give). When he tempted Christ to throw Himself down so that God's angels would catch Him, Satan was tempting Him to throw off weakness and embrace power. And when Satan tempted Jesus to turn the stone into bread, he was tempting Him with disobeying the will of His Father—for God had led Jesus to fast in the wilderness.

In all these temptations (and others) during our wilderness periods, Satan causes us to think and/or feel that God has abandoned and forsaken us. In essence, he is tempting us to question the honesty and faithfulness of God to keep His Word, where He says: "I will never leave you nor forsake you." (Hebrews 13:5)

Sounds like a familiar challenge, doesn't it? It goes all the way back to Genesis 3:1, when Satan said to Eve, "Did God really say . . ." As Jesus did, we must resist this temptation by proclaiming our faith in the Word of God, despite all appearances, thoughts, and feelings to the contrary. When we do, Satan will respond the same way he did with Jesus—he will withdraw until a more opportune time (ref. Luke 4:13).

Wounds of Injustice

Most of us have suffered wounds of injustice. During each of them, Satan's henchmen demons were there, not only inciting our wounding, but also planting thoughts of doubt about the goodness and fairness of God in our heart during the intense emotions of the moment. At such times, their voice whispers: "It's not fair . . .

- that You (God) put me in this family,
- that You put me in this body,
- that You let my child die,
- that You allowed me to be molested,
- that You let the innocent suffer!"

When we read God's reply to similar cries from Job, our frustration gets compounded. His answer to Job was: "Where were you when I laid the foundation of the earth?" (Job 38) Instead of directly answering Job's question about why He was allowing all of those terrible things to happen to him, God addresses the attitude of the heart behind Job's remarks. In God's mind, the greater problem was the doubt in Job's heart about God's goodness and the arrogance behind his presuming to be able to have enough information to even begin to make such charges against God.

When we suffer wounds of injustice, we often bury anger, judgment, and bitterness against God deep inside, too afraid to acknowledge their existence. And so it makes us even madder when God doesn't answer our question, "Why did You let me be hurt?" In fact, His silence can be the most maddening thing of all, for it is then that we discover that we cannot command answers from Him, nor can we control or manipulate Him into answering our angry tirades. This reminds us that we are not sovereign gods, that we are wholly dependent on Him, and that inflames our pride, which does not die easily. When we respond to wounds of injustice with angry, prideful ultimatums rather than humble accedence to the unseen wisdom of God, we open up large tracts of ground for Satan to take in us.

The Immediate, Temporal, Finite Perspective

One of Satan's most effective tricks is to so monopolize our attention with the tyranny of the now that we forget the true dominance of the eternal. He immerses us in the sensate, which *Webster's New Collegiate Dictionary* defines as being, "preoccupied with things that can be experienced through a sense modality." He exploits this predominance of the physical senses, our common inexperience with spiritual discernment, and the dearth of faith found in our sinking culture to deflect our attention from eternal realities and perspectives. He gets us so preoccupied with the complexities of modern life that we fail to give much attention to practicing or reinforcing the greater reality of the kingdom of God in our midst.

In this manic, self-focused world, we must aggressively apportion time to focus in on the eternal. We must pursue the transcendent. We must consciously maintain facility with the sights and sounds of that greater reality of God's kingdom and purpose that exists unseen all around us. We must immerse ourselves in those things that strengthen faith and an awareness of God's presence.

Our battle against this satanic "hit," more than any other, requires an aggressive posture toward the kingdom of God and against the kingdom of darkness. It is not sufficient to wage a defensive battle against sin, waiting unprepared for its onslaught. Instead, we must live vigilant, proactive lives, knowing ahead of time what Satan's schemes are and what our response will be when they are employed against us. I must make up my mind once and for all what my response to each temptation will be. Is yielding to it going to be considered an option? It is at this level that I must make an irrevocable decision that the answer will forevermore be "No", understanding that God will honor my commitment only when, by faith, I turn to Him at each moment of temptation and call upon His power to enforce the decision.

It is important to understand that my dependence on His holiness to empower my decision must be accompanied by the faith of knowing that God will do so every time I truly want Him to. And the thing that keeps my will yielded to His is maintaining an intimate love relationship with Him. When I abide in Him, temptation loses its allure in the glory of His presence and my desire to live in holiness stays resolute.

God has called us to be violently aggressive in taking the kingdom (Matthew 11:12). It does not just happen to us. We must fervently pursue and take it by the force of a passionate will and desire for the things of God. (That passion comes from being in His presence.) And we must refuse to live solely by the evidence of the immediate, the temporal, and the finite.

Pride

Pride is an insidious, unseen killer, more like a hit done with a slow-working poison rather than a brutal frontal assault. It hides itself in the independent spirit of americanism. It flaunts itself in sports, in business, in entertainment and other arenas where successful heroes become the models for our culture. In the west, pride is seen as a virtue. It is all the more difficult to resist because it is championed by almost every structure of modeling and authority—even ecclesiastical ones. And it follows quickly on the heels of even our righteous thoughts and acts.

There is only one effective approach to this problem. We must continuously ask God to show us if there is any such wicked way in us (Psalm 139:23-24). Pride must be ruthlessly and immediately attacked with the weapons of our warfare the instant it is detected. Its opposite must be aggressively sought and practiced. We must purposely teach, model, and reward humility and the seeking of it—for God gives grace to the humble and opposes the proud (James 4:6). He esteems the humble (Is 66:2). And so, we must live in the reality of Galatians 2:20:

"I am crucified with Christ and I no longer live, but Christ lives in me. The life I live in the body, I live by faith in the Son of God, who loved me and gave Himself for me."

The Flesh

Romans 7:18 says, "Nothing good lives in me, that is in my flesh." This seventh chapter of Romans describes what seems to be a hopeless battle that rages within the heart of every man—wanting to do what is right and not doing it, wanting not to do what is wrong and doing that instead. Satan's trick is to persuade us that this is the unchangeable state of man in this world—that we have no hope of living any other way before Jesus comes. Once again, the devil is saying, "Has God really said . . . " He's hoping that our love of sin will cause us to ignore the answer found in Romans 8 and use Romans 7 as an excuse for a compromised, unfaithful life.

In Romans 8, we are told that Jesus Christ has set us free from the law of sin and death described in Romans 7. It tells us that walking by the Spirit makes the difference. When we yield ourselves to the Spirit, He overcomes the enemy for us and enables us to walk in the ways of God. A big part of yielding ourselves to the Holy Spirit has to do with the moment by moment decisions we make to consider ourselves dead to the flesh (the sinful nature) by not feeding it, not believing it, and not following after it, and instead, receiving God's continual flow of life within us to keep us from falling. If we will do this, 2 Peter 1:3-11, Galatians 5:16, Jude 24, Titus 2:11-14, 2 Corinthians 1:21, 1 John 2:1-6, Romans 8 and Galatians 2:20 all conspire to suggest that God will live His righteousness through us, conquering our flesh for us, and progressively move us deeper into a life of faithfulness to His ways.

Fear

Finally, one of Satan's most effective strategies against us is to assault us with thoughts and feelings of fear. In fact, he may be trying to pull this one on you right now. If you have found yourself guilty of the first nine "hits" described in this chapter, you may be experiencing feelings of fear and hopelessness. This is a trick of the enemy. You must stand against it and call it the lie that it is. You must put it away just as aggressively as the other tricks. 1 John 16b, 18 says:

"God is love . . . . There is no fear in love. But perfect love drives out fear, because fear has to do with punishment. The man who fears is not made perfect in love."

Fear is often an element of Satan's first great hit—performance orientation. If your sense of acceptance by God is based on having lived free from Satan's schemes, and if this chapter has uncovered levels of compromise that you didn't realize you had, you may be experiencing feelings of worthlessness, fear, and rejection. Remember, such feelings are based on the lie of performance and are deceptions of the enemy! Run back into God's arms as did the prodigal son and experience the healing grace and love that is there for you. Let God's love quench your fear.

- Performance orientation
- condemnation
- unforgiveness
- idolatry
- wilderness trials
- wounds of injustice
- the immediate perspective
- pride
- the flesh
- fear

As you can see, these ten of Satan's greatest hits are quite sophisticated and extraordinarily clever. But our God is infinitely wiser and has a perfect way for you to escape them all.

Let's first determine in our hearts that by God's power we are going to stand against the schemes of the devil, that we are going to plan ahead of time what our response to these temptations will be, that we are going to wage an aggressive, offensive war against the enemy rather than a defensive one, always dependent on God's power and promises to see us through.

Second, understanding that all of Satan's schemes depend on unbelief, let's commit once and for all to trust in God and be led by His Word. His is the greater power! All the forces of evil combined cannot hold a candle to it. When God comes to vanquish sin and evil, just the breath of His mouth will destroy all of Satan's power (2 Thessalonians 2:8). In writing "A Mighty Fortress is Our God," Martin Luther had it right when he proclaimed,

".... one little word shall fell him!"

*   *   *   *

Next we're going to look at the situation from another angle. Now that we've examined Satan's most brilliant schemes to defraud us of the life that Jesus has won for us, let's zero in on how we sometimes unilaterally derail ourselves from pursuing and realizing the high call of holiness in this life. Let's look at the problem with holiness from a human perspective. Let's look at how very important it is to understand God's ways, so that we don't undermine our path to freedom from sin by operating in the wisdom and ways of this world.

6

The Problem With Holiness: How to Make it Work in the Real World

The subject of how to walk in holiness has been the most central theme of healing that God has given me in ministry. It seems that most Christians have not been made aware that the lion's share of what Christ offers them for this life lies beyond the initial point of salvation—that, in fact, salvation is an ongoing process whereby we are transformed into the image of Christ in ways practical and supernatural.

I see people becoming comfortable with the idea of being "saved" and "eternally secure" to the point where there remains no compelling vision to call them to holiness and, in fact, no faith that it is even possible to any significant measure. The Book of Ephesians has always been a beacon to me regarding this issue. There can be traced the theme of the promise for holiness in this life.

> For He chose us in Him before the creation of the world to be holy and blameless in His sight (1:4). . . .
>
> . . . the purpose of His will, . . . that we, who were the first to hope in Christ, might be for the praise of His glory (1:11c-12). . . .
>
> . . . I pray also that the eyes of your heart may be enlightened in order that you may know the hope to which He has called you, the riches of His glorious inheritance in the saints, and His incomparably great power for us who believe (1:18-19a). . . .
>
> . . . As a prisoner for the Lord, then, I urge you to live a life worthy of the calling you have received (4:1). . . .
>
> . . . So I tell you this, and insist on it in the Lord, that you must no longer live as the Gentiles do, in the futility of their thinking. They are darkened in their understanding and separated from the life of God because of the ignorance that is in them due to the hardening of their hearts. Having lost all sensitivity, they have given themselves over to sensuality so as to indulge in every kind of impurity, with a continual lust for more. You, however, did not come to know Christ that way. Surely you heard of Him and were taught in Him in accordance with the truth that is in Jesus. You were taught, with regard to your former way of life, to put off your old self, which is being corrupted by its deceitful desires; to be made

new in the attitude of your minds; and to put on the new self, created to be like God in true righteousness and holiness (4:17-24).

. . . And do not grieve the Holy Spirit of God (4:30a), . . .

. . . Be imitators of God, therefore, as dearly loved children and live a life of love, just as Christ loved us and gave Himself up for us as a fragrant offering and sacrifice to God. But among you there must not be even a hint of sexual immorality, or of any kind of impurity (5:1-3a) . . .

. . . For of this you can be sure: No immoral, impure or greedy person—such a man is an idolater—has any inheritance in the kingdom of Christ and of God (5:5). . . .

. . . For you were once darkness, but now you are light in the Lord. Live as children of light (for the fruit of the light consists in all goodness, righteousness and truth) and find out what pleases the Lord. Have nothing to do with the fruitless deeds of darkness, but rather expose them. For it is shameful even to mention what the disobedient do in secret. But everything exposed by the light becomes visible, for it is light that makes everything visible. This is why it is said: "Wake up, O sleeper, rise from the dead, and Christ will shine on you." (5:8-14) . . .

. . . Christ loved the church and gave Himself up for her to make her holy, cleansing her by the washing with water through the word, and to present her to Himself as a radiant church, without stain or wrinkle or any other blemish, but holy and blameless (5:25b-27) . . .

. . . Finally, be strong in the Lord and in His mighty power (6:10).

It should be noted that beyond the problem of getting people to believe that holiness is possible (though sinless perfection in this life isn't) is the problem of what we use to motivate the desire to be holy. Essentially, where much religious teaching has gone wrong in the past has been in what has been used to motivate holiness: the law imposed externally, guilt, shame, approval of men, earning God's love and approval, repaying Him for His salvation, etc. People fail largely because, when they are exhorted to lead holy lives, they are usually motivated to do so from guilt, from duty, from obligation—from law. From such motivations, people are left in their own strength, blind to the fact that God stands ready to do it all for them if they will but renounce the self-righteous fantasy that lies behind those ways of thinking and follow His lead.[1]

Thus, concomitant with casting the vision of holiness "in this present age"[2] is the need to stimulate the proper internal motivator for that goal —that being love for God, in response to His demonstrated love on the Cross. In this, we see that holiness and intimacy with God have been inextricably bound together. The former springs from, as well as deepens, the latter—Christ being our life (2 Corinthians 4:10-11; Philippians 1:21; Colossians 3:3; 1 John 5:12)—we no longer living but Christ (Galatians 2:20)—holy as He is holy (1 Corinthians 1:2; Ephesians 1:4; 1 Peter 1:15-16).

Leanne Payne's continuous theme of practicing God's presence is on target for eliciting that proper motivation for being holy.[3] It is only by direct, intimate communion with God that we become properly motivated. Such is a natural by-product of "knowing" Him. To our peril we ignore the great importance of this perspective. It should always be the central theme in ministry. The knowledge that one gains of psychology and human behavior during years of counseling can often have an insidiously undermining effect on such awareness. We become proud and puffed up by our own experience and learning, and lose our dependence on God. We must regularly examine our motivations and realign our priorities accordingly. No wonder that even King David, who was said to be a man after God's heart (1 Samuel 13:14; Acts 13:22), still continued to ask God to search his heart and show Him if there was any wicked way in him (Psalm 139:23).

One of the greatest devotional compilations (and interpolations) of the writings of Christian "mystics" was done by Fr. Gabriel of St. Mary Magdalene in the middle part of the twentieth century. On this subject of intimacy with God, he writes:

> God is jealous of a heart which has been consecrated to Him, and He will not admit it to intimacy with Himself as long as He finds it occupied with some affection which prevents it from concentrating on Him all the love of which He has rendered it capable. St. Teresa of Jesus says, "As He refuses to force our will, He takes what we give Him but does not give Himself wholly to us until He sees that we are giving ourselves wholly to Him" (Way, 28). "God will not have a divided heart; He wants all or nothing" (T.M. Sp). If we do not give our hearts entirely to God, we cannot enjoy divine intimacy. Jesus said, "Blessed are the clean of heart: for they shall see God" (Matthew 5:8). This vision, this enjoyment of God, is in a certain way anticipated even in this life for those who keep the integrity and purity of their heart for Him. St. Thomas says, "A heart which is free from thoughts and affections alien to God is like a temple consecrated to the Lord, in which we can contemplate Him even in this world" (*Commentary on St. Matthew*). A pure heart, like a limpid eye, can comprehend God and to a certain degree penetrate the depths of His infinite mystery. For this reason theologians teach that the gift of understanding corresponds to the beatitude "blessed are the clean of heart." By this gift, the Holy Spirit enables the soul to read within, "*intus legere*," that is, to penetrate divine truths. One who loves ardently desires to know the loved one more and more, not only exteriorly, but also intimately, sharing his thoughts and secrets; he is willing to sacrifice every other satisfaction in order to attain this end.[4]

Fr. Gabriel later provides an even more compelling meditation on the centrality of pursuing intimacy with God, not only as the purpose of life but also the path to holiness:

> St. Thomas teaches that "in the pursuit of the end, no limits should be set" (IIa IIae, q. 184, a. 3). Sanctity is the end of the spiritual life; that is why we must propose it to ourselves, not in a reduced, restricted manner, but in all its fullness—fullness which speaks to us of intimate union with God, of the complete invasion of grace, and of entire conformity to the divine will, to the extent that it

becomes the only motive of all our actions; for when the soul becomes totally purified of everything contrary to God's will, "then the Lord will communicate His supernatural Being to it, in such a way that it will seem to be God Himself and to have what God possesses" (AS II, 5,7). Sanctity is the plenitude of love and grace; it is transformation in God by love, it is deification by grace . . . , the secret of reaching the goal is never to stop: . . . , because even if we were to grow in love indefinitely, we would never be able to love God as much as He is to be loved; . . . , and the more we give ourselves to Him in the exercise of intense love, the more He will give Himself to us by grace.

The measure of loving God is to love Him "without measure"; . . . This is the indispensable condition for loving God with our whole heart. . . .

. . . this treasure is not given to us in a short time [-i.e., quickly] because we do not give ourselves to God entirely and forever.[5]

When Holiness Fails—Why it Fails

Following are a few observations on what can subvert a person's attempt to walk in holiness, with supporting insights found in the writings of Leanne Payne and Larry Crabb.

I. Failure to Receive the New Birth in Christ (where the effects of the Fall begin to be reversed).

Many with whom we minister (even in our churches) have not yet received the new birth from Christ even though they believe that they have (cf. Matthew 7:21-23).[6] Part of the problem is our modern penchant for dumbing salvation down to its lowest and most socially acceptable denominator, and the other part of the problem is a loss of accurate focus on the means and end of holiness.

We have become masters at cosmetic salvation, where only the appearance is changed, but not the heart. And so we fool ourselves. Televised crusades have taught us how to act repentant, but they have not necessarily conveyed the heart of repentance.[7] Like so many of the actors who have portrayed Jesus on the screen, they have provided the lines to read, but have not always changed the character of the one who delivers them. That said, without that supernatural restoration of union with God through genuine repentance and salvation, true and lasting transformation of life cannot take place.

So many of our "Christian" counseling and healing methods train their sights on helping a person maintain sobriety from their besetting sin rather than entering into a dynamic, transforming, intimate relationship with God through Christ. To rephrase the comment of a very wise man: What good is it for a man to control his behavior and lose his soul? It is therefore incumbent upon healing ministers to first try to determine if the person has truly been converted. If not, their progress in behavioral change will ultimately be meaningless and may even be the means by which they convince themself that all is right with God. In other words, we will have given them the rope with which to hang themselves, pretty though the rope may be.

The new birth is critical not only for substantive progress toward obtaining the prize of union with God, but also as the means by which a true, metaphysical, and ontological change is effected in us by God. Our nature is transformed from being internally bent toward (or at peace in) sin, to being bent toward (or at peace in) holiness. That empowers our will to the point where making moves toward holiness in our behavior becomes natural and delightful to us rather than an obligation imposed from someone other and outside. Leanne Payne describes the importance of the new birth:

> The first and primary healing out of which all other healing proceeds is the new birth. Once Christ abides within, one with our spirits, then His life can radiate throughout our souls—that is, our minds and hearts —including our memories, our willing (volitional) feeling, intuitive, and imaginative faculties, and beyond that, even to our sensory and physical being. Then, as His light encounters dark places of unforgiveness and woundedness within us, healing can take place.[8]

Without the new birth, the best a person can hope for is a self-empowered, "maintenance program." With it, Christ offers a transformation program. Rather than simply changing the outward behavior, Christ transforms their interior heart and its desires. They go from following God because they're supposed to, to following Him because they want to. Obedience becomes the natural desire rather than one imposed from the outside on an unwilling subject. Christ, in effect, writes His law on their very heart (cf. Jeremiah 31:33b).

II. Failure to Understand How to Live by the Spirit and Thus Crucify the Deeds of the Flesh.

"So I say, live by the Spirit, and you will not gratify the desires of the sinful nature" (Galatians 5:16).

Many of those who have received Christ have never been taught that a passionate pursuit of holiness is required in order for the sanctification process to proceed. Many assume that the great and precious promises of Scripture for the believer are just supposed to happen to them—to fall on them as they dutifully sit in church week after week. The Bible teaches something very different (italics mine):

> "But if from there you seek the LORD your God, *you will find Him if you look for Him with all your heart and with all your soul*" (Deuteronomy 4:29);

> "*You will seek Me and find Me when you seek Me with all your heart.* I will be found by you," declares the LORD" (Jeremiah 29:13-14);

"For the eyes of the LORD range throughout the earth to strengthen *those whose hearts are fully committed to Him*" (2 Chronicles 16:9);

"The sluggard craves and gets nothing, but *the desires of the diligent are fully satisfied*" (Proverbs 13:4);

"Blessed are those who *hunger and thirst for righteousness*, for they will be filled" (Matthew 5:6);

"And without faith it is impossible to please God, because anyone who comes to Him must believe that He exists and that He rewards *those who earnestly seek Him*" (Hebrews 11:6).

It's the old "don't cast your pearls before swine" principle[9]—God only gives what is precious to those who treat it as precious. Many sit waiting for God to answer prayers for deliverance from sin when in their hearts they are not yet fully committed to permanent deliverance from sin. Rather than cast the pearls of holiness before someone who will trample them underfoot, God waits for the trials of life to deepen His work of holy desire in them.

Holiness doesn't just happen. Although the judicial standing of being "set apart" unto God, (set apart = holy), occurs when we make covenant with God through faith in Christ, the capacity to be holy in the daily struggle with temptation is imparted in direct proportion to our sincere, daily desire for and faith in being rendered so by God. And the core source for it all is our intimacy with Him, which elicits from Him an infusion of His own holiness into our very being (cf. Galatians 2:20).

The ongoing, practical manifestation of holiness requires a second cross —our cross.

Then he said to them all: "If anyone would come after me, he must deny himself and take up his cross daily and follow Me. For whoever wants to save his life will lose it, but whoever loses his life for Me will save it" (Luke 9:23-24);

If anyone comes to Me and does not hate his father and mother, his wife and children, his brothers and sisters —yes, even his own life —he cannot be My disciple. And anyone who does not carry his cross and follow Me cannot be My disciple (Luke 14:26-27).

Since it is our natural inclination to avoid pain at all costs, we keep climbing down from our cross. What then is God's provision to keep us motivated to stay on it? The only thing that can achieve that goal successfully is that which motivated Jesus to stay on His Cross: He became one with the Father (one mind, one purpose, one heart) and in so doing, became a channel of the Father's love.

Now He wants to become one with us so that we can become channels of God's love to the world (cf. John 17). That occurs through an ongoing intimate relationship with Him, where He exchanges His life for ours. He becomes greater, we become less. We no longer live, but Christ lives His righteous life in and through us.

> I have been crucified with Christ and I no longer live, but Christ lives in me. The life I live in the body, I live by faith in the Son of God, who loved me and gave himself for me (Galatians 2:20).

Another way of seeing this is to differentiate between the old man and the new creation in Christ. Both currently reside within us. The old man is the flesh, the sinful nature, whom we must continuously crucify, starve, and deny. The new spiritual man is what was made alive when we were born from above—upon putting our faith in Christ. This new man is united with Christ, fed by His Spirit, infused with His life, including His righteousness.

We remain separate from God in the sense of being created, individual persons, yet in another sense, we are united with Him, have become one with Him in heart, purpose, and a shared life—we in Him and He in us.[10] In this way, we participate in the divine nature.

> Through these he has given us his very great and precious promises, so that through them you may participate in the divine nature and escape the corruption in the world caused by evil desires (2 Peter 1:4).

And while all of this is literally true now, and becoming even more so as we cooperate with the divine plan, this life of God in us manifests itself only when our will gives consent—when we express a passionate desire for Him to do so and believe that He will. It is not an imposed life. It expresses itself only to the degree that we deeply desire for it to be expressed.

The process of sanctification, therefore, is the process of training our soul and body to switch its allegiance from the old man to the new. As that identification with Christ deepens, we become persuaded to forsake our fleshly desires, counting as worthless the discomfort that our cross brings, for our sake and for the sake of those Christ died for—those who are headed toward an eternity without Him.

It is a deeper knowledge and experience of the Cross (both His and ours) that we need. And we get it by pursuing it with all our heart.

Turn back to the Cross. Meditate on what God did there. Ask God to deepen your understanding and appreciation of Christ's sacrifice. Dr. John Stott has written:

> The essence of sin is man substituting himself for God, while the essence of salvation is God substituting Himself for man. . . Man claims prerogatives which belong to God alone; God accepts penalties which belong to man alone.[11]

See the evil of sin on that Cross and you will be drawn closer to Him. Jesus was the innocent lamb of God, perfect and sinless in all His ways. How severe evil must be to mercilessly assault such an innocent.

See the love of God on the Cross and you will be filled with a love for the one who suffered so. He did not have to go to the Cross. He suffered and died for you.

See the power of God on the Cross and you will be persuaded to cling to Him. In His weakest possible posture (a lamb to the slaughter), God utterly defeated all the power of the enemy.

See the genius of God on the Cross and you will be persuaded to surrender your unanswered questions to faith in His greater wisdom. At the pinnacle of Satan's most ingenious and elaborate scheme to destroy God's chosen people and their Savior, God achieved the redemption of mankind by using Satan's own scheme against him. By urging the authorities to crucify the Son of Glory, not only did Satan unwittingly participate in the redemption of mankind, he signed his own death warrant for his crime. As with men, his wisdom was made utterly foolish by the brilliant mind of God.

Harold St. John once wrote, "The Cross of Christ means nothing until it takes your breath away."

Has the Cross taken your breath away lately? Let it infuse you with love for God. Let it transform your will. And let His indwelling presence make you holy, as He is holy.

Living by the Spirit entails having a deeper experience of God's life flowing through us—that river of living water that Christ and Ezekiel spoke of:

> Jesus answered, "Everyone who drinks this water will be thirsty again, but whoever drinks the water I give him will never thirst. Indeed, the water I give him will become in him a spring of water welling up to eternal life" (John 4:13-14).

> On the last and greatest day of the Feast, Jesus stood and said in a loud voice, "If a man is thirsty, let him come to Me and drink. Whoever believes in Me, as the Scripture has said, streams of living water will flow from within him." By this He meant the Spirit, whom those who believed in Him were later to receive (John 7:37-39a).

> The man brought me back to the entrance of the temple, and I saw water coming out from under the threshold of the temple toward the east (for the temple faced east). The water was coming down from under the south side of the temple, south of the altar. He then brought me out through the north gate and led me around the outside to the outer gate facing east, and the water was flowing from the south side. As the man went eastward with a measuring line in his hand, he measured off a thousand cubits and then led me through water that was ankle-deep. He measured off another thousand cubits and led me through water that was knee-deep. He measured off another thousand and led me through water that was up to the waist. He measured off another thousand, but now it was a river that I could not cross, because the water had risen and was deep enough to swim in —a river that no one could cross. He asked me, "Son of man, do you see this?"

> Then he led me back to the bank of the river. When I arrived there, I saw a great number of trees on each side of the river. He said to me, "This water flows toward the eastern region and goes down into the Arabah, where it enters the Sea. When it empties into the Sea, the water there becomes fresh. Swarms of living creatures will live wherever the river flows. There will be large numbers of

fish, because this water flows there and makes the salt water fresh; so where the river flows everything will live. Fishermen will stand along the shore; from En Gedi to En Eglaim there will be places for spreading nets. The fish will be of many kinds —like the fish of the Great Sea. But the swamps and marshes will not become fresh; they will be left for salt. Fruit trees of all kinds will grow on both banks of the river. Their leaves will not wither, nor will their fruit fail. Every month they will bear, because the water from the sanctuary flows to them. Their fruit will serve for food and their leaves for healing (Ezekiel 47:1-12).

Unfortunately, we too often exchange that Holy Grail for a deeper experience of the world.

At the beginning of my coming to Christ, the Lord gave me an experience of the literal reality of this "living water" that He spoke of in the Scriptures. I was following Guru Maharaj Ji at the time, but had come to the place where I was beginning to doubt that he was God, and wanting to follow the one true God no matter who He was, I said so, crying out one night. Suddenly a rush of living energy began pouring into my heart. An aperture to the spirit realm opened in my chest and a literal river of living water began surging into the opening, straight into my heart. It had the sound of rushing waters, almost voice-like—a raging torrent, as though I were lying at the bottom of Niagara Falls with the water directly hitting me full force. The difference, however, was that as the river hit my chest, it entered the dimension of the spirit and disappeared from my three-dimensional perception. If it hadn't disappeared, I expect that I would have exploded into trillions of atoms from the force of it. Another distinctive feature of the river was that despite its destructive force, it felt like liquid love. It was as if someone had turned pure love into a liquid and was pouring it all over me. It was frightening, yet healing. It was Lewis' Aslan.[12]

I was being sealed unto salvation by the Holy Spirit of God,[13] though at the time I did not understand what was happening. I only knew that God existed and that His river of living water was real. It is the most powerful force in existence and it flows through every born-again believer. It is God Himself. Since most take Biblical references to God's "river of living water" as merely symbolic, it has got to be the most untapped resource in the universe.[14]

Leanne Payne has the gift of calling up our faith to believe in God's river and has inspired me to hold back no longer in boldly declaring its "true presence." The power of Satan and the things of this world are nothing in comparison to it. They are ridiculous. They are ludicrous!

In truth, God is not trying to eliminate pleasure. He is trying to provide superior pleasures—those that have been consecrated for His holy people. Pastor Mike Bickle has also written well on the subject:

We are on a treasure hunt to know the richness of the beauty and the glory of the personhood of God. . .

. . . Our heavenly Father's enjoyment of us . . . never diminishes, even when the

Father disapproves of our behavior and disciplines us. With God, correction is not rejection; disapproval is not despising. . . .

. . . God's method for the inward transformation of His people has never been to warn us against pursuing sinful pleasures and then tell us to just hang in there. Rather, God provides *superior pleasures* to replace and give us power over negative pleasures.

He doesn't tell us to deny pleasure in and of itself. He says to us: "Let Me give you a superior pleasure as the power source to help you deny those lesser pleasures." In His grace, God uses superior pleasures to cause us to want to walk away from the sinful ones.

What are those superior pleasures? They are that we feel valuable, beautiful and successful before Him. We feel enjoyed by God.

Such knowledge empowers us emotionally like nothing else. Happy people obey God readily and love Him deeply.[15]

Many of those who have received Christ misunderstand how holiness is brought forth. They see it as a state they have to achieve (with God's help, of course).

They see it as self-produced—a by-product of their own (naively, well-intended) efforts to wage war against sin.

The vision that they have of themselves, once successful, is of a self-made, self-contained entity of holiness (albeit with the help of God).

When this vision ultimately fails to materialize, some conclude incorrectly that the promises of being holy must be for the next life, and they settle into a lukewarm, compromised life with little passion to pursue a goal that they now believe cannot be achieved. (Perfectionism plays havoc here.)

We often refuse to fervently seek and allow God to make us holy, because it is impossible to achieve such a goal this side of heaven. The perfectionists among us are particularly at risk. If we can't do something perfectly, we don't want to do it at all. The avoidance of failure is our priority. It is curious though, that many a perfectionist will not allow that fear to stop them from pursuing a worldly career or dream. A tennis player knows that there will never be a day when they will play every shot perfectly, yet they pursue the virtue of excellence anyway. The difference between perfectionism and a fervent pursuit of being made perfect, is that perfectionists are performance-oriented people who seek to establish their worth and value through what they achieve. A person who is on fire to be made holy by God is someone who is responding to a worth and value already given them by God's love poured out on the Cross and reacts to the call to obedience and faithfulness from an inner delight and desire. The law has been written on their hearts and is now part of their own will.

In essence, out of stubbornness, anger, or pride, many refuse to put the law written on stone tablets in submission to the law now written on their hearts, and so it never emerges to bring victory.

"For I will take you out of the nations; I will gather you from all the countries and bring you back into your own land. I will sprinkle clean water on you, and you will be clean; I will cleanse you from all your impurities and from all your idols. I will give you a new heart and put a new spirit in you; I will remove from you your heart of stone and give you a heart of flesh. And I will put My Spirit in you and move you to follow My decrees and be careful to keep My laws. You will live in the land I gave your forefathers; you will be My people, and I will be your God" (Ezekiel 36:24-28).

The law of his God is in his heart; his feet do not slip (Psalm 37:31).

"This is the covenant I will make with the house of Israel after that time," declares the Lord. "I will put My law in their minds and write it on their hearts. I will be their God, and they will be My people" (Jeremiah 31:33).

Another possibility is that some have never gained a deep "knowledge" of Christ's suffering on the Cross and been changed by it. Their motivation to good works is earning God's love and approval rather than a love for Him birthed from a deep knowledge of His love for them.

In ministry, I will often tell the story of the night that God came to me in a most unnerving way as I meditated on the Cross. Having read the crucifixion accounts in the gospels, I was asking the Lord to deepen my understanding and appreciation of what happened there, when suddenly God the Father let me feel the incredible pain of His own heart as He watched His Son be tortured and die on the Cross. The pain was so intense, that He mercifully allowed me to feel it for only a few seconds.

I had never considered the pain of the Father before—the pain of the Son being so dominant in the story. But the Father's pain was excruciating. He had to watch His purely obedient and loved Son be tortured by godless men and not lift a finger to stop it, even though He had all the power in the universe to do so.

In giving me such experiential knowledge of His heart, I was branded. I now knew too much to cavalierly romp through this fallen world. A greater capacity to say "No" to sin was imparted simply by the intimate knowledge of the love and the pain of the heart of God. Such knowledge enables holiness like nothing else can, and it can be obtained in no other way but by being in His presence.

The result of failing to obtain such knowledge is, too often, legalism and eventually, Phariseeism. People never come to terms with their abject helplessness against evil and they never learn how to let Christ do it for them. They live in the pride of self-achievement, self-effort and performance-orientation—and thus, independent of God's power. Eventually, no matter how strong-willed they are, life gets too tough, the house of cards collapses, and they return to their old ways. In essence, the problem is a refusal to die to self and to embrace wholesale dependence on God.

Such people have never grasped how to "live by the Spirit"—how to let the righteousness of Christ be reflected through their life.

Of this, Leanne Payne writes:

To walk in the Spirit is to cease striving in our own strength and goodness, and to walk in His. It is to celebrate our smallness, our inadequacy apart from Him. It is to admit that He alone is our righteousness. We cannot keep the law. Another, the Holy Other, must do it for us. To walk in the Spirit is to live in the present moment, always looking to Christ, always practicing His Presence, always moving in tandem with Him.[16]

III. Failure to Accept Oneself.[17]

Some might object to the idea that a Christian should develop a sense of self-acceptance, pointing to the Apostle Paul's statement in Romans 7:18 "that nothing good lives in me." They really must read the qualifying second half of Paul's statement, however—"that is, in my sinful nature." In one brief sentence, Paul has summed up two very important truths that must be kept in tension. Our sinful nature is bereft of good, but the new self, which has become the true self for believers, is very good. God declared it so before the Fall and repeats the judgment for those He has redeemed through Christ.

"Self-acceptance," Payne writes, "denotes an authentic and necessary Christian virtue."[18]

Again, we must take note: Self-acceptance is not the same as saying that everything about me is good. It is, rather, a deliberate focusing in on the new creation part of me, accepting that as good, and reckoning dead the old nature.

Payne continues:

Today, there is a multitude of Christians whose failure to accept themselves is accompanied by a needless and ongoing sense of guilt and shame, or even more critically, an intense and even pathological self-hatred.[19]

The sin of pride . . . is bound up in . . . self-hatred.[20]

. . . In rejecting and hating (ourselves), (we fall) into pride. Herein is the pride: (We) want to be good enough on (our) own. . . . (We need to) come to terms with the depths of sin in (our) heart and acknowledge (our) self-deception.

Just as sons or daughters often will try the rest of their lives to win the love of an unaffirming parent—by great exploits or accomplishments or whatever—so people try to keep the law on their own and thereby win God's love. . . They want, in short, their own righteousness, not His. And this is where the pride comes in.

The humility that acknowledges ourselves as truly fallen is a first priority in coming to accept ourselves. You may be asking, "Stress humility to the one who hates himself?" Yes, for self-hatred in the Christian is a substitute for humility; it belongs to pride. . .

. . . When we are properly related to God, we silence the accuser of our souls by admitting, "Yes, I am capable of the petty; I am capable of the monstrous; and if

He should leave me but for a moment, I should do yet worse."

The humble acceptance of myself as fallen but now justified by Another who is my righteousness is the basis on which I can accept myself, learn to laugh at myself, be patient with myself. And then, wonder of wonders, be enabled for at least part of the time to forget myself."[21]

How then can such pride be overturned?

It is imperative that we begin earnestly listening to God the Father, the One who waits to bring us out of fearful, dependent relationships and into right relationship with Himself and others. This will occur quite naturally as we spread out before Him every diseased thought and attitudinal pattern. Then, as His precious chosen ones, we listen and receive the truth and reality He gives to replace them. That is how we bring dysfunctional, sinful, prideful patterns in the thought life and the imagination into submission to Christ. It is in this way that fleshly and demonic strongholds in the mind and imagination are torn down. . .

. . . In this stance of listening prayer, every thought of the mind, every imagination of the heart, is brought captive to Christ.[22]

We must differentiate between the self that collaborates with the principle of evil and selfishness, and the self that abides in Christ and collaborates with Him. That is the true self. That is the justified new creation, the soul that is saved and lives eternally. The former self we deliberately and continually die to; the other we joyfully and in great humility and thankfulness accept. . . .

. . . it is only with the full acceptance of this new self that we find our true center, that place of quiet strength and solid *being*, that center from which we know and see ourselves to be white-robed in the very righteousness of Christ Himself.[23]

If I fail to accept and become identified with the new self, Payne writes:

I will be dependent upon others, perhaps grievously bent toward them; I will be seeking their affirmation, their validation, and even their permission for my every move. Failing to accept myself, I will have no solid center, therefore I will "walk alongside myself." . . . and will be a "man-pleaser" rather than a "God-pleaser."

. . . the failure to accept oneself is an attitudinal block. It has to do with how we perceive and feel about ourselves and others.[24]

To achieve a healthy personality, we must pass from this self-centered stage [which occurs in puberty and adolescence] to the self-acceptance that is full, secure. Whoever does not accept himself is engrossed with himself.

. . . the key to stepping from adolescence into self-acceptance is the love and affirmation of a father.[25]

It is important that we help people realize that this fatherly love and affirmation is available from God the Father. Those who never received it from their earthly father can still look forward to these most necessary of ministrations if they will only spend the time to develop an intimate relationship with Him.

At the same time, we can do other things that help bring about a change in our negative self-image. We can make a deliberate renunciation of self-hatred each time it rears it's ugly head. We can resolve to deny the attempts by diseased thoughts and feelings to control us and practice operating from our true self rather than the old man who has been buried with Christ. We can declare instead the affirmations of God found in the Scriptures about ourselves as His new creation.[26]

Payne quotes the Catholic philosopher-theologian Romano Guardini, who declares:

> I must agree to be the person who I am. Agree to have the qualifications which I have. Agree to live within the limitations set for me.[27]

Payne notes that the evil one uses the failure to accept and celebrate the new self in Christ to tempt us to sin. How does he obtain the right to so tempt us? He acquires his right by virtue of our sin of unbelief—when we refuse to believe what God has said about who we are in Christ and instead elect to bathe in the condemning thoughts suggested by the evil one.

Gaining a secure identity in Christ is crucial. Otherwise, we are left with shame, self-pity, and self-hatred which the enemy uses to oil our slide into sin.

Praying a prayer of forgiveness for the ways our parents and others may have failed us is also crucial. God will even impart to us the capacity to forgive when we are faced with memories that seem too egregious for our own resources.

Payne writes:

> It is our grievous reactions to the shortcomings and sins of others against us that make up so much of the matter to be dealt with in healing prayer. Once these subjective reactions are identified and we set out with the help of God to change them, we are on our way to wholeness.[28]

Leanne Payne recommends praying a prayer of renunciation of self-hatred. See Him dying on the cross to take those things into Himself. Then see Him risen again, ascending to the Father, there to intercede to the Father for you, to pour out upon you His Spirit, to send to you words of life that engender in you new and wholesome feelings and attitudes. And give thanks.[29]

She then quotes C.S. Lewis as having written:

> Your real new self will not come as long as you are looking for it. It will come when you are looking for Him. . . .[30]

> In love we escape from our self into Him and into one another.[31]

She continues:

> It is only after we have accepted ourselves that we are free to love others. If we are busy hating that soul that God loves and is in the process of straightening out, we cannot help others—our minds will be riveted on our-

selves—not on Christ who is our wholeness. When we hate the self, we in fact practice the presence of the old self; we are *self*-conscious rather than *God*-conscious.[32]

How are these people healed? . . . Their crying need is to exchange old patterns of relating to life for new ones, to build in new patterns of thinking about themselves and others, of seeing themselves and others, of relating to themselves and others. In order to do this, they must learn to listen—to God and to their own hearts. There is nothing that will bring these souls through the failure to accept the self more quickly and thoroughly than the practice of "listening prayer." Through it, they will begin seeing themselves through the eyes of the Master Affirmer, our Heavenly Father. This listening involves, of course, coming into the Presence of God and there receiving His Word and illumination as to why we feel the way we do, why we do the things we do. It involves writing down every negative, untrue, and irrational thought and attitudinal pattern as we become aware of it. . . . When we write down our diseased patterns of thought, we must always listen to Him for the healing, positive, true words and patterns that are to replace the dark, negative ones! That is how we gain the mind of God and get rid of diseased patterns of thought. We first *acknowledge* we have them; then we find what they are rooted in and why we have them. Finally, we confess and get rid of them by yielding them up to God and taking in exchange the true word He is sending.

In the doing of this, we begin to realize that we are holding onto some of these old patterns, that we have a real resistance to letting them go. We find that they are often, in fact, defense mechanisms against the pain of growing up, of being vulnerable, of being responsible.[33]

These words from Leanne Payne are perfectly on target. They bear reading three and four times. She has, in fact, distilled the nature of the beast and called out the true focus and method for growth and healing.

One incident in my own life illuminates the roots of human brokenness that underlie all of the psycho-emotional dynamics that modern man has become so obsessed with. I was complaining one night to God that His process for setting me free from the various things that had me bound was awfully repetitive, laborious and grueling. Clear as a bell, He said back to me, "David, I'm just trying to get you to grow up." And that's really all it is. God is using the occasion of our sin and brokenness to teach us how to grow up and be responsible adults. The world is in the throes of inventing new ways to stay young, carefree and irresponsible while God is trying to teach us maturity, character, and integrity. Why? Because it's the only lifestyle that restores intimacy between God and man. It's the only lifestyle that will ever bring us joy, fulfillment, and contentment.

Many of us never received a clear message that we were valuable, redeemable, and beautiful as children of God. This great void of knowing God's favor has been the field in which the enemy has sown self-hatred, anger at God, and consequent rebellion. The damage from such a lack must be healed.

Toward this end, Leanne Payne writes:

> It is in the love and affirmation of those around us as we are growing up that we gain a reasonably self-assured view of ourselves. . . . (However) this affirmation is never fully adequate to get the job done. Even if the love is there, the rejections we experience in a fallen world can hold us back from being able to receive it until we are healed. . . .
>
> We all must eventually turn to the Master Affirmer, God the Father, for our true identity, our real, authentic selves. He heals the unaffirmed by sending His affirming word. . . . We are all unaffirmed in the higher sense until we find ourselves complete in Him. . . .[34]
>
> . . . In the Presence of God the Master Affirmer, the real self in union with Christ comes forward. He sees His Son in me. He calls us forward.[35]

Affirmation must also come from fellow believers, though it will be more unpredictable from this quarter. We need to become a community of affirmers. Leanne Payne and other writers, such as Dr. Larry Crabb, suggest that we need to see what is right and good in people and praise it.

> Affirming persons praise the good wherever they see it, and they are always looking for it. . . The truly affirming person, . . . , sees the good and the true in a person and calls it forth.[36]

Dr. Larry Crabb, in his book, *Connecting*, offers a new paradigm for the church as a healing community. He notes that:

> God helps us become more like Christ by doing three things:
>
> First, He provides us a taste of Christ delighting in us—*the essence of connection*:
>
> • Accepting who we are
> • Envisioning who we could be . . .[37]
>
> . . . In our flesh dwells no good thing, but Christians are more than flesh. We are now supernatural people, absolutely forgiven, clothed in Christ's spotless apparel, and gifted with a new heart brimming with wonderful desires to do good. . .
>
> . . . Good urges are created in us when we're forgiven. . . . And good urges are *released* in us now as we get to know Him better.
>
> Until we realize that there are no legitimate longings in our souls beyond His power and intention to satisfy, all change is cosmetic. But as we grasp how tenderly committed He is to our well-being, we feel more inclined to obey. Good urges become stronger. . . .
>
> . . . Change depends on experiencing the character of God.
>
> Until we thrill in the Father's embrace after admitting we've been prostitutes, until we watch Him jump up and down with delight every time He sees us, until we hear Him ask, "How can I help?" when we expect Him to say, "I'm sick and tired of putting up with you!" we will not change, not really, not consistently, not deeply.

Do we see the good in people, . . .

. . . Without this foundational element of offering others a taste of Christ's delight in them, all our skillful techniques, our wise counsel, our insightful interpretations, even our warm encouragement, will add up to nothing. If there is no love, no supernatural delighting in who we are and who we one day will be, every effort to help people change will fall short of its potential. . . .[38]

We need to let people know we delight in them as Christ does.

Second, He diligently searches within us for the good He has put there—*an affirming exposure:* . . .

. . when a friend meets our meanness with kindness, something better often comes out of us. . . .

We can impact others by: . . .

• eagerly looking for the goodness in someone's heart and identifying the passions that are prompting loving, strong choices;[39]

Third, He engagingly exposes what is bad and painful—*a disruptive exposure:* . . .

. . . There are times . . . when goodness is most fully released only when badness is first resisted. That resistance may require the special encouragement of seeing grace at work when judgment is most deserved. Connecting helps not only to enliven the good but also to destroy the bad, and it does so by surprising us with forgiving love. . .

. . . God . . . exposes the bad to reveal the good. That's what we therefore must do as well.[40]

IV. Failure to Forgive Others

This is the second great barrier to wholeness in Christ, according to Leanne Payne, (failure to accept oneself being the first). She sees a causal relationship between the chasm that divides head and heart in western, rationalistic cultures, and the failure to forgive others.[41] Certainly it is a large part of the problem, for when we are out of touch with our heart, we sometimes lose touch with the reality of deep, interior strongholds of unforgiveness. Even when such strongholds are acknowledged, the overblown pride that we harbor in our capacity to reason is employed to justify them. In other words, when our finite capacity to accurately judge a matter unites with a philosophical commitment to human reason as the highest good, we either rationalize fair excuses for holding unforgiveness or we deny it a place in our consciousness altogether. Either way, it lies hidden, like some land mine, ready to blow up in our face when properly triggered.

Possibly the most prevalent reason that we continue to harbor unforgiveness is that we misunderstand what it means to forgive. Many are faced with having to "forgive the unforgivable" (Payne's term). Their sense of ultimate justice has been severely damaged and their raw sensibilities make them vulnerable to misunderstanding what it means to forgive.

We need to try and help such people see the difference between what they may have thought forgiveness is and what it really is, as we spoke of in the previous chapter.

V. Failure to Receive Forgiveness for Oneself

This is the third great barrier to wholeness in Christ, according to Leanne Payne. Receiving forgiveness for oneself is critical in the healing process for those who have suffered emotion-based trauma or neglect, yet they are often the people least willing to believe that God still loves them and that they can still be forgiven.

Their problem? Many still live under the law. In other words, they still see God's love, forgiveness, and acceptance as something they have to earn. Part of this is ignorance and part of this is pride—the pride that insists on being good on our own.

Many will not accept something they did not earn. Many others will not value something they didn't work hard for. And then there are those who won't accept the free gift of salvation through Jesus Christ because it will obligate them to Him. They want to remain free, independent and disconnected from anyone and anything that might expect a commitment or a deep and intimate relationship. They live off of a concoction of pride, fear, selfishness, and mistrust. And so they refuse the free gift of pardon from God and live in a prison of their own making. Our job is to help them see that their fears and mistrust of God are unfounded and that intimacy with Him is the most glorious thing imaginable. Our job is to be vessels of Christ Himself.

Part of the solution, according to Payne, is to acknowledge the "Bad Guy" within—to acknowledge our competing natures or identities, (old man and new man), and learn the "rhythm of repentance and reception of forgiveness" so that we deliberately "rise up from confession in our prime identity, having received forgiveness."[42]

In my seminars, after praying a prayer for forgiveness of sin, I will always take the time to pause so that people can, by faith, receive the forgiveness that they have just asked for. What does that mean? It means deliberately taking the time to consciously assume that God is keeping His promise, (found in 1 John 1:9), and declaring the forgiveness just sought, from His throne in heaven.[43]

The important thing is that Jesus has provided grace to forgive us our sins by His death on the Cross. In the world, people suffering under the relentless onslaught of sinful choices have no other conclusion to draw but that they are defective. The hopelessness of such a conclusion is what drives them habitually and addictively to worldly remedies for the pain of their own existence. In Christ, we have the power of grace to cleanse us from our sin and so restore us to a right relationship with our Holy God. Provided we keep short accounts with God, and go to Him for pardon quickly after we fail Him, this provision of grace enables us to maintain a positive view of ourselves and a grateful view of God. The power of sin to condemn has been circumvented, and so our recidivism rate declines with each cleansing from sin. It becomes too hard to wage war against someone who keeps cleansing and forgiving you.

Leanne suggests the posture of King David, who regularly went before God and asked to be shown if there was any wicked way in him.

She warns us to examine our patterns of going to God, to see if we suffer from what she calls, "the disease of introspection" (an unhealthy self-focus that keeps one's face turned from God and fixed on self).[44] We all have suffered from this disease at one level or another. Some of the great Christian "mystics" have written of our penchant to posture a seeking after God when in fact we are seeking the fulfillment of our own needs (e.g., Teresa of Avila and St. John of the Cross). We focus on God only to the degree that He serves our needs. In truth, it is a manipulative focus on God, not a true focus. Eventually, this predilection is remedied through the dark night of the soul, where God removes the consolations of His presence so that we learn to seek His face and not just His hand.[45]

Another problem that Payne uncovers is what she calls the "inability to name the sin," which is a conscious sense of guilt that stems from sin at unconscious levels of the heart. It is a problem of being "too out of touch with our hearts and feelings to notice" that we haven't yet resolved our sense of guilt over a sin even though we have just emerged from the confessional.[46] The remedy is to ask God to show us our heart and the underlying attitudes and beliefs that may still be holding guilt hostage within our mind and heart.

Finally, Payne suggests that some of us fail to settle the "sin" question, meaning, we have not yet decided to forsake our sin and so retain feelings of guilt for harboring a compromised heart in the face of God's grace. In other words, we don't really believe that we have been forgiven because we know that we have every intention of committing the sin again. She relates the story of one case:

> I asked him if he was willing to repent of his adultery and turn from it, and he said no. I then told him it would do no good to pray for him, that he was probably depressed over that and other sin in his life that he had failed to "put to death." I asked him to leave and make a decision about this matter and then return for prayer only if he decided to repent. . . . To pray for such people apart from repentance is to waste precious spiritual energy and power. It merely singes them with the flames of God rather than allowing His holy fire to burn away all their impurities. Their hearts are left even more hardened than before.
>
> There are many whose consciences are so seared they no longer feel guilt. They too can receive forgiveness as they *will* to confess their sins, knowing that

besides the fact that their consciences have been seared, their feeling being is also out of order. God can restore consciences and the capacity to feel compunction as they confess and deliberately turn from sin.[47]

VI. Failure to Forsake the World and the Things of the World

Compromise. It is deadly to a healthy spiritual life. It quenches holiness and even the desire to be holy. It is the offspring of an unforsaken stronghold of love for the world that many harbor in their heart. Its genius is in how subtle and reasonable it appears. Cloaked by man's fear of man, it insinuates itself in a most presentable way into our everyday life—even into our most accepted ecclesiastical enclaves.

Many saints throughout history saw the reality behind its facade and took radical action to distance themselves from it. They entered into levels of wholesale commitment to God not demanded by Holy Writ so as to keep far from it, and considered the charge of "fanatic" by their contemporaries as praise and comfort.

Precious few souls truly forsake the things of the world anymore. Hence our limpish spiritual punch and our bare-limbed fruit trees.

Passion for Jesus is missing! In Mike Bickle's wonderful book on this subject, he points to intimacy with God as the antidote to love of the world:

> While we are discovering His beauty and delighting ourselves in Him, the Lord is sealing our spirits. We will never again be content with a life of compromise that neglects spiritual intimacy.[48]

VII. Failure to Pursue and Embrace Humility

Holiness of life requires humility of heart. You can't have one without the other. Oh, you can exhibit seemingly pristine actions on the surface, but without humility of heart, they will be centered in a pursuit of the praise of man and of no value in the Kingdom of God.

Humility is a very dangerous thing to ask for because the obtaining of humility usually comes through humiliation.

Fr. Gabriel of St. Mary Magdalen writes:

> Before seeking humiliations on our own initiative, we should prepare to accept those which will come to us against our will. . . . they must be willingly accepted in order to bear fruit. It is not the humiliation itself which makes us humble, but the act of the will by which we accept it. . . . everyone, in one way or another, receives humiliations in this life. Not many, however, become humble because very few accept humiliation and submit to it patiently. . . .
>
> . . . If, in spite of all the repugnance and resistance of nature, we accept a humiliation by an act of the will, and assure God that we want to be content with it and to savor it thoroughly, we will gradually become humble. The hard, bitter bread of abasement will become, little by little, sweet and pleasant, but we will not find it agreeable until we have nourished by it for a long time.[49]

Jesus expressed Himself only once in these words: . . . "Learn of Me, for I am meek and humble of heart" (Matthew 11:29). Knowing how much the practice of real humility would cost our proud nature, He seemed to want to give us special encouragement. The example He gave in the extraordinary humiliations which made Him "the reproach of men, and the outcast of the people" (Psalm 21:7), those humiliations by which, out of love for men, He was "made sin" (2 Corinthians 5:21) and the bearer of all our iniquities, even to being "reputed with the wicked" (Mark 15:28), is certainly the strongest stimulus and the most urgent invitation to the practice of humility.

Jesus speaks directly to us about humility of heart, because every virtue, every reform of life, if it is to be sincere, must come from the heart, whence come our thoughts and our actions. The exterior attitude and the humility of our words are useless unless accompanied by lowliness of heart; many times they are but the mask of a refined—and therefore all the more dangerous—pride. "First make clean the inside," said Jesus when He was branding the Pharisees' hypocrisy, "that the outside may become clean" (Matthew 23:26). St. Thomas teaches that "an interior disposition to humility puts its seal upon the words, gestures, and acts, by means of which that which is hidden within is manifested on the outside" (IIa IIae, q. 161, a.6).

Therefore, to be truly humble, we must apply ourselves first of all to humility of heart and continue to deepen the sincere recognition of our nothingness, of our weakness. Let us acknowledge our faults and failings without trying to assign any other case for them than our misery; let us recognize the good that is in us as a pure gift of God and never claim it for our own.

Humility of heart is a virtue which is at the same time both difficult and easy. It involves hardship because it is totally opposed to pride, which is always urging us to exalt ourselves; it is easy because we do not have to look very far to find grounds for it; we find them—and how abundantly—in ourselves, in our own misery. However, it does not suffice to be wretched in order to be humble—only he is humble who sincerely acknowledges his own unworthiness and acts accordingly.

Man, proud by nature, cannot reach this acknowledgement without God's grace, but since God never refuses necessary grace to anyone, we have only to turn to Him and ask Him with confidence and perseverance for humility of heart. Let us ask for it in the Name of Jesus who humbled Himself so much for the glory of His Father and for our salvation; "ask for it in His Name, and you will receive it" (cf. John 16:24). If in spite of our sincere desire to become humble, movements of pride, vain glory, or idle complacency arise in us, we must not become discouraged, but know and admit that they are the fruit of our fallen nature and use them as a new motive for abasing ourselves. . . . We must humble ourselves within, the more we are praised by others. If humility of heart is practiced in this way, it will give us such a low opinion of ourselves that we will not be able to prefer ourselves to anyone; we will consider others better and more worthy of esteem, respect, and consideration than we are. Thus we will be in peace, undisturbed by the desire to be better than others, undisturbed by the humiliations which may come to us. The fruit of humility is interior peace, for

Jesus has said: "Learn of Me, for I am meek and humble of heart, and you shall find rest to your souls" (Matthew 11:29).[50]

To some, it may seem contradictory that we began this chapter by extolling the great virtue of self-acceptance and end it with exhortations to self-abasement. This is another of the many paradoxes of Scripture—two truths that appear contradictory but which are both true and must be held in tandem. The key, I believe, lies in the differing foundations from which each virtue proceeds.

Self-acceptance is rooted in the foundation of God's unconditional love for us, His view of our worth and value, His miraculous work to recreate us in righteousness, and His adoption of us into His royal family through Christ. It is a corrective to the false image that sin has cast upon our soul.

Self-abasement, on the other hand, is a corrective to the false image that pride has cast upon our souls. It's foundation is our creatureliness—a reminder that though we have been given great favor and honor by God, that favor does not spring from any merit in us, but from His unwarranted grace. And in relation to our fellow man, it is an attitude of honor and respect and an acknowledgement of equal standing before God.

VIII. Failure to Nurture the Marriage with God

The single greatest reason for failing to live a holy life is our unwillingness to nurture the marriage with God—a calling so important, so vital, so central to the purpose of life that we will devote the next chapter entirely to exhorting the reader to focus on this as the primary goal of their existence.

George Butron has written a song for the Vineyard label entitled "One Holy Passion," that sums up the destination for all Christian healing:

Let me burn with holy fire
Marked by purpose and desire
Set apart unto Your name
My life, my heart, my strength You claim.

Now in Your holiness I see
Intense desire calling me
Away from what possessed my soul.
You have captured me and made me whole.

Holy, holy, holy Lord
God Almighty, I adore
Your glory, now my eyes can see
You're the King who reigns in majesty.

One holy passion now I know
As to a ruined world I go
To kindle fire, spread a flame

That will reveal Your holy name.

Holy, holy, holy Lord
God Almighty, I adore
Your glory, now my eyes can see
You're the King who reigns in majesty.[51]

How then do we make the call to holiness work in the real world? We recognize and aggressively embrace the high calling of the believer. We practice the faith of believing that with God, it is possible, even if mitigated by our fallen condition. We regularly sit in God's presence, develop an intimate relationship with Him, and learn how to walk by the Spirit so as to crucify the deeds of the flesh. We accurately divide the old man from the new. We accurately divide the old image of God that we grew up with from the true image of God. We embrace maturity—learning to make the hard choices for the greater good, and crucifying our flesh by faith in the Son of God and the goodness of His will. We forgive ourselves and others with God's help. We embrace humility and the things that cause it to grow in us. We forsake the things of this world while simultaneously nurturing the marriage with God. It is at once a work of our will and a product of His power. It is the purpose of our lives.

*　*　*　*

Part one of this book has examined the hidden problems that disable the modern Christian walk. We ignore the true purpose of life, clearly outlined in the Scriptures, for a life of no eternal purpose at all. Many of us have never learned what love is and how to express it in all its aspects. Others of us have been so befuddled and disappointed by the wilderness periods of life that we have developed anger and judgments against God Himself. And most of us have still not discerned and lived the difference between performing for God's love and living out of gratefulness for it. Satan has worked his tricks against us in clever and subtle ways, and many of us have not noticed because we were not living in an ongoing intimate relationship with God where we could have heard God's warning. And finally, we have not picked up the gauntlet of holiness thrown down by God, who challenges us to believe in His power and His grace and to have our wills transformed by His love, so that we pursue holiness with both faith and passion. Now let's turn to that very act by which it all comes together—the marriage of Christ and His Church.

Part Two:
The Corrective Vision

7

$\mathfrak{Sacred}$ $\mathfrak{Mystery}$:
$\mathfrak{The}$ $\mathfrak{Heavenly}$ $\mathfrak{Marriage}$

Did you know that God wants to marry you?—that in fact, the end for which you have been created is just such an intimate union with God?—that the marriage starts when you give your life in covenant commitment to Him at salvation?—that what God hath joined to Himself, no man is to put asunder? This is one of the great mysteries of God. It is for this, that you were born and that Christ died and rose again.[1]

What then does the Bible mean by the term, mystery? The *Doxa Quarterly Review* gives this definition:

> In the Christian Tradition—in the Bible, in the Fathers ancient and modern, and in the Liturgy—*mystery* is a very important word. But in the Bible its meaning is quite distinct both from ancient Greek, where mystery simply meant *secret*, and from the modern popular definition, where it signifies a scary tale or a problem to be solved. In first century Greek (*Koine*) the term *mysteries* had come to connote secret teachings and sacred rites. In the New Testament this pagan usage of *mysterion* was Christianized. Thus in biblical Greek *mystery* (as well as terms kindred in function, such as *symbol, sign,* and *word*) signifies an *external manifestation* of otherwise unknowable secret or hidden reality (e.g., Matthew 13:11; Romans 16:25; Colossians 1:26; 4:3).

> In a biblical/traditional *mystery* the incomprehensible is revealed in terms of everyday experience. The invisible and non-material is made known in terms of matter, time, and space. The ineffable (the unspeakable) is communicated in sense-perceivable symbols (including words). For that reason the sacramental rites of the Church are known traditionally as "the Holy Mysteries" (see Ephesians 5:32; 1 Corinthians 4:1). The basic teachings of the Church, outward symbols of hidden truth, are called "the mysteries of the Faith" (1 Timothy 3:9; 3:16).[2]

The Bible teaches that there are mysteries that are to be revealed only to those who love Him. The central mystery is, of course, God's saving grace through the birth, death, and resurrection of Jesus Christ—sometimes referred to as "God's secret wisdom" and "a wisdom that has been hidden" but which is now revealed to us by His Spirit (1 Corinthians 2:7, 10). That mystery of God reconciling men to Himself through Jesus Christ is referred to again in Romans 16:25 as "the mystery hidden for long ages past." In fact, it is this core mystery that God speaks of when He says in Isaiah 64:4: "No eye has seen, nor ear has heard, no mind has conceived what God has prepared for those who love Him." In other words, man was clueless until God revealed the plan to us and enabled us to believe it.

In Colossians 1:25-27, Paul repeats the idea again and then expands on it, saying:

> I . . . present to you the word of God in its fullness—the mystery that has been kept hidden for ages and generations, but is now disclosed to the saints. . . . the glorious riches of this mystery, which is Christ in you, the hope of glory.

So we see a second facet of that same mystery—that God is reconciling men to Himself through Jesus Christ by imparting Christ into our very being. Later we see in Scripture even more facets of that mystery which reveal how Christ in us inspires, enables, and empowers a holy life, so that we can say with Paul, "I no longer live, but Christ lives in me" (Galatians 2:20b).

Another facet of this core "mystery of salvation" is found in Ephesians 1:9, which says:

> And He made known to us the mystery of His will according to His good pleasure, which He purposed in Christ, to be put into effect when the times will have reached their fulfillment—to bring all things in heaven and on earth together under one head, even Christ.

And so, the plot thickens. Not only has God established a way for man to be reconciled to Him through believing in Christ; not only does Christ enter such men to enable a holy life, in Christ also, God has brought together previously inseparable and opposing forces, both earthly (Jews and Gentiles) and heavenly.

Paul refers to this in Ephesians 3:3-6 as:

> . . . the mystery made known to me by revelation, . . . the mystery of Christ, . . . This mystery is that through the gospel the Gentiles are heirs together with Israel, members together of one body, and sharers together in the promise in Christ Jesus.

These are sacred mysteries!

Another mystery is the fact that not all men will die. Paul writes in 1 Corinthians 15:51: "Listen, I tell you a mystery: We will not all sleep, but we will all be changed—in a flash, in the twinkling of an eye, . . ."

We also discover in Romans 11:25-26, the mystery of the hardening of Israel "until the full number of the Gentiles has come in" so that "all Israel will be saved." Later, the passage sheds a bit more light by describing it more broadly as the binding of "all men over to disobedience so that He may have mercy on them all" (Romans 11:32).

There's also the "mystery of holiness," ("godliness," NASB), referred to in 1 Timothy 3:16 and only there. Paul states:

> Beyond all question, the mystery of godliness is great: He appeared in a body, was vindicated by the Spirit, was seen by angels, was preached among the nations, was believed on in the world, was taken up in glory.

Sacred mysteries!

Finally, there is the astonishing mystery concerning the relationship between Christ and the Church, referred to in Ephesians 5:32:

> This is a profound mystery—but I am talking about Christ and the Church.

In this Ephesians 5 passage (which has thematic roots all the way back to chapter one), Paul arrives at the supreme example and end for God having saved us. It is the overarching theme and teaching of the Book of Ephesians—the great and high calling of the believer, the primary reason for creating and redeeming mankind.

He wants to marry us!

He wants us to be His lawfully wedded wife, to have and to hold, from this day forward and forevermore. And in the Upper Room, with a towel wrapped around Him and a basin of water in front of Him, He knelt down to propose marriage.[3] And what God hath brought together, let no one put asunder!

Admittedly, this is a secondary meaning to the passage in Ephesians 5:29-32. The primary and more obvious meaning is that Jesus Christ is the Bridegroom of the Church corporate. However, throughout the ages, some Christian leaders have suspected that the metaphor can be taken further to suggest that there is an individual "mystical marriage" between Christ and each individual believer. In fact, many believers have claimed to have experienced just such a reality.[4]

Let's take a closer look at this truth revealed to us in the Book of Ephesians. In 4:1ff Paul exhorts us to "live a life worthy of the calling you have received." He calls for unity and humility in the Body of Christ. He calls for us to put off the old self, to "be made new in the attitude of your minds" and to "put on the new self, created to be like God in true righteousness and holiness."

In Ephesians 5:1ff, he asks us to "Be imitators of God" through a life of sacrificial love, to "live as children of light," to "be filled with the Spirit." Then, beginning in 5:21, he delineates several kinds of relationships through which we are to "Submit to one another out of reverence for Christ"—relationships between husbands and wives, children and parents, and slaves and masters.

It is in the description of how a husband and a wife should interact (5:22ff) that Paul reveals what he calls "a profound mystery—. . . Christ and the Church" (v 32).

The relationship that is to illustrate the interaction between Christ and the Church is the marital relationship. Note that in verse 31, Paul quotes Gen 2:24—a passage which lays out the intention and purpose of God in creation—a passage that Christ Himself used (in Matthew 19:5) to draw a definitive conclusion about God's design for marriage:

> For this reason a man will leave his father and mother and be united to his wife, and the two will become one flesh.

The description that is given in Ephesians is one of selfless giving and sacrifice, honor, and respect in ways that are consistent with the role that each have been given by God in creation.

In some mysterious way then, the uniting of a man and a woman in a one-flesh, covenant bond of unconditional love is a reflection or a depiction of the uniting of Christ and the Church.

Now we see why Satan is so intent in defacing and destroying human sexuality and marriage. He is trying to mock God. He is trying to mar the very image of God expressed on this earth through the marital bond, sexual and otherwise. He is trying to rob God of His deepest and most passionate intention—that of marital union with man—because if he can destroy the beauty of the earthly bond, he can destroy in us any desire for the heavenly bond.

You and I, and every believer, were created to live in marital union with God, both now and in the age to come. Everything about a healthy marital union on this earthly plane has been designed by God to be a reflection of the interaction that we are meant to have with God Himself:

- the covenant that is struck to bind us together eternally;
- the signs and symbols of that covenant that are a public declaration of that bond;
- the keeping pure of oneself for the other;
- the wedding party, with a host of invited guests looking on, rejoicing in the display of our mutual love and affection;
- intimate moments of sharing our deepest self with the other, resulting in new life being born and a oneness of body, soul, and spirit;
- over time, the development of a oneness of heart that produces a unity of thinking and even appearance (cf Romans 8:29; 2 Corinthians 3:18; 1 John 3:2—"when He appears, we shall be like Him").
- the parallels are endless.

God desires that we develop and nurture a personal, interactive relationship with Him.

When you marry someone, you don't go live in separate houses and never talk to each other from that day forward, do you? That's not the way it's supposed to happen!

It's the same with the church. A lot of people think that they're just supposed to say the marriage vows, ("I accept Jesus as my Savior"), get born again, and then go about their merry way.[5] They've got their ticket to heaven, but they have every intention of continuing to live their life the way they want to, (albeit cleaned up a bit more), without any serious effort at having intimacy with the one to whom they've just given their life.

Perhaps that's the problem. Perhaps most Christians don't realize that getting born again is just the starting point of a rich and deeply intimate life in union with God. And so they miss out on the very heart of what they've been given. They remain focused on themselves and the things of this world and lose the very purpose of their life!

God did not save us just so that we could escape the fires of Hell and sit on some cloud somewhere pondering our navels. He wants to set His affection on us and love on us for all eternity. He wants us to gleefully pursue Him with the ardor and fervor of a new bride, embrace Him, and share intimate moments of deep unity with Him.

I'll never forget the day—it was the first time that the Lord had told me to give my full testimony in public. It was excruciatingly difficult because I was convinced that if people knew what I had been in my past, they would reject me. But I did it because I knew God was asking me to. And at the end, as I awaited the final verdict of the crowd (which turned out to be very positive and supportive), I felt God inside of me jumping up and down and clapping His hands as a child would, going, "Yeah! You did it! You did it!" I felt the pleasure of God responding to my sacrificial act of love for Him— and I will never forget that moment as long as I live. We had an altar call and they flooded to the front to be cleansed from their sin. New life was born!

The mystery of Christ and the Church is the mystery of God bearing new life through intimate communion with man. There is the husband, Christ, becoming one with His wife in an act of covenant-making, and we become born again. The marriage is then consummated and in the act of sowing spiritual seeds within us, new life is born around us. People see our passion for God and turn to Him. They hear the word of our testimony and learn how to overcome the enemy. They experience the life of God in us being expressed through unconditional love and sacrificial action, which kindles a flame for God within them.

There's personal growth happening, as well. We are transformed into His image, with ever increasing glory. In fact, there's so much spiritual fruit being born from our intimacy with God that, half the time, we don't even know it's happening.

It is so very important that we not stop with the initial moment of salvation, but that we go on to the exchange of selfless love and service, to the giving of ourselves to God. We, the Bride, must bear and nurture that new life into fullness. If we don't nurture it by taking a daily swim in the

Scriptures, by singing love songs to the Lover of our souls, if we don't pursue Him with all our heart, mind, and soul, the great harvest of spiritual fruit that God wants to produce with us will never come to life. There's mutual responsibility involved in our marriage with God just as there is with any marriage.

Consider this. The image of both husband and wife is passed on to the life that they create together. When a man and a woman come together and a baby is formed, the image of that man and woman is in that baby. It looks like one of them and acts like the other!

The same thing happens spiritually. When Christ plants His spiritual seeds in us and we give birth to new life, the spiritual children that we have are going to look like us. This is why it is so important for us to remain faithful in our walk with the Lord and to be conformed to His image through our own intimate relationship with Him.

The people that are born to new life from our love relationship with Christ are in many ways going to look like you and me. Why? Because we are the enfleshed model that they will see, day in and day out. They may never attain to a greater image of God than the one you and I reflect to them. And so, the image of both husband and wife gets passed on to the new life.

We have been made to reflect the image of another. If God isn't the love of our life, we will reflect what is.

Some ten years ago now, I had a vision while in worship. Suddenly, in the midst of my singing, I found myself in heaven in the presence of God. An instant later, I realized that I was in the middle of a wedding ceremony and that I was the one getting married—to God! A jolt of joy and wonder shot through my heart.

Several years later, I asked Leanne Payne what she thought the vision had meant. She told me that it was important for everyone to marry God, even those who marry someone here on earth. In fact, she said, they should enter into a marital union with God first, so that their earthly marriage doesn't become an attempt to get something from a person that they can only get from God. Only then will they be adequately prepared to be the spouse of another.

There is a wonderful book called *The Good News About Sex & Marriage* by Christopher West that I'd like to reference. Mr. West has a really great way of describing how earthly marital unions have been established by God to be a type and shadow of the greater marriage between God and man.

He writes:

> From beginning to end, the Bible itself is a story about marriage. It begins in the Book of Genesis with the marriage of Adam and Eve, and it ends in the Book of Revelation with the "wedding of the Lamb"—the marriage of Christ and the Church. Throughout the Old Testament, God's love for His people is described as the love of a husband for his bride. In the New Testament, Christ *embodies* this

love. He comes as the heavenly Bridegroom to unite Himself forever to His Bride—to us.

Yes, God's plan from all eternity is to "marry" us—to draw us into closest communion with Himself. God wanted to reveal this eternal plan to us in a way we couldn't miss, so He stamped it right into our very being as male and female. This means that everything God wants to tell us on earth about who He is, who we are, the meaning of life, the reason He created us, how we are to live, and even our ultimate destiny is contained somehow in the truth and meaning of sexuality and marriage. This is important stuff. . . .

. . . [The Scriptures say that] a man will leave father and mother and cling to his bride, and the two shall become one flesh. . . . [Likewise] Christ left His Father in heaven. He left the home of His mother on earth—to give up His body for His Bride, so that we might become "one flesh" with Him. . . .

. . . God created Adam from the dust of the ground and breathed the breath of life into him. . . . remember that the Spirit of God is the very love between the Father and the Son. God is breathing *His love* into the man. . . .

. . . the man is a person called to live in a relationship of love with God. The man, having received the love of God, is called to give himself back to God. He's also called to share the love of God with others. It's stamped into his very being, and he can only fulfill himself by doing so. As the Second Vatican Counsel put it, "Man, who is the only creature on earth that God created for His own sake, cannot fully find himself except through the sincere gift of himself."

This is why the Lord said, "It is not good that the man should be alone; I will make him a helper fit for him" (Genesis 2:18). That is, God said, "I will make someone he can love.". . .

. . . Adam looked at himself; he looked at Eve. He realized this profound reality: "We go together. God made us *for* each other. I can give myself to you, and you can give yourself to me, and we can live in a life-giving communion of love"— the image of God, marriage. . . .

. . . Satan sets out to keep us from God's life by convincing us that God doesn't love us. . . .

. . . In offering us His body, Christ offers us a "marriage proposal." All we need do is say yes by offering our bodies—our whole selves—back to Him. . . .[6]

. . . Marriage in this life is meant to point us to heaven, where, for all eternity, we will celebrate the "marriage of the Lamb" (Revelation 19:7), the marriage of Christ and the Church. This is the deepest desire of the human heart—to live in the eternal bliss of marital intimacy with God Himself. As wonderful as marriage can be in this life, it's only a sign, a foretaste, a *sacrament* of this joy to come. Earthly marriage is simply preparation for heavenly marriage. . . .

. . . In heaven, all that separates and divides us on earth will be done away with. We'll all live in a heavenly *communion of persons* as the one Bride of Christ.[7]

But first, we must marry God—not just legally and judicially, but in truth. This is the sacred mystery of the ages! As Leanne Payne says—all of us should marry God, for it is from that foundational relationship that the power and inspiration for all other relationships is to flow.

We don't love one another because we don't love God.

We don't serve one another because we don't serve God.

We don't die to self and sacrifice for one another because we don't first do those things with God.

And so we live with a veneer of Christianity, much like those cheap, gold-colored souvenir trinkets that we buy at vacation spots that tarnish before we even make it home.

But the real gold—the true "mother lode" is found only in the heart of God and only by those who seek Him with all their mind, heart, soul, and strength.

Let me close with a story.[8]

One day a beggar saw a magi and his entourage approaching from a distance. He was quite poor, owning only the bowl of rice in his hands. As the magi drew near, the beggar cried out "Oh magi, if you would please share with me out of the bounty that God has placed into your hands, I might live another day." The magi stepped down from his carriage and said to the beggar, "I am so very hungry today. Would you give me your bowl of rice?" The beggar was astonished and a bit peeved that such a rich man would be asking him for anything when he was the one in need. So he ran his fingers through the rice in his bowl and finally brought two grains to give to the magi. The magi thanked him, mounted his carriage and rode off down the road. By then, the beggar was fuming and ran his fingers through the rice once again, suddenly noticing a piece of gold the size and shape of a grain of rice. He frantically scrounged around some more and found a second grain of gold, but no more. Looking up as the magi began to fade from sight in the distance, he cried, "Magi—if I had only known, I would have given you the entire bowl!"

Now we know!

*　*　*　*

With any marriage, there are going to be moments when one person is doing something the other does not understand or appreciate. Let's develop that more deeply.

8

Spiritual Passages

s I reflect back on my spiritual journey thus far, some of the more vivid memories have come from the disappointments. Nobody likes surprises, especially unhappy ones. Satan loves to confuse us with them. He loves to use them to cast doubt into our minds about God's faithfulness, about what we believe, and about the goodness of God.

So I thought it a valuable thing to lay before you what many Christian thinkers and writers throughout the ages have observed about the course of a person's spiritual journey. And to help us, I've decided to include insights from J.I. Packer's book, *Knowing God*, and Benedict Groeschel's book, *Spiritual Passages*.

If you're like me, you tend to focus on the romantic, pleasure-giving elements of the spiritual path to the point where you are ill-prepared for the more earthy, mundane, and downright confusing parts of it.

And in truth, at the beginning of the journey, a focus on the pleasurable elements is what is needed to provide the spark that motivates the heart to persevere. But if one isn't prepared for the more difficult elements, it becomes so very easy for the enemy to lure us off the path.

St. Bernard of Clairvaux once wrote:

Jesus hope of the penitent
How kind You are to those who ask
How good You are to those who seek
What must You be to those who find?[1]

God has beckoned us on an incredible journey—the eternal uncovering of His glory. Like the trials of Jason and the Argonauts, there are dangerous sirens along the way that can deflect us from the true quest, even angels of light (2 Corinthians 11:14-15). And so, a successful journey requires the same level of dependence on God that we saw in Jesus, who moved only as He was directed by the Father (John 5:19). Of the study of God, J.I. Packer, in his classic book, *Knowing God*, writes:

No subject of contemplation will tend more to humble the mind, than thoughts of God. . . .

It is a subject so vast, that all our thoughts are lost in its immensity; so deep, that our pride is drowned in its infinity. . . .

. . . We need to ask ourselves: What is my ultimate aim and object in occupying my mind with these things? What do I intend to do with my knowledge about God, once I have it? For the fact that we have to face is this: If we pursue theological knowledge for its own sake, it is bound to go bad on us. It will make us proud and conceited. The very greatness of the subject matter will intoxicate us, and we shall come to think of ourselves as a cut above other Christians because of our interest in it and grasp of it; and we shall look down on those whose theological ideas seem to us crude and inadequate and dismiss them as very poor specimens. For as Paul told the conceited Corinthians: "Knowledge puffs up. . . The man who thinks he knows something does not yet know as he ought to know" (1 Corinthians 8:1-2). . . .

. . . there can be no spiritual health without doctrinal knowledge; but it is equally true that there can be no spiritual health *with* it, if it is sought for the wrong purpose and valued by the wrong standard.[2]

So, then, how can we make sure that we are approaching this subject in a godly manner, so that our search will result in truly knowing Him more intimately? Packer writes:

How can we turn our knowledge *about* God into knowledge *of* God? . . . It is that we turn each truth that we learn *about* God into matter for meditation *before* God, leading to prayer and praise *to* God. . . .

. . . A little knowledge *of* God is worth more than a great deal of knowledge *about* Him.[3]

What are the signs of truly knowing Him? Packer writes:

when people know God, losses and "crosses" cease to matter to them; what they have gained simply banishes these things from their minds.[4]

I'll never forget the time, several years ago in Nashville, when we had a tornado that flattened a great many houses and other buildings near the downtown area. There were dozens of interviews on the local TV news of the victims of the disaster. It was interesting to see that there was a notable difference in the responses of those who had a deep, intimate relationship with God. I'll never forget the interview of a poor, black lady standing next to her demolished house. The reporter asked her the same, lame question that they always ask: "How do you feel after losing everything?" The lady looked straight-faced into the reporters eyes and said, "All I know is, God is good all the time. That's what I've got to say about that!" Her loss was her cross and in the face of the knowledge she had of God, her loss of everything material didn't really matter.

Jesus indicated that the eternal life that He came to give was more than just an infinite number of days. It was intimate fellowship with God. In John 17:3, He said: "This is eternal life: that they may know You, the only true God, and Jesus Christ, whom You have sent."

I don't think most folks know that! I don't think most folks even in the church know that. I think most believe they were saved for the singular purpose of getting into heaven without punishment. The church has missed the boat big time in teaching new converts what lays ahead for them in Christ.

God saved us to have fellowship with us. He saved us to have a love relationship with us. He rescued us not to put us in the guest house on His estate, but to put His signet ring on our finger, His royal robe on our shoulders, to provide us with a room in His mansion, and a seat at His table.

This is the love story to end all love stories. There can never be a love for you as perfect as the one God has for you. There can never be a heart of passion as fervent as God's heart for you. There can never be a promise so grand, so complete, so certain and irrevocable as God's intentions for your future in relationship with Him.

Satan's grand scheme is to persuade us to not believe this. He wants us to believe that God's promises are exaggerated, enticing come-ons designed to manipulate and control us. He wants us to believe that God's heart toward us is as fallen and devious as our heart often is toward those we try to love.

If he can succeed in causing us to doubt the goodness and the promises of God, Satan can ruin that portion of our love relationship with God that takes place on this earth—a segment of time that is so critical, so potent, so significant to God's plan, that all the forces of Hell are massed against it in a continual pitched battle. The evil one wants to render us unfruitful in bringing to term the new life that God has given birth to in us by blocking the intimate relationship between God and man through which it is realized. He wants to sully and cheapen, for a season, the greatest love story ever told and turn it into a cheap dime store romance novel, that has a form of godliness but denies its power (2 Timothy 3:5); that professes a love that is barren and devoid of any substance or reality.

Packer writes:

> Our point [that we were made to know God intimately] is one to which every Christian heart will warm, though the person whose religion is merely formal will not be moved by it. (And by this very fact his unregenerate state may be known). . . .
>
> the main business that you are here for is to know God.[5]

Don't let the enemy of your soul get away with it! Don't let him ruin it for you. Don't let him rob you of the abundant life and eternal reward that has been designed for you as a natural fruit of a deep and abiding love relationship with your Creator.

Often we draw back from intimacy with God because we think that He is going to find something in us that will repulse Him, and we fear His rejection. Packer counters:

> [God's] love to me is utterly realistic, based at every point on prior knowledge of the worst about me, so that no discovery now can disillusion Him about me, in the way I am so often disillusioned about myself, and quench His determination to bless me.

His love is not based on qualities in us that provide Him with a benefit or payoff. His love is grounded in His perfect nature, and it is pure and unchanging.

Packer writes:

> God is actually opening His heart to you, making friends with you and enlisting you as a colleague—. . . It is a staggering thing, but it is true—the relationship in which sinful human beings know God is one in which God, so to speak, takes them onto His staff, to be henceforth His fellow workers (see 1 Corinthians 3:9) and personal friends. The action of God taking Joseph from prison to become Pharaoh's prime minister is a picture of what He does to every Christian: from being Satan's prisoner, you find yourself transferred to a position of trust in the service of God.

What does knowing God involve then?

> knowing God involves, first, listening to God's Word and receiving it as the Holy Spirit interprets it, in application to oneself; second, noting God's nature and character, as His Word and works reveal it; third, accepting His invitations and doing what He commands; fourth, recognizing and rejoicing in the love that He has shown in thus approaching you and drawing you into this divine fellowship.[6]

For those who would like to take advantage of God's offer of deep, intimate friendship, Benedict Groeschel (a Franciscan Friar in New York), has written a book, *Spiritual Passages*, that will keep you from being surprised by the sirens and Cyclopes along the way. And by virtue of the fact that you are serious about embarking on this journey, he writes:

> When the individual has decided to respond to the call of God experienced within, and strives to make this call the center of activity and choice, he or she may be called a truly spiritual person.

The Four Voices of God

There are, however, many different kinds of spiritual people, each looking to obtain very different things from God. Out of His infinite aspects, they tend to focus in on one or two that are particularly important to them.

Groeschel notes that there are four classifications of what people expect when they journey toward God—what he calls the "four voices of God." The first voice is *God as One*. "God known as the One, the Supreme, and Living Unity will attract a person whose life is an intellectual and emotional pursuit of integration." Those who are struggling to overcome abuse, addiction, or intellectual confusion are often found seeking this voice of

God. Groeschel writes:

> The contemporary French writer, Jean Genet, is . . . [an] example of a person in conflict.

> . . . Genet attempted to find unity in a total commitment to evil. He tried to bring to this pursuit of evil the same purity of heart which characterizes the life of a mystic. He was even called the devil's saint. However, since evil can never totally satisfy, his life deteriorated into ever greater conflict. Genet represents those who have not been able to find that unity which would bring them peace because the pursuit of evil, of its nature, leads to disintegration of personality.

Groeschel goes on to note that it is not unusual for alcoholics or others in search of psychological equilibrium "to find that the scars of a difficult life bring them to their knees before the one God."[7]

The second voice of God that some are drawn to is known as *God as True.* Groeschel writes:

> A passion for truth often subsumes other passions so that seekers of the truth are usually more calm, methodical, and curious than others. They love to question and delve. They delight in discussing their insights with others. Such people feel called by God as He is ultimate reality, Truth itself, unlimited Being, that which simply *is.* . . .

> St. Thomas Aquinas is certainly an example of one of those summoned by truth. . . .

Toward the end of his career, this man who was perhaps the greatest theologian the world has ever known, experienced a personal revelation of truth, after which he stated: "Such things have been revealed to me that all I have taught and written seems quite trivial to me right now."[8]

Groeschel notes that the real danger for such a person is that they will become so immersed in the discovery of truth that they will become enveloped in "a labyrinth of ideas wherein they hide from the voice of the Living Truth," dulled by their own imagined, intellectual prowess.[9]

The third voice of God that some are drawn to is known as *God as Good.* Groeschel writes:

> Those who seek Him as the Good are at once the most beloved and affectionate of human beings. . . , they are usually cheerful, compassionate, and gregarious. . . . [but] often manipulated, deceived, and even betrayed. . . , if they remain faithful to the pursuit of the Good, they become spontaneously involved in a life of generous service. . . . they (often) experience a constant penitential sense that they have not served [God] as well as they might have.

> A danger for such seekers of the Good is a kind of stunned disillusionment. . . [and over time, a temptation] to run away . . . from all that is ugly and damaged.

> St. Francis of Assisi was such a person, but one who persevered through his varying moments of disillusionment by focusing on the horror of the Cross and glorying only in that Cross.[10]

The fourth voice of God that some are drawn to is known as *God as Beautiful*. Groeschel writes that the best example of the seeker of Divine Beauty is the young Augustine, who in his *Confessions* simultaneously rejoiced and lamented, saying:

> Late have I loved Thee, O Beauty so ancient and so new; late have I loved Thee! For behold Thou wert within me, and I outside; and I sought Thee outside and in my unloveliness fell upon those lovely things that Thou hast made. Thou wert with me and I was not with Thee. I was kept from Thee by those things, yet had they not been in Thee, they would not have been at all. Thou didst call and cry to me and break open my deafness; and Thou didst send forth Thy beams and shine upon me and chase away my blindness; Thou didst breathe fragrance upon me, and I drew in my breath and do now pant for Thee; I tasted Thee and now hunger and thirst for Thee. Thou didst touch me, and I have burned for Thy peace.[11]

Groeschel notes:

> Almost every fiber of the human being cries out for some pleasure or beauty. The lover of divine beauty has to be constantly vigilant. . . , [lest] he or she escapes into mindless religiosity or unreligious hedonism, becoming a sad clown whose smile is a mask for the tears within.[12]

There we have the four voices of God that call to us. In concluding the matter, Benedict Groeschel says:

> The first step toward understanding one's spiritual life is to recognize what beckons us: the One, the True, the Good, or the Beautiful. . . . We are all led by the divine and by one, or perhaps two, of the four voices of God, although the others are never entirely absent.[13]

What then can we expect along the road to spiritual union with the heart of God? Great Christian minds have studied this throughout the centuries, and there is basic agreement on the stages that a person can expect to go through, provided they persevere. In understanding them, we can more successfully weather the potholes along the way and maintain our resolve not to settle for less than what God has made available to us.

The Apostle Paul wrote in Philippians 3 that nothing could happen that could outweigh the supreme advantage of knowing Christ Jesus. In fact, he considered everything as so much rubbish if only he could have Christ. He concluded, "I want to know Christ and the power of His resurrection and the fellowship of sharing His sufferings, becoming like Him in His death" (Philippians 3:10). Wow! In that third heaven experience of his, Paul had evidently seen so much of God's glory that he literally invited God to give him a share in the sufferings of Christ. When was the last time you prayed that?

Groeschel notes:

> when the faith of which St. Paul speaks in Philippians takes hold of a person, life itself becomes a series of good works performed by Christ living within the

person and increasingly operating through his or her acts. The essential personal good work is to consent with all one's being to the knowledge of Christ within.[14]

Religious Development

In many ways, the development of our spiritual life mimics that of our physical life. In fact, the parallels can be quite striking. Our first steps in the spiritual life are as fraught with the same hesitancy, weakness, and immaturity as were our first steps after being born physically. You've probably witnessed a baby or two taking their walking legs for a spin the first time—right into a wall.

Groeschel notes that our earliest attempts at the religious life are "a matter of attempting to control or manipulate the Divine Being by prayer, supplication, and good works." This, he refers to, as the *religion of childhood*. Fortunately, God knows and understands our immaturity and graciously works with us.

In *religious adolescence*, we finally begin seeing God in abstract terms as an omnipresent, invisible spirit. Our faith becomes intellectual and speculative. Although at times still powerfully driven by emotions, the religious adolescent "increasingly uses the mind rather than the emotions to make sense out of life."

When we have grown into *religious maturity*, we have finally learned to die to self and love truth, no matter where it takes us. We even allow truth to take us into regions where reason cannot reach. Rationalists (those who believe that God can be apprehended solely through man's reason) never make it this far, as Cardinal John Henry Newman noted: "The Rationalist makes himself his own center, not his Maker; he does not go to God, but he implies that God must come to him."[15]

I remember the day God unveiled that very fault in me. I was demanding an answer to the perennial question "Why God allows the innocent to suffer?" when the Lord showed me that I was making an idol of that question and demanding that He bow down to it—that I had to give myself in trust to Him without the answer that I wanted and that I needed to base that trust solely on His demonstrated love on the Cross.

Of this problem, Groeschel notes:

> The childish impulse to control God by prayer and works and the attempt of the adolescent mind to control Him by speculation and understanding must come to an end.
>
> The fundamental anxiety expressed by these two attitudes must be rooted out. The energy expended in the emotional need to control God must now be transformed into trust; the intellectual obsession with reducing God to one's categories of thought must now give way to the act of faith. These two changes constitute a real *metanoia*, i.e., a basic change of attitude made possible by grace. The *metanoia* takes place on two levels: that of the heart and that of the head.

Neither faith nor trust destroys the mental process nor the emotional dynamism, but each directs these primary human powers away from their impulse to dominate God. The individual surrenders to grace, an act which is impossible without direct divine assistance because it goes completely contrary to the human personality. "No one can say that Jesus is Lord except in the Holy Spirit" (1 Corinthians 12:3). Faith and hope are theological virtues; they are not self-given. They do not originate from the being of the individual. They are gifts and like all gifts must be received. They prepare the way for an even greater gift of charity or love. They make an effective termination of self-centered aspects of childhood or adolescent religion, and prepare the way for contemplation, or listening to God. Faith and hope do require an inner act of the will. This is a choice on the part of the individual to step beyond the narrow confines of personal security. In their mature form, faith and trust (which is ultimate hope) imply a death of the child and adolescent self. The impulse to do good works or to speculate about the divine does not come to an end. It is transformed so that the builder of temples and the writer of books may say with St. Thomas, "Nothing but Thee," or with St. Teresa, "God Alone!"[16]

Spiritual Development

Groeschel notes that our spiritual life begins with one or more experiences of awakening, where we come face to face with intangible, spiritual realities.

I remember my first such experience. When I was 12, during a solo anthem of "O Holy Night" a strong, exquisite sense of Jesus' presence suddenly was made known to me in the church service. I knew that God existed and that I had a real choice to make.

Groeschel notes that once this awakening is either accepted or rejected by a person, their life is never the same again. He also notes that it may take years for the initial awakening to God to take hold, but once it does, the person knows they must change their life to be consistent with the knowledge they have now embraced. Then begins the journey of the Christian spiritual life.

Theologians and mystics throughout the ages pretty much agree that it has three stages—Purgation, Illumination, and Union.

The first stage—*Purgation*—includes the various processes known as repentance, the renewing of the mind, the healing of the memories, deliverance, the disciplining of one's life, the reckoning of the old man as dead, and various sundry operations.

It is not easy, mostly because believers have usually not yet learned to let Christ live His life through them. They have often not yet learned how to die to self, to hate evil, to forsake the things of this world or to live by the Spirit. In this stage, they learn spiritual warfare and how to use the weapons God has placed in their hands against the enemy. In this stage, they become persuaded little by little to be faithful to God and to reject compromise, lukewarmness, and half-heartedness. They learn how to stop playing games with God and get with the program. Their faith and their actions become integrated into a consistent whole. Internal attitudes and beliefs are brought into alignment with the mind of Christ. Moral virtues such as faith, hope, love, temperance, and justice begin to dominate the person's behavior under the influence of the Holy Spirit. Intimate contact with God increases.

Often this first purgative stage of the spiritual journey culminates with a time of significant trial, when the person loses control of something or someone they've needed. Someone dies, a job is lost, or perhaps they are betrayed. Groeschel says:

A decision to cling to God in the darkness is demanded. . . .

. . . One has nothing: . . . One is fortunate at that time to be able to cry. In a very real way one dies. Many important things are laid aside as trivia. One becomes detached, objective, "disinterested," to use Loyola's word. There is a dead person lying on the stage of life; he or she looks familiar: "Oh yes, it's me!". . .

For most, this darkness ends rather abruptly. In an hour, or a day, or a week, a new world dawns—sharp, clear, free.[17]

Many of us imagine a Disney version of the spiritual journey and are caught off guard by this sudden downturn of fortune. We're caught assuming that because we have been faithfully following after God, He owes us a certain level of happiness, protection, and prosperity. Having gathered teachers around us who have tickled our ears with such fantasy, we bear a heavy burden of shock and dismay when things start unraveling, wondering if we have offended God, committed some unpardonable sin, not performed up to standard or in some other way subverted the normal processes of the spiritual life. Such despair can drive us to forsake the Lord and the ways of the Lord.

So—be forewarned. There are dark places along the road in drawing close to God. And sometimes such dark times actually signal progress rather than failure. If you leave God when they occur, you'll never find out which it was. By all means, stay committed to God and trust Him.

The second stage of the spiritual life is called *Illumination*. Oddly enough, some will draw back from the gate at this point because they have become perversely accustomed to the comfort of suffering, temptation, and misery, and fear the loss of them. They refuse to trust the safety of the unknown passages that God now beckons them down and opt for what has been familiar. Some fear the responsibility that greater light brings and prefer to live in the comfortable shadows of compromise.

Oh how it breaks the heart of God when, in the face of being offered a mansion, we elect to crawl back into our dumpsters and scrounge around in the refuse of this rotted world.

In his book, *Spiritual Passages*, Benedict Groeschel mentions other reasons why some balk at the door of the Illuminative way. He writes:

> Others . . . misinterpret the illuminative way, thinking it will be without sin or struggle. They experience both, so they suppose that they must be deceiving themselves. . . . [Others] fear . . . a life without self-seeking. Augustine encountered the threat of this possibility: "You will never have us again. Can you live without us?" his vices called out. . . .
>
> . . . As one moves on, . . . Not only the past with all its failures, but also the present with its imperfections are mercilessly enlightened in this illumination. The love of God, the loving call to Christ, the gifts of the Holy Spirit combine to make the presence of egotism,cupidity, spiritual immaturity, and lack of social responsibility almost unbearable. There is a growing . . . awareness of the obstacles one places in the way of being in love with God. . . . One is frustrated by the inability to do more—. . . good works, . . . , become the hallmark of the illuminative way. . . .
>
> The prayer life . . . is much changed. It flows like a God-given spring from the earth rather than through the valves and pumps of a human-made fountain, says St. Teresa. It has a gentle joy and release in it. God is everywhere. . . . Techniques are discarded; they become "excess baggage" because He is there.
>
> The Christian in the illuminative way lives on Scripture and is fed on the writings of the saints. Reverence and awe are growing in his inner life and the soul is now seen not so much as a shadow being but as the inner place where the Trinity abides in glory. . . .
>
> As the illuminative way proceeds, a silence and calm envelop the individual. . . . A gentleness . . . becomes the individual's salient emotion. . . . Such opposites as creativeness and destructiveness, attachment and separateness, masculinity and femininity begin to be resolved. . . . The resolution takes place in the presence of the infinite, simple Being of God. God appears to have become the *All* of the individual.[18]

Then comes what St. John of the Cross christened "The Dark Night of the Soul," which we have previously examined. It begins as a sense of aridity. Before it is over, all felt consolations and reminders of God's favor and presence disappear. Groeschel writes: "The childish ego, thought to have died so long ago, returns like a specter. It wails, pitifully in the night, with a repressed need to be satisfied."

He adds:

> If prayer can take place at all amid these distractions and strong feelings, it is a prayer of aridity. . . . It is really the beginning of the prayer of simple union with God. . . . Gradually, as this Dark Night is dispelled, very advanced souls may come to so profound a union with God that it is referred to as ecstasy. . . .Those who have experienced the Dark Night say that they become almost dissociated from their work, so that the Holy Spirit puts into their mouths words and wisdom which help others but never touch their own hearts.
>
> Worst of all, the sweet penitence of the illuminative way, the healing tears for

having sinned and failed to love God, are now dried up. . . .

. . . What has happened is that everything is lost and gone. All that is left is the stripped human will, unsupported, unadorned, without reinforcement or reward. One preserves the *desire* to remain loyal to God. T.S. Eliot in the *Four Quartets* suggests that this experience is unlike any other experience of faith, hope, and love in the past. It is a simple "yes" to the simple presence of God; the simple acceptance of the grace to love.

The inner icon is gone.[19]

The third and final stage of the spiritual life is called *Union* or the *Unitive Way*. Groeschel says you can only describe what it is not.

It is not spectacular in any sense. Rather, it is like the sun at high noon in a cloudless sky. . . .

According to Augustine, it is a single Word spoken by God, with neither beginning nor end, and containing all.

. . . [It's like the love of] an elderly couple who are quite at peace and tranquil in each other's presence. . . . [It is] a simple childlike hymn of praise.

. . . St. Augustine [writes:] "If this experience could continue, and all others so inferior be taken away, and this one so wrap the beholder in inward joys, that all of life might be like that single instant in which we had come to touch (the Divine Reality), would this not mean 'enter into the joy of the Lord.' "[20]

So there is a bit more to this journey, with its three stages and various sub-stages, than we may have thought. Loving God is a bit more multi-dimensional than a simple tune sung from a puffy white cloud. And, yet, when the maturation process draws near its end, there are many ways in which the product does indeed resemble that simple tune sung from that puffy white cloud. It's just that the voice singing the tune is far richer and deeper.

A word of caution. A danger in writing of such things is that the author may create in readers an obsession with where they stand on the spiritual path. This examination is rife with possibilities for reigniting a dormant performance orientation or pouring gas on an existing one. The purpose of this chapter has been to alert those who have recently embarked on the spiritual journey to the unexpected twists and dark nights along the way, so that they won't lose hope when they occur. It is indeed a marriage with God containing many of the varied dimensions that one struggles through with any healthy marriage. Some will most surely need the comfort of knowing that what is happening to them is normal and healthy, and that God will never leave nor forsake them no matter what things may look like. Let us all take caution from the words of Fr. Gabriel of St. Mary, who, in describing spiritual growth, aptly points to the need to ruthlessly excise any preoccupation with spiritual standing from one's mind and imagination, lest one not grow at all. He writes:

In order to enter the fullness of the hidden life, it is not enough to hide oneself from the attention of others; we must also hide from ourselves, that is, forget ourselves, avoiding all excessive concern about ourselves. We can be preoccupied with self not only from a material point of view, but also from a spiritual point of view. To be overly concerned about one's spiritual progress, about the consolations which God gives or does not give, about the state of aridity in which one may be—all this is often the sign of a subtle spiritual egoism, a sign that the soul is more occupied with self than with God. We must learn to forget ourselves, to hide from ourselves, by refusing to examine too minutely what is happening within our soul, and by not attaching too much importance to it, renouncing even the satisfaction of wanting to know the exact condition of our own spiritual life. It is well to understand that God often permits painful, obscure states just because He wants the soul to live hidden from itself. . . . But in order to avoid turning one's thoughts inward, the soul must focus its aspirations elsewhere; hence the *negative* exercise of not thinking of itself must accompany the *positive* exercise of fixing its *center* in Christ, of "burying in Christ" every thought, every preoccupation with self, even in the spiritual order. No one can succeed in turning away from himself unless he concentrates all his attention on the object of his love. . . .

A soul entirely oblivious of self is also completely disinterested. It no longer serves God in a mercenary spirit, with more regard for the reward which it may receive than for His glory, but it is "at His service,". . . as great lords serve their king. This should be the attitude of an interior soul called by God to a life of intimacy with Him. Such a one should act not as a hireling, but as a daughter or a spouse. Here we have one of the most beautiful fruits of the hidden life. . . .

This total purity of intention makes the soul act for God alone and never for personal interest, even of a spiritual nature. God will certainly reward our good works, but concern about this is wholly abandoned to Him as long as the soul is intent only on giving Him pleasure. The hidden life thus finds its culminating point in a complete disinterestedness, not only concerning human rewards and praises, but also in regard to spiritual consolations; our soul seeks God alone and God alone is sufficient for us. Even if, apparently unaware of our love and our service, He leaves us in aridity and abandonment, we do not worry nor stop on this account, since the one motive which actuates us is to please God alone.

O my God, teach me how to forget myself, to bury every preoccupation, all excessive care of myself in You. . . . I understand that if You lead me by an obscure and arid road, if You often permit the darkness to deepen around me, it is only because You want to teach me to serve You with a pure intention, seeking nothing but Your satisfaction, not my own. If You allow me to continue to practice the interior life and virtue without seeing any results, if You veil my eyes to my slight progress, it is to establish my soul in humility. If I had more light, or if the workings of Your grace were more evident in me, perhaps I would glorify myself and halt my progress toward You, the one object of my affection. . .

Blessed be this interior obscurity which protects me from the dangers of spiritual pride! . . . , teach me how to serve You out of pure love; show me how to forget myself entirely, to hide all concern for myself in You, to put my soul in Your hands with complete abandon.[21]

Do not miss this journey. It's laid out perfectly so that at the end of the road, you will have fulfilled the very purpose of your life—the very reason you were born—in all its richness, color, and fullness. God created you to have a love relationship with you. He wants to marry you. And remember, no matter what happens along the way, no matter what things look like, or how you feel, God is faithful. He will never leave you nor forsake you from this day forward and forevermore.

*   *   *   *

How then should we live? Knowing the astonishing depth of God's love and intentions for us, how then can we please our Bridegroom? The Scripture is clear: We please Him by living a holy life, one that is in sync with His heart, His nature and His character. What seems impossible to man is possible with God, though imperfectly realized until we are completely transformed into His image in the next life. Let's then examine what is possible now and how it can be practically achieved. Let's look at how sin can be successfully resisted right now.

Part Three:
Walking It Out Practically

9

Taming the Wild Horses Within

Preparing the Ground for Battle

God has indeed built analogy and simile into creation. Though we try to generate wisdom through the rational mind, it continues to lay hidden before us in earth, branch, and toil.

In Florida, for example, keeping a lawn and garden is all out war! You literally have to create a toxic environment in the soil that will destroy any of a hundred different enemies that may come to attack it (ants, chinch bugs, moles, etc.).

Knowing how each pest operates—the food it eats, the conditions in which it thrives—is very important.

Concurrently, you need to give attention to preparing that same ground with those things that strengthen the grass that you want to grow and flourish (fertilizer, water, iron, etc.). So there is a great paradox in having to maintain an environment that is simultaneously toxic and friendly.

In our war against the lusts that Satan and our fallen human nature bring, we have to make the same preparations and institute the same protective measures that we do with a Florida lawn and garden. We must keep the environment toxic for enemies and healthy for friends.

We also must remember that Satan continually trespasses into our turf, like wind-blown dandelion seeds that transgress the solemnity of our domain, contrary to our most ardent wishes and intents. He is a thief, who has come to steal, kill, and destroy.

One of his most effective strategies is to, almost imperceptibly, till the ground of our heart and mind in advance of any major frontal assault—often, way in advance. As we first noted in chapter five, he does this by persuading us to repeatedly compromise righteousness in seemingly minor and unimportant ways. He convinces us to lie to the traffic cop, or the IRS, or one's spouse—little lies, mind you. He persuades us that a lustful look in secret will not be a problem for us; that continual viewing of movies, magazines, or TV programs that preach the gospel of the world will have no lasting effect; that briefly entertaining sinful fantasies is no more than a harmless diversion.

These and other minor compromises are the gruel for fortifying the sinful nature. They slowly, but surely, empower the enemy's influence in our lives. He tills the ground of our hearts, little by little, with small matters so that when he sends the big temptation, there is no root left in us and we fall flat on our faces.

Then a herd of wild horses is let loose—unchecked erotic fantasies and other sins that wreak havoc with our ability to believe that we are lovable, redeemed children of a holy God.

Each wild horse that runs loose in our mind has a belief behind it. You see, Satan is out to tempt us to more than just sexual sin. He wants us filled with self-hatred; doubts about God's goodness; unbelief; and an independent, self-reliant spirit.

He wants us isolated, believing that we're the only ones with such thoughts, that no one could ever love us, that we are beyond God's love and grace.

Sexual (or other) sin has been a surface manifestation of much deeper and darker inner beliefs—evidence of a more systemic disease.

The War

We have two enemies: our fallen human nature and the Prince of Darkness—Satan, who comes in many guises, and commands an army of demonic spirits.

Satan's minions have a proven strategy that they've perfected over the past 6,000 years of human history. They are very good at what they do, and if it weren't for the fact that we have the King of Kings on our side, we wouldn't stand a chance.

Therefore, cling to Jesus Christ! The Bible teaches us to hate evil and cling to what is good (Romans 12:9).

But with the King of Kings on our side, as long as we are cooperating with God's Kingdom (and battle plan), Satan doesn't stand a chance. Why? Because all power and authority reside in our God (Matthew 28:18).

What is the battle plan for the kingdom of God? "The reason the Son of God appeared was to destroy the work of the devil" (1 John 3:8). *Webster's Dictionary* definition of *destroy* is "to ruin the structure, . . . [to] demolish . . . to put out of existence . . . [to] kill . . . [to] neutralize . . . to subject to a crushing defeat . . . [to] annihilate."[1] Dr. John Stott has noted that the Greek word (*lysë*), means "to deprive of force; render inoperative; conquer; and overthrow." Therefore, he says, "Christians must not compromise with either sin or the devil, or they will find themselves fighting against Christ."[2]

Have you been losing your battle? It might be time to look at whom you have been fighting. It may even be necessary to take one step back from that to recognize that your actions are, indeed, acts of war—missile launches either against the Kingdom of Darkness or against the Kingdom of God. When I have experienced a consistent period of defeat in my life, it has often been the case that, to my awakening horror, in some area of my life, I have been fighting against God Himself.

The Secret Weapon of Darkness

One day I was complaining to God about a particularly stubborn sin that did not seem to have a remedy. I screamed at God: "Why can't I get free." His reply, "Because you love it." Rooted deep in my soul was a love for the sin. On the surface, I was convinced I wanted release, and it took the searching eyes of God to see through my duplicity. Though unconscious on one level, it was still very much a part of my will. It is one of our greatest enemies—this duplicitous heart, wed with an amazing human capacity to deny the obvious and to tell ourselves lies.

On another occasion, when I was complaining to the Lord about something that had just gone wrong, God said to me . . . . "Have you ever noticed that every time something goes wrong in your life, your first and immediate thought is to question Me?"

Nailed again!

It is a propensity born in the Garden of Eden, from which we have not yet escaped—this autonomic response to trials which instantly questions, even blames, God—that assumes an error on His part, a lack of concern, that "doubts His goodness," as Oswald Chambers put it.

If I can then briefly state the obvious. This is no minor skirmish. It is all-out-war to the death. There are no neutral parties in the conflict. There will be no prisoners. The enemy of our souls is about to go down in a hail of bullets, and we had best be on the right side when it happens.

Fortunately, the only power that the Prince of Darkness has is that power which we abdicate to him, by believing his lies, by giving into his enticements, by doubting the goodness and the power of our God.

Lies form the foundation of Satan's kingdom and his power. Jesus called him the father of lies. It was with a lie that he brought about the fall of man. It was with a lie that he enticed one-third of the angels to rebel with him against God. And it is with lies that he continues to sow sin and rebellion in the heart of man.

Why are we so prone to seek comfort in the idols of modern addiction rather than the arms of Jesus? The bottom line is that we have believed things that are not true and acted according to those erroneous beliefs.[3]

In our formative years, many of us were implanted with lies, often at the point of intense emotional pain or trauma, when Satan whispered in our ears: "How could a good God let this happen to you? If God really loved you, this would never have happened. You can't trust God. You're on your own. You're going to have to make it all by yourself!"

Or perhaps you believed that it was your fault that you were molested. "After all, everyone loves daddy, so I must have made him do it. And besides that, since God is all powerful and can do anything He wants, He could have intervened and chose not to. It's because I'm too bad, not worth it, a mistake, unacceptable, too ugly, too stupid, unlovable, unredeemable"—NONE OF WHICH IS TRUE!

You believed lies. You were a little kid, without any capacity to accurately process what was happening to you, and you drew the wrong conclusions. Or you naively and innocently believed people who told you lies. Or without realizing it, you listened to the voice of the evil one, who will say and do anything to keep you from becoming the powerful saint of the Most High God that you are meant to be.

You began to see the Father as an angry tyrant against whom you had to protect yourself—an ogre who stands in heaven with a whip, eager to find an excuse to crack someone over the head.

Or maybe you believed that even though Jesus saves, that you are an exception to the rule—that your sins are too grave to be cleansed by the blood of the Lamb. You went too far; committed the unpardonable sin; lived a life that was too perverse, that you knew better and did it anyway and, therefore, are without excuse and cannot be forgiven.

Why do you see God this way? Perhaps the authority figures in your life were that way; or you saw a movie that portrayed God that way; or, again, you unwittingly listened to the voice of the evil one who spoke such lies into your heart and mind during lonely hours of failure, shame, anger, and bitterness.

What lies are you believing?

If you have a personality that is prone to addiction, you've undoubtedly painted God in the image of some authority figure who did you wrong. You've probably constructed a path to holiness that eliminates the need for an intimate relationship with God the Father. And so you have a thoroughly erroneous idea of how being holy works.

Let's look at a few more examples of life-controlling lies. Upon being molested as a child, you may have taken up the belief that:

- it was your fault
- you are now damaged goods
- you are unlovable
- sex is the only way to get people to love you

Upon seeing pornography for the first time as a child, you may have concluded that:

- to become a powerful person, you must do what those people were doing

- to get a girl like that, you must be a guy like that
- to be a normal man, you must learn to do the things in those pictures
- since you aren't like they are, you are doomed to failure in love
- that to love someone means to use them sexually
- that you can lust over people without even having to risk getting close to them
- that you must be an evil person because you are turned-on by such perverse behavior
- that no one who finds that out will ever accept you, so you must keep it a secret

Again, these are all lies that we believe and with which we build a fortress of anger, self-hatred, and rebellion. From this castle of internal lies, we justify rebellion against the fiction that an unreasonable God has left us to such an unhappy fate.

Fortunately, God knows that we're easily fooled and prone to wander. He knows that even though we may have given our lives to Him, we are still weak vessels. His patience remains everlasting and His grace ever-reaching through Jesus Christ.

Jesus Christ is the Truth. Everything He is, everything He does, everything He says is Pure Truth. The Christian life is very much a matter of learning to trust Jesus rather than our own thoughts, feelings, internal belief systems, and memories. How is that done? By getting to know Him directly in prayer, worship, and the reading of His Holy Word. By learning to recognize and obey His voice. By making the choice, moment by moment, to believe Him rather than any other thought or any other voice.

In general, and all things being equal, we tend to fall under the power of that Kingdom and that King whom we love most; the one we believe in most; the one we trust most; and the one whose claims and whose ways we identify with the most. So, God sent His Word and His Son to tell us the truth and show us the way. He is the exact representation of the Father (Hebrews rews 1:3).

Rather than sending you off to achieve righteousness on your own, He has designed the Christian life so that His life can be impressed into yours (just like the boy in Acts 20:10 who came back to life when the Apostle Paul laid upon him). The Christian life is not a matter of self-manufactured righteousness, but is one of God's righteousness being impressed, formed and released in and through us. His very presence living in born again believers is what makes this possible. But it only happens to the degree that we will it to happen. God will not force Himself on anyone.

For those of us who have already given our lives to Christ, the process begins by uncovering the lies that we have believed that have served as internal justification for yielding to sin. Since we have buried many of these lies deep in our subconscious, we need to ask God to uncover them—to show us the truth about what we really believe.

Next, we must ask God to show us the truth that has been denied by such lies. We need a present word of truth spoken directly into our souls by God Himself, so that we'll believe it. (I can tell you "God loves you" until I'm blue in the face, but to you, that's just my opinion. However, when God Himself says it directly into your soul, that word has supernatural power to heal and to transform your life). Then, each time the lies reappear, we need to resist and counter them by standing on the truth that God has spoken. The wild horses of temptation are thus tamed by the power of truth applied by faith and conviction.

It's really a matter of choosing which voice you are going to believe. Has Satan's voice been reliable? Have your own thoughts been accurate reflections of reality? Or is the voice of our slain and risen Savior the better choice?

We need to receive the truth even if we cannot understand how it can be true—by establishing a new foundation upon which our beliefs rest. Instead of a rational, intellectual foundation, we need to establish as our foundation the Cross of Christ. Why? Because what we really are doubting is God's love for us, and the answer to that is found at the Cross. P.T. Forsythe has said: "The cross of Christ . . . is God's only self-justification in such a world as ours."[4] When the Cross becomes enough proof of God's love for us, then we will be free.

Lies are convenient because they give us excuses to pursue sinful pleasures, but their fruit is death and ruin. They provide pleasure for the moment, and then they take your life.

Dying to Self—The Old Man/New Man Battle

How much holiness can we expect to achieve in this life? If we win the battle of lies and learn to let Christ live His righteousness through us, will we then be holy as He is holy?

Theoretically, the answer is "Yes." But unfortunately, our situation is a bit more complicated than that. We are strangers in a strange land, living in a hostile environment, with forces that are quite skilled at undoing our most valiant efforts to be holy. We are on a mission from God, left in enemy territory with a mandate to rescue the lost and retake territory for the Kingdom of God. Yet, in the wisdom of God's plan, our susceptibility can become a strength, if we will discipline (and humble) ourselves to turn to Him for empowerment when attacked.

Sometimes we fail to do that. Sometimes we decide to fraternize with the enemy. Though we are called to move toward the goal of perfect obedience to God, we remain incapable of achieving that goal perfectly until He returns and makes us perfect. What then? The Apostle Paul writes:

Not that I have already obtained all this, or have already been made perfect, but I press on to take hold of that for which Christ Jesus took hold of me. . . . I press on toward the goal to win the prize for which God has called me heavenward in Christ Jesus.[5]

In other words, rather than lowering the bar, as the world does, in order to make ourselves feel better (which reflects a focus on pleasing self), we must continue to lift high God's standard of holiness and press toward it even in the face of failure (which reflects a focus on pleasing our heavenly Father), and soothe our wounded egos with the love and grace of God upon each and every setback.

Fortunately, God is more clever than our enemies and has provided a judicial writ of holiness for those who have received Jesus Christ as Lord and Savior, and who have meant it. And so, in the midst of periodic failure, those who are committed to the King of God's Kingdom are given the status of "holy" through the merits of Jesus Christ.

Why is this important? Because without such a writ, we would indeed fall prey to the deadly force of condemnation and the siren song of our crucified old man, who weeps and wails pitifully from his grave, kept barely alive by the remnants of love that many of us still have for him and for the world.[6]

God has provided us a boat that keeps us above the waters of eternal death. It is a vessel constructed from the body and blood of our Savior. As long as we stay in the boat, we are safe. Outside of the boat, we sink back into death. It is God's hope that during our times of being in communion with Him, we will lose our desire to return to the things of the world, so that what has been given us judicially will be embraced by us unconditionally and exclusively. Thus, we work out our salvation with fear and trembling (Philippians 2:12).

To return to our first analogy, though we have been provided with a lovely new garden to till, there still remain toxins in the soil. Lies believed and temptations loved still linger, trying their best to breathe life back into our old man, the flesh—the one who was judicially crucified with Christ.

Dr. Francis Schaeffer, in his book, *True Spirituality*, writes:

Romans 6:4a: "We were buried with Him by baptism into death."

Romans 6:6a: "Knowing this, that our old man was crucified with Him."

Galatians 2:20a: "I am crucified with Christ."

Galatians 6:14: "But God forbid that I should glory, save in the cross of our Lord Jesus Christ, by whom" (or whereby) "the world is crucified unto me, and I unto the world."

In these statements we find that as Christians we died, in God's sight, with Christ when we accepted him as Savior; but there is more to it than this. There is also very much the demand that in practice we are to die daily. . . .

the Bible gives us a very sharp negative indeed—one that cannot be made an abstraction but which cuts into the hard stuff of normal life. . . . ; it is a negative of saying "no" towards the dominance of things and of self.[7]

Schaeffer also points out the positive side of the issue. Quoting Romans 6:4:

"Therefore we were buried with Him by baptism into death; in order that as Christ was raised up from the dead by the glory of the Father, even so we also may walk in newness of life."

This is the way it should be read: "that we *may* walk in the newness of life."

. . . There is a possibility of walking in newness of life in the present life, right now, between the new birth and our death, or the second coming of Jesus. In Romans 6:6 it is the same: "Knowing this, that our old man was crucified with Him, in order that the body of sin might be made powerless, that henceforth we should not serve sin." So we died with Christ, but we rose with Christ. That is the emphasis. Christ's death is an historic fact in the past and we will be raised from the dead in future history; but there is to be a positive exhibition in present history, now, before our future resurrection. . . .

. . . The true Christian life, true spirituality, does not mean just that we have been born again. . . . [or] that we are going to be in heaven. . . . it means much more than that. . . .

Our desire must be for a deeper life. . . .

True spirituality . . . is not just outward, but it is inward—. . . it is positive; . . . inward reality, . . . [with] positive . . . outward results. . . , there is to be a positive manifestation externally. It is not just that we are dead to certain things, but we are to love God, we are to be alive to Him, we are to be in communion with Him, *in this present moment of history*. And we are to love men, . . . *in this present moment of history*. . . .

Anything else is trifling with God, and because it is trifling with God, it is sin.[8]

Taming Wild Horses Means Aiming for the Right Target

Often, we confuse being healed with being holy. Out of an obsessive focus on self, we mistake a pursuit of healing for a pursuit of holiness. The problem is, when self is at the center of the issue, holiness is never the result. We are not the focus of the universe. God is. Any path toward healing must have that as a primary tenet lest the healing be subverted by a more sophisticated and occluded form of spiritual dysfunction. Dying to self is really the crux of the matter.

Dr. Larry Crabb, in his book, *The Safest Place on Earth*, writes:

I have given up on healing, if healing means a repair job on what is wrong inside me that will lessen my struggles. I am now searching for a path to maturity that doesn't focus so intensely on all that's wrong with me, on all the unsatisfied longings of my heart that seem to require a self-protective style of relating, on whatever traumatic memories still sting. . . .

. . . We moderns tend to think of our spiritual journey as a God-directed adventure until something goes seriously wrong or until certain problems persist past the time we give God to take them away. Then we think about solving the problems more than about finding God in the midst of them. We focus more on using God to improve our lives than on worshipping Him in any and every circumstance. We think more about pathology—what can be fixed—than about the journey we're on.

As we listen to each other tell our stories, we switch categories from progressing *spiritually* to healing *emotionally* or improving things *circumstantially*. The journey toward knowing God takes a detour. We get off the narrow road of glorifying God and go searching for a rest stop or a refreshment stand or a hospital to make us more comfortable. . . .

. . . Somewhere near the center of our approach to community is a failure to see dark valleys for what they are. We don't realize that they do not primarily represent problems to be solved, but are rather *opportunities for spiritual companionship*, for experiencing a kind of relating that is better and different from any we've known before. . . .

. . . For too long, we've been encouraged by a solution-focused, make-it-work culture to flee to human mountains when life gets tough, . . . We've been counseled, medicated, religiously entertained and inspired, exhorted, distracted, and formula-directed long enough. We've lost our focus on spiritual living. . . .

. . . *It's time to build the church*, a community of people . . . who know the only way to live in this world is to focus on the spiritual life—. . .

. . . When members of a spiritual community reach a sacred place of vulnerability and authenticity, something is released. Something good begins to happen. An appetite for holy things is stirred. For just a moment, the longing to know God becomes intense, stronger than all other passions, worth whatever price must be paid for it. . . .

. . . The first thing is to find that room, that place in your heart where the Spirit is alive, and to release the spiritual energy He has put there. To abandon yourself to God's purposes. To listen to the Spirit speak through His Word. To think after Him.[9]

Dr. Crabb notes how easy it is for us to lose spiritual focus and to return our attention to the pain of our personal situation. He says:

Counselors spend wasted time trying to improve what God has abandoned. Sorting things through often has the purpose of understanding what's gone wrong and how to fix it. The Spirit, however, has created another room in our souls, a room that is always clean and well furnished. We need to leave the fascinating room of complex psychological dynamics and find the room where spiritual forces from God are alive. . . .

. . . Unless you want to be in that . . . room with all your heart, and unless you're willing to literally wait on God to make it real, you won't get there. Your appetite for that new room needs to be nourished.[10]

What is the result of seeking God rather than knowledge concerning our brokenness? The result is that God reveals to us depths of knowledge that we never could have uncovered via man's wisdom. He targets the roots of problems. He reveals powerful solutions. He shows us how to find healing through our knowledge of Him rather than through our knowledge of good and evil. He unites us one with another in a bond of authentic love.

Dr. Crabb writes:

> When we appreciate Christ for the kind of Person He is and the sort of love He extends to make us lovable, we begin to realize we really do want to follow Him. We experience the Passion to Obey. . . . [11]

> Addictions are the expression of distracted desire. . . .

> . . . Perhaps if we once see that beneath every desire is a yearning for God, we will do a better job of providing the safety of hope. Perhaps then we will realize that our desires are not to be laughed at, derided, or put away, but to be traced to their source and given full expression.[12]

He concludes:

> A shift is in order, a radical shift that most of us rarely consider. We must shift from management to mysticism, from operating as managers in that tense moment to living as mystics. Only then will [spiritual] passions be aroused. . . .

> . . . The road to becoming a Spirit-led mystic begins with seeing the Cross as our opportunity to relate with God, intimately, passionately, enjoyably. The starting point for spiritual community is not learning and practicing relational skills. It is relating with God, drawing near to Him through the door opened by the New Covenant.[13]

Letting God Do It For You

The Bible tells us in Galatians 5:16 that if we live by the Spirit, we will not carry out the desires of the flesh. Many of us have an inability to grasp how to "live by the Spirit." In essence, it is to forsake the striving to become righteous by our own wisdom and strength and to allow the Spirit of God to release the righteousness of Christ through us. It is to willingly and cooperatively become a reflector of His holiness. It is to fix our focus on Him as the center of life and to allow His Spirit to freely pour forth through us to accomplish the purposes to which He has called us. And it is to do all of this with the peace and knowledge that as we look through this glass darkly the results will be imperfect until Christ returns in glory. Yet, we will do it anyway, because the love of Christ compels us (2 Corinthians 5:14).

The Bible is clear that if it is the hunger and thirst of our heart (Matthew 5:6), then God will send forth His righteousness to tame the wild horses for us. Note the repeating theme in 2 Corinthians: (the pressures of the Christian life) "happen that we might not rely on ourselves but on God (1:9b), . . . it is God who makes both us and you stand firm in Christ (1:21).

. . . it is by faith you stand firm (1:24c). . . . our competence comes from God (3:5b). . . . we have this treasure in jars of clay to show that this all-surpassing power is from God and not from us (4:7). . . . We always carry around in our body the death of Jesus, so that the life of Jesus may also be revealed in our body (4:10). . . . we are the temple of the living God (6:16b). . . . (Jesus said), 'My grace is sufficient for you, for My power is made perfect in weakness.' Therefore, I will boast all the more gladly about my weaknesses, so that Christ's power may rest on me" (12:9).

And also note 2 Peter 1:3, which says: "His divine power has given us everything we need for life and godliness through our knowledge of Him who called us by His own glory and goodness." Notice that he says we already *have been given* everything we need for godliness. It's not out there somewhere. The power has already been deposited within by virtue of the presence of God Himself in the life of a believer.

So for those of us who really want to be taken into progressive levels of holiness in this life, though it will never be achieved perfectly this side of the second coming, God will make it happen at levels far beyond anything we could have ever achieved on our own. The level to which He takes us is a function of how desperately we *hunger and thirst* (Matthew 5:6), how immensely we value the gift (Matthew 7:6), and how deeply we love the One who gives it (John 14:15). If we're in it for our own glory, it won't go very far. But if we seek holiness from a pure delight in the person of Jesus Christ, the sky's the limit![14]

The Bible also teaches that for those who are in Christ Jesus, God screens every temptation that comes our way and provides a way out (1 Corinthians 10:13). And so, God will not only tame the wild horses, He will harness them to work on our behalf. He will cause evil and unrighteousness to pave the way for our journey into God's holiness.

Strategic Warfare Tips

What God has designed for us is a collaborative effort. Our part is to position ourselves in Him, in love, in dependence, in obedience to His voice. His part is to respond to any pure desire in us to be kept in holiness. We do the wanting, He does the fighting. However, along the way, He gives us minor assignments that test our resolve and give us a sense of participation. But the power to win is all His. The actions that win are also His, often cleaving to the deeds He has asked us to perform.

Let me share with you then a few pointers that God has taught me along the way concerning the kinds of things that we are usually responsible for doing.

When you oppose a temptation at its strongest point, you gain the maximum spiritual benefit from your decision. In other words, the more powerful the temptation, the more powerful the spiritual growth and blessing when properly resisted. Thus, should you find yourself seemingly lured to the point of no return, and make the choice to turn to God anyway, great spiritual power will pour forth from the Kingdom of God, not only to defeat the enemy, but to fortify your spiritual man for future battles. (See Ephesians 3:16 and Colossians 1:11 for the concept of being strengthened in your inner man.)

Should you find yourself drawn to someone in an idolatrous manner, (whereby you are trying to feed off of their image in order to complete yourself—their image symbolizing a perceived deficit in your heart), stop in that very moment of maximum temptation and ask God to fill that need with Himself. Once again, turning to God at the most alluring moment of Satan's foothold in your life brings forth the maximum power and response from God. Cap it off by praying for the salvation of the person whom Satan used to try to bring you down.

Temptations come from one of two sources—Satan or your own heart. Learn the difference, because the way you respond will vary depending on the source. A demonic-borne temptation has an element of power to it. It comes unexpectedly, with great force and cannot be tied to a pattern of careless thoughts or actions. If a temptation is demonic in origin, aggressive spiritual warfare prayer is often in order—casting the powers out in Jesus' name and commanding them to go where Jesus sends them.[15] If the temptation is from your own heart (which is usually evidenced by a trail of compromises, wrong choices, or an ongoing failure to set one's mind and actions on the Kingdom of God), the response needs to be quite different. It is to repent, to humble yourself in sorrow over your divided heart, and to ask for God's renewed power to be faithful.

Though they are linked, make certain to carefully divide and rightly order the difference between finding intimacy with God and your personal healing process. Most of us get this one backwards—we see holiness as the carrot that will create in God a desire to be intimate with us. And so, we try to fix the broken areas of our lives first in an effort to gain a sense of being accepted by God. In essence, we try to create our own foundation for having an intimate relationship with Him. It's a very sophisticated game of works-righteousness and, by playing it, we not only deny the unconditional gift and sufficiency of the Cross, we also divert our attention from God to us. Thus, even our attempts to "know" Him become focused on ourselves, and we end up using Him rather than loving Him.

Larry Crabb writes in his book, *Finding God*:

> When I value God only because I regard Him as useful to my purposes, He will not let me find Him.
>
> If we are to find God as He wants to be found, if we are to know Him in a way that frees us to live with joy and purpose and self-control, then we must not work primarily to solve our problems. Instead, we must work to dismantle our

fallen structure, replacing the foundation of doubt with a rock-solid trust in God.[16]

Approach God humbly and allow Him to dictate the terms of reconciliation and sanctification. Larry Crabb writes:

> We come to God believing that He rewards those who earnestly seek Him, but then insist that we be rewarded right away with what we think we deserve.
>
> The seeking that gets rewarded, however, allows no spirit of negotiation. It is a trusting passion that emboldens us to ask for everything our hearts desire, like children before Christmas, but at the same time frees us to remain deeply content with whatever comes. . . .
>
> . . . Maybe the problem is not too much desire, but rather too little. The core problem . . . is not that we are too passionate about bad things, but that we are not passionate enough about good things.
>
> We will not overcome our addictions by looking for ways to weaken them or by focusing on our need for power to resist them. Uncovering the roots of homosexuality in the hopes of reducing their intensity will not, in the long run, prove helpful. And drawing strength from one's community simply creates another addiction, this one to the community.
>
> Something must be released within us that *wants* to resist more than to yield. We must become caught up in a larger, compelling purpose that strengthens good passions. When holiness becomes more attractive than sin, when knowing God seems more important than finding self, when no cost seems too great to pay for the privilege of intimacy with Christ, then we will find the strength to resist sin meaningfully—not perfectly, but meaningfully. Then our obedience will be sincere rather than manipulative. Then our efforts to live properly will seem more like *going after* something good than *giving up* something good.[17]

Be careful that feelings are not allowed to dictate reality to you. They are often based on the system of lies that we talked about earlier in this chapter. I'm not suggesting that we deny or suppress what we are feeling, but that we discern whether each feeling is accurately reflecting truth. If we find a feeling to be in opposition to what God has said, we need to reject it and stand on the truth that God has shown us.

We must also recognize the fact that truth is not signaled by intensity of emotion. Many false emotions are quite intense because they are linked to lies that emerged from significant, life-changing traumas out of our past. Others are intense simply because they are linked to the things of this world, which are more tangible and visceral.

Larry Crabb writes:

> Bad passions are often more sensual, but noble passions are more appealing.
>
> We may be *ruled* by a passion for God but *feel* bad passions with a stronger intensity. The measure of what rules us is not which passions *feel* stronger but rather which passions we are *obeying*. . . .

Maturing people are sometimes miserable (Hosea 5:15) [-i.e., the emotions that are telling them the truth are sometimes not as pleasant as those that are telling them lies]. . . .

. . . until we actually see Christ, our natural appetites and fears may seem more urgent and compelling.[18]

Set your mind on what God loves and ask Him to deepen that love in you. Dr. Crabb writes:

God reveals Himself to people whose passion to know Him makes them supremely uncomfortable with whatever grieves or offends Him, not only because they fear reprisal but far more because they long for intimacy. Godly passion develops when we face what is true about the way we relate to others, including God, and yearn to relate differently.[19]

A Working Model for Responding to Temptation

The subject of temptation is overwhelming for most people. They have gotten so inundated with information on the dynamics of sin, the reasons for sin, and on and on that it is hard for them to imagine that there might be some simple steps that they can learn as a defense against these "wild horses" that come charging through the mind without warning. I have found, however, that the most effective strategies are the simplest, so let me suggest seven simple steps for you to use when temptation strikes.

- **Step One**—Simultaneously acknowledge your weakness and the absolute power and desire of God to defeat the temptation for you.[20]

- **Step Two**—Remember the destruction that sin has brought into your life and those you love. Remember that Satan is a liar, that he is trying to make a fool out of you again, trying to destroy your relationship with God and your effectiveness for the Kingdom. Let righteous anger and indignation arise within you and put passion into your prayers for God's help.

- **Step Three**—Ask God to send His power to defeat the enemy and to convert your love for the thing tempting you to a greater love for Christ's purity.

- **Step Four**—Remember that temptation and trial for the believer are opportunities to grow in righteousness and in intimate oneness with the lover of your soul. Oswald Chambers once said that temptations are allowed by God "in order that a higher and nobler character may come out of the test." Leanne Payne has said that "temptation and trial compel us to face honestly what is in our hearts."

- **Step Five**—Envision the result. See God leaning down to listen to you. See in His face a determined passion and jealousy to oppose anything that might be trying to harm you and your relationship with Him. See Him giving orders to angels and them going forth to battle on your behalf, or see Him just speaking a word and the enemy being scattered.

- **Step Six**—Stand in place and wait on the power of God to quench the fiery dart. Listen for any directions from the Holy Spirit (e.g., He may prompt you to pray aggressive spiritual warfare prayer; He may ask you to pray for the salvation of the one tempting you; He may ask you to fix your mind on things above; He may prompt you to recite certain Scriptures). Do whatever He tells you, knowing that His power will imbue your obedient efforts with effectual force.

- **Step Seven**—Praise and thank Him for defeating the enemy. Listen for any advice He may give you concerning what brought on the temptation. Sometimes it was something you did or failed to do. Ask Him to forgive you for the love that remains in you for the thing that tempted you (which is what made it a temptation in the first place) and ask Him to put in you a deep love for what Christ loves and to make you strongest in that very area by the power of His Spirit.

*   *   *   *

Everyone needs encouragement along the way. In order to stay passionate about our cause, we need to see signs that we are progressing—that our efforts are bearing fruit. This is especially true in the Christian life. Let us examine then what some of those signs might be. We will use as our illustration the same issue of sin and brokenness that we used in chapter two—the struggle with homosexual confusion. That walk out of darkness aptly illuminates the many signposts that we all share in our struggle against sin.

10

What does it Look Like to be Healed?

The healing of the human condition is a lifelong process. When we finally get serious with God and conscientiously enter into the process whereby we are transformed into His likeness, it is a journey that lasts the rest of our life. The advances often are unseen to us, being internal and spiritual. The more broken we have been, the longer and more difficult will be the transformation. Sometimes we become impatient along the way and want to see evidence that we are changing. Especially in the first few years, we want to see tangible proof that what we are putting ourselves through is actually worthwhile and that it is working. Most everyone, at some point along the way is going to ask, "Am I healed yet?" or "How long is this going to take?" or "When can I consider myself healed?" or "What is it going to look like when I am healed?"

Because it can be so very important for young Christians to find encouragement in signs of their progress, I thought it would be helpful to discuss what some of those signs might be. In order to enumerate signs that could be expected to be universally found (no matter what area of brokenness was involved) I have had to look at the broadest possible categories - the big picture. It has been the point of this book to do that in any case.

First, let's start with some common assumptions that often stymie the healing process.

The Assumption That I Can Find Healing Without Entering Into a Loving and Dependent Relationship with God Through Jesus Christ

Knowing God is what brings permanent healing and transformation. Many believe that they do not need a savior—that they have divinity within them that only needs to be mined and tapped in order to bring about results. Some believe that a god or "higher power" of their own choosing is sufficient for the task. They have missed the point of being made whole, of being made right in God's eyes. They have looked at being made holy as though they were the focus of the command. Eventually, they will need to learn that this world isn't about them. It's about Him.

The truth is that intimacy with God through His Son Jesus Christ is the true focus and the goal of every divine command. Achieving right behavior is not an end unto itself, but rather a fruit of what truly is the goal of life—a personal, deep, and loving relationship between God and man. Holiness is birthed from such intimacy with God. It is a fruit of right relationship, not the achiever of right relationship. Hence, the healing of any condition that is unholy will never be permanent if someone attempts to achieve it outside of that relationship. For the person who refuses to enter into intimacy with God, who refuses to give their life to Jesus Christ, healing will always be temporary and incomplete. It will never be established in the foundation of their souls. It will always be an effort, a burden, and an ongoing cause of fear and insecurity. It will be a maintenance program rather than a transformation program.

The Assumption That I Have to Achieve Healing Through My Own Will, Power, and Effort

Even those who are in the process of coming to know God can be tripped up by the incorrect assumption that God expects them to achieve the transformation. It's the old, "God gave you a mind, He expects you to use it;" "Pull yourself up by your own bootstraps," ethos that many of us were taught. We adopt this self-effort, religious perversion of the truth not only because it is the way Americans think, but also because it sounds so righteous. After, all, if we have sinned, then certainly God expects us to make up for it; otherwise, justice is not being served. Ironically, the assumption is based on a proper view of justice, but one that has failed to take into account the abject inability of man to correct the damage that he has caused. It also fails to take into account the redeeming grace of Christ that has been provided to correct the damage.

We also resist because to accept grace means we are beholden to the giver of that grace. It means that we have lost control and become dependent. It's humbling and excruciatingly uncomfortable to the spirit of independence that has driven our fallen nature since the garden of Eden. And what is worse, it is thoroughly unamerican!

The reality of God's provision for healing is this—we are completely dependent on Him for the power, for the knowledge, the wisdom, and direction for our healing. And what is more, we will remain completely dependent on Him to be kept from falling until that day when Christ returns and we are then fixed in our chosen state. This means we must not only go to God for healing, but that we must remain in Him, committed to Him, dead to self, and a bondslave of Christ. Nothing grates more against our natural man than that!

The Assumption That There is a Common Time-Frame
and Order for Seeing Results

When we try to heal ourselves, or utilize the services of a psychotherapist or some other human "expert" *in place of* entering into relationship with God, the Bible says that we are made foolish through the very "wisdom" of man that we have chosen *in place of* God. A good trained professional (particularly a Christian one) may be able to outline the necessary issues that need to be faced and addressed in any given healing process, but he or she cannot look into your heart and soul and provide them all. Nor can any professional accurately predict the timing and the order of how those issues must be addressed without specific revelation from the Holy Spirit. And while some will give lip-service to God when starting a counseling session, many aren't truly reliant on His leading during the session. Their reliance is more often on their expertise, their training, and a prideful sense that they can accurately "read" you and your problem. It is a propensity that afflicts all of us who counsel others. We will look at that in more detail in a later chapter.

Every broken person is unique. How they became broken and enmeshed in sinful lifestyles is unique to them. A human counselor can at best guess at what is wrong and how to fix it. God the Holy Spirit knows exactly what to do and when to do it. Many people abort their healing process simply because they have never done it properly. They charge ahead (with all good intentions), but in their own wisdom (or the wisdom of some therapist), and fail to wait upon the Lord for that "still small voice" that tells them what to do and when to do it. They often do the right thing, but in the wrong timing and, when it fails, assume it was the wrong thing to have done. Or they may do the right thing, but fail to do it in concert with other things that must be done simultaneously in order for the desired results to be achieved. Again, because it fails, they conclude that they did the wrong thing, or worse, that they have done the right thing and can now move on to others things in order to bring about the desired results. Can you imagine making a cake that way—throwing whatever ingredients together in whatever order and timing suits your inclination of the moment?

"Faith" is a good example of a necessary ingredient that must accompany other more obvious actions. I can do and say all the right spiritual things, but if I do not believe God's promises in connection with them, none of those actions or words are going to achieve anything.

One day I was in worship when the Lord asked me if I believed 2 Corinthians 3:18, which says, "As we gaze upon the Lord's glory, we are being transformed into His likeness." I replied, "Yes, Lord, I believe all of the Bible!" He said to me, "No you don't. As you worship me, consciously and deliberately set your mind on assuming that what 2 Corinthians 3:18 promises is actually happening. For example, assume that as you are worshipping Me for my purity, that My purity is being transformed into you—literally!"

It was like night and day after that. When I assumed that the things I worshiped about God were literally being transformed into me, they actually began to be. I could see measurable changes every few months. The difference was startling.

Most of us believe that if we intellectually agree with something in Scripture that we are believing it. That is a western concept of "faith." To believe something in the Biblical sense means to assume it is happening! It means that you change your life to become consistent with that belief, whether you see evidence of fulfillment for the promise or not. So you can see how this extra ingredient of Biblical faith is critical to the effective working of other actions in our life with God. Without it, right actions may not work right, and we may erroneously conclude that those actions were not the right ones.

When well intentioned Christians fail to rely on the leading of the Holy Spirit, who is the Counselor, and instead rely exclusively on another human's expertise or education to lead them on a healing journey, all manner of confusion and misunderstanding can be created. Strewn along the path are all sorts of right actions done at the wrong time or not in concert with other necessary things, now ignored as having been accomplished, when in fact they still need to be done at the right time and with other right things.

This is why the fallen Christian is much harder to help than the fallen nonbeliever. The Christian who has fallen into a bondage to sin easily convinces himself that he has done most of the "spiritual" things and embarks on a desperate search for some new psychological clue, some new angle that's going to be the key for setting him free. The odds are, he has never truly done the first things under the direction of the Holy Spirit, but has done them as self-led, religious acts that have no power by themselves.

The Evidence for a True Relationship with God

If Spirit-led healing is occurring, over time you will see primary shifts in behavior, identity, fantasy, and attraction.

The Holy Spirit is God. If you have given Him permission to be the Lord of your life, He will do exactly that. That means, when you pursue sin, He will bring conviction and correction. The idea that true believers can blithely continue in a sinful lifestyle for the rest of their lives is contrary to the witness of Scripture. The book of 1st John claims to be a treatise on how you can know if you truly love Jesus and have eternal life (1 John 5:13). What is the evidence of having been saved? We are truly repentant when we sin (1:10); we do not love the world anymore (2:15); willful, knowing, and habitual sin is progressively being eradicated from our life (1:5-7; 2:4; 3:6,9-

10; 5:18); we have a growing love of the brethren (2:9-11; 4:7-8,12,20-21); we believe that Jesus is the Messiah (5:1), the Son of God (5:5), and our Savior (5:6-12); and we love God and are progressively more and more obedient to His commands (2:17,29; 3:24; 4:13; 5:1-3).

The Book of James also makes the point that faith without the expected fruit of good works is not true faith at all. In other words, slow start or fast, there will be a changed heart and life after one truly gives their life to Jesus Christ.

If we have truly given our life to Him and then repeatedly resist this process of sanctification, God may allow calamity to come upon us (1 Corinthians 5:1-5), but all for the purpose of preventing the dominance of evil in our lives and bringing us back into relationship with Him. In other words, whatever discipline is required, it is no longer focused on punishment (since Christ has taken our punishment upon Himself) but rather reconciliation and our ultimate good.

The Bible is very clear that many who have named the name of Christ, even having done miracles in His name, have never known Him (Matthew 7:21-23; 22:11-14). Their profession of faith never came from the heart, was never born from true repentance. The Bible also indicates that although no one has the power to take a believer out of the Father's hand (John 10:27-29), there will be some who taste of the knowledge of God through the Spirit of God who will willfully walk away from Him (Matthew 26:21-25; Hebrews 6:4-6; 10:26-29; 2 Peter 2:20-22) and be lost.

The Process of Healing Described

Why does the picture of the healing process vary so widely? Multiple elements account for the variety.

People begin their healing process at different places of mental and spiritual knowledge and health. Some don't know a blessed thing about God. Others were raised in the Church. Some are so psychologically and emotionally messed up at salvation that it takes a while for them to get to the place where they can see and think clearly enough to respond appropriately to the new impulses of the Holy Spirit within them. Others have been so damaged in their ability to trust, so taken advantage of by authority figures in their past, that it takes a while for them to learn to trust the internal proddings of the Holy Spirit. The battle within is not a matter of hating the holy impulses, but more one of learning to trust them and learning how to let them take charge.

We sometimes make the mistake of looking only at the outside—at the visible achievements and progress being made. We want to see tangible fruit and sometimes demand to see it before it is ready to emerge. God looks on the heart. He is interested in new desire and new intent. His interest is in the direction that the heart is set on, not the perfect accomplishment of that intent.

And so, the length, the extent, the details, and the outward success of the process varies.

Some people fail to understand that God's goal for them is a progressive walk toward greater and greater levels of holiness. They see salvation as a ticket to heaven without much else required. And so, they settle for less than God offers and stunt their own growth through the ingratitude of compromise and continued identification with the world. Having removed "the big sin" from their life, they feel they have pleased God enough and done all that anyone can be expected to do (except, of course, for special saints whom they see as having a higher calling).

Other people grow weary in the battle and give up. (In a sense, these folks have a stopwatch on God, and when He doesn't make everything better or easy within their timeframe, they give up on the call that He has placed on their lives.) They have never changed their focus from their own comfort to living for the glory of God. So, when the pain of healing or the fray of the battle intensifies, they shrink back in order to avoid the pain and/or the conflict.

Some never come to see a partial healing as a danger because they have taken their cues from the lukewarm Christian culture around them. If others are getting by without much effort (especially leaders), they assume that that's an acceptable way of doing things. They never lift their eyes to the higher call in Christ Jesus.

There are many factors that play a part in how extensive the transformation will be for any given individual in this life. If God were to just zap the believer and instantly heal everything, he or she would not grow. The believer would still be the same immature person and, thus, extremely vulnerable to reverting to previous behavior. Only in the slow process of healing each contributing issue can a believer be set free and grown up into a mature, Christlike human being.

God certainly has the power to achieve complete healing in everyone. However, He allows us free will to decide how committed we're going to be to the process. We reap a result consistent with that level of commitment.

So the commitment of the person to do whatever it takes to be healed is necessary. In many ways, this is similar to the commitment required of alcoholics and drug addicts. Most failure to realize complete transformation can be found in a reluctance to go the distance, no matter how long it takes, and no matter how difficult it becomes.

Like the alcoholic, the person must recognize that he (or she) cannot heal himself and that he must pursue an intimate and dependent relationship with God for the power and direction necessary for healing.

Many people find that they do not have this level of commitment when it comes to working through the more difficult issues.

Why?

Many people are motivated out of a performance-orientation rather than genuine love for Jesus Christ.

Many people find it difficult to rely on God, to believe what He says, and to commit fully to His Kingdom, and they refuse to give up their anger at Him in order to obtain this ability. They listen to other voices and get side-tracked—the voices of their own internal self-hatred or self-doubt, self-effort birthed in misguided family creeds or certain psychological theories, their compromised friends, or even of a doubting church.

Some put a timetable on God's promises. If He doesn't heal them in such and such a period of time, they're going back to their old lifestyle. God won't bow to their manipulation. To do so would be for Him to sin.

Others don't approach God's promises with faith, but with an attitude that says "I'll try this and see if I want to commit to it" or "I'll try this, but I won't believe it until I see it." This is not faith! The Kingdom of God is not a supermarket from which you pick what you would like and what you don't like.

Some simply love the idolatry and the pleasure of their sin and refuse to completely forsake it. They try to hold on to a piece of it as an option. In essence, they are trying to remain the god of their life instead of submitting to the One who is God.

Am I saying then that everyone who gets with the program will become completely transformed without any temptations from the past?

That's what the world would like you to think is the criteria for being healed. It's an argument continually used against those who claim healing from alcoholism or homosexuality, for example. But it's a false criteria, selectively imposed in order to justify someone's desire for a particular sin. For example, if I haven't smoked in 20 years, but today am tempted to, according to that criteria, I would still have to call myself a smoker, even though I've successfully abstained from smoking for 20 years! Even with cancer, you are declared healed after five years.

The truth is, there will always remain memories of past pleasures and, in moments of weakness and distraction from who you are, a desire to return to being who you used to be. Temptation isn't the criteria but rather a consistent history of how you see yourself, how you operate, what primarily drives you, and with what you identify yourself.

There are a number of factors that make one person's transformation longer and more arduous than another's. Let's take, for example, the case of the homosexual. In my more than 20 years experience of observing the process, the turnaround occurs more quickly in cases where: they refused to adopt the identity of homosexual (having considered themselves a broken heterosexual rather than inherently gay); they refused to enter into the darker and more perverse activities found in the gay subculture; they had some positive experience with heterosexual sex prior to changing over to homosexual partners; they started the healing process rather early on in their life.

And so, an older man who has been deeply identified as a homosexual for 30 or 40 years, who has engaged in the darker aspects of homosexual life with countless partners, and who has had experiences in life that gave him a revulsion for the female body may not live long enough to see the complete transformation (although I don't want to say that is a hard and fast rule, considering the power of God). There may simply be more to overcome than that person has years of life left to work through. It should be said, though, that those years of working through will reap great rewards for him in heaven. Despite the fact that he may retain a significant level of homosexual orientation for the remainder of his life, his commitment to abstinence, to celibacy, to turning from homosexual fantasy, and to pursuing a holy life will bring great joy to the heart of God.

For others, especially those who begin the turnaround in their teens and twenties, and for some, even thirties, there exists a hope that their healing can be significant enough for them to marry, have kids and realize many of the blessings that God has designed for those who love Him and who live according to His Word.

The length of the healing process can also be affected by the number of factors that need to be overcome. Some have a homosexual orientation simply from having failed to bond with their same-sex parent on an emotional level. Others have the orientation simply as the result of the trauma of childhood sexual abuse. Others, however, may have multiple factors, including emotional incest with the opposite sex parent, a history of humiliating attempts at relating to the opposite sex, intense parental or peer misconduct, etc. Such cases may take more time because there are more issues that need to be healed.

In short, the transformation process is affected by several broad categories: knowledge; commitment; the time frame; and the number of elements to overcome.

So, What Does it Look Like to Be Healed?

As I've mentioned already, for someone who has been in the healing process a while, there comes a day when they ask themselves, "Am I healed yet?" or "How will I know when I'm healed?" In that moment, it is helpful to understand some of the earmarks of what being healed looks like so that one can take comfort in seeing the progress that God has wrought in them.

These criteria are not meant to imply that there is a state at which the capacity to be tempted by a sin no longer dwells in us. (That state will only be brought about when God fixes believers in a state of perfection after the second coming of Christ.) Although there is testimony from a few rare saints that they have achieved such victory over particular sins, the more common picture is one where impulses to sin remain (to one degree or another), but are kept in check by the means God has designed.

In the following list of signs of being healed, I have included one that is particular to the issue of homosexual confusion (IX), but otherwise, these criteria can serve as guidelines for anyone's path to overcoming sin.

I. You effectively keep perfectionistic tendencies in check.

Many people refuse to try something that they cannot perfectly perform. Since the path toward holiness is riddled with periodic failure, they refuse to give it an honest shot. They have performing tied up in their minds with being loved and accepted by God.

A healed person has learned that God's love and acceptance is based on Christ's work on their behalf, not their flawless performance. They have learned that God's love and acceptance can never be earned and can never be repaid—it can only be humbly received as a free, unmerited gift.

God's call to be holy as He is holy is not based on some unreasonable expectation in Him that if we try hard enough, we will somehow perfectly achieve holiness. He doesn't expect instant flawless perfection from fallen human beings anymore than He expects a child whom he has called to become a tennis pro to be instantly and flawlessly perfect at tennis. He understands the learning process. He also learned obedience from what He suffered (Hebrews 5:8) and grew in wisdom, stature, and favor with God and men (Luke 2:52).

God's pleasure is not solely focused on our achieving the goal. He gains pleasure from our love-inspired desire to cooperate with Him in moving toward the goal. His joy comes as much from the relationship of the moment, as from any prospect of the future. A healed person has come to understand this and is committed to putting perfectionistic tendencies to death when they attempt to reassert themselves.

II. When temptations come—you consistently and quickly put them away.

Notice I didn't say "if." I said "when." You will always have memories of past sinful pleasures and old mental videotapes of events that once brought great excitement and thrills, no matter what the sin has been. The difference in a "healed" person is that they have had such a change of heart and have acquired such a level of discipline that such temptations are consistently rejected upon arrival. A healed person doesn't give temptation any time or any consideration. In their mind and heart, that sin is no longer an option.

III. When temptations come—you effectively and efficiently turn the battle over to God on a consistent basis.

A healed person has learned how to let God fight the battles. Long past are the self-righteous attempts to prove oneself holy and above sin. Dead and buried is the idea that anyone can become a self-contained, self-made entity of holiness. A healed person has learned that the only power over sin that is available comes from the throne of God and must be sought immediately and relied upon completely upon being tempted. A healed person understands that without Christ, they can do nothing. Those who are healed have come to terms with being dependent on God to keep them from falling and are committed to allowing Him to do so.

IV. The tyranny of thoughts and feelings has been conquered with only minor skirmishes remaining.

A "healed" person has learned that thoughts and feelings lie on a continual basis, that they are completely unreliable sources of truth. With only minor and infrequent exceptions (that happen to everyone during times of stress and defeat), a healed person does not allow them to dictate reality anymore.

A healed person has come to grips with the autonomic tyranny of thoughts, feelings, and emotions. A healed person has learned how to assess and discern the true ones from the false, settling on God's Word as the only infallible source of truth and refusing to allow thoughts and feelings to be a god anymore. When lies and emotions from the old life try to take control again, the healed person meets them head-on with the Word of God.

Understand that I am not suggesting that we *suppress* or *deny* our feelings. That would be very unhealthy. We must always honestly acknowledge what we are thinking and feeling. What I am suggesting, however, is that we train ourselves, with God's help, to discern thoughts and feelings that are lying to us. This means, among other things, immersing ourselves in the study of Scripture.

Once identified as lies, we reject them either by simply ignoring them, by countering them (out loud if necessary) with what is true, or in cases where the Holy Spirit has alerted us to a demonic power behind the lie, using aggressive spiritual warfare prayer and commands to cast them away.

V. You wisely and habitually guard your heart and mind against whatever has power to resuscitate the old nature.

Immature and unhealed people play games with God. They try to keep one foot in the world and one foot in the Kingdom. They engage in very

cleverly devised games of self-deception, whereby they convince themselves that they must give in to one sin or another, or that considering their
lot in life or their past brokenness, they deserve to be able to give in every
once in a while. They convince themselves that a life of obedience and holiness is only for priests, nuns, and saints, but not for the average person.
They convince themselves that considering how far they have come and
how much they have given up, God understands and approves of their
dalliances with sin. They "supermarket shop" for holiness—i.e., they retain
the lordship of their life by telling God where He can make them holy and
where He must leave them alone. As though they were shopping in a gro-
cery store, they pick and choose what seems most attractive to them in the
Kingdom and reject what seems unattractive, thus keeping certain areas of
their life "off-limits" to the Spirit of God.

Healed people have forsaken all such games, to the extent that God has
given them awareness.

Even though the rest of life may be an ongoing discovery of the darker
and more cleverly hidden parts of their fallen nature, healed people are set
on facing those moments of truth and listening to God. In the process of
identifying those elements of the sinful life that are fuel to further sin, they
take very seriously the need to eradicate such things from their lives.
Anything that may bring to life the desire for a sin is ruthlessly removed
from their environment to the extent that it is up to them.

**VI. Your love for Jesus, born out of an abiding intimacy with Him, is
now your strongest inner resource for deciding to turn to God to be
set free.**

Love must become the single motivating factor for obedience. Any other
motive is religion, is death. The person who is healed has developed a deep
and abiding love relationship with Jesus—one that compels holy pursuits.
When temptation comes, the central reason for turning away is that the
thought of hurting the Lord they love is too grievous to consider. During
moments of intimacy with them, God has succeeded in writing His Law on
their heart. In other words, the desire to be obedient, to be holy, has become
their natural desire, replacing the previously natural desire to rebel.

As we have seen, grace is what produces this fruit in our lives. Titus 2:11-
14 tells us clearly that it is the grace of God that teaches us to say "No" to
ungodliness and to live upright and godly lives in this present age. In other
words, it is in being forgiven again and again and again that we finally
acquire the desire to be faithful to such a Lord as that. Therein lies the value
in seeing how dark is our heart, how fallen is our nature. When God's grace
continues in the face of that reality, our rebellious heart is conquered by
such love and we become persuaded that He has nothing but good in mind
for us. We go from obeying Him because we're supposed to (though not yet

trusting Him fully), to obeying Him because we want to (trusting Him completely). And that is all the difference in the world to Him.

VII. The mind, heart, and perspective of Christ consistently guides you.

Behavior associated with arrested emotional development has decreased considerably—e.g., magical thinking or fantasy thinking. Romance and reality have struck their happy balance. An understanding and appreciation of the complexity of life has blossomed. The self-centered, impulsive, impatient ego is regularly submitted to the Lordship of Christ.

An intimate connection with God has grown to such an extent that you think His thoughts after Him, know what He's going to say before He says it, experience His heart for others, see things through His eyes and with an eternal perspective rather than a temporal one.

VIII. Your experience in knowing Satan's schemes enables you to resist him from an offensive posture rather than a defensive one.

God has taught you how Satan operates and strategies to overturn his attacks. Your will has been engaged to such an extent that you now fight from an offensive posture rather than a defensive one. Knowing ahead of time what he is likely to do, you have already prepared battle plans for every contingency. There are few surprises and even those are met with an aggressive relish for the opportunity to take ground for the Kingdom of God rather than defending besieged territory. You know well the weapons of warfare and value each opportunity to strike another blow against the enemy of, not only your soul, but the souls of all those who are perishing.[1]

IX. For those who have struggled with homosexual confusion . . . Your heterosexual identity is now the predominant one and the one you have irrevocably embraced. You use the occasional reappearance of the waning homosexual persona as a lever to send you back into greater dependence and refuge in God.

Like the ongoing struggle between the old man and the new creation in Christ, you recognize old thoughts and temptations as a defeated foe trying to come back to life while also recognizing that the only thing that's going to bring him back to life are your own poor choices. You understand the lie behind the old persona. You understand the destruction that it wrought not only in your life and the lives of those around you, but also in the suffering of Christ, and you are dead set against allowing him to resurrect himself ever again.

You have taken great delight in the formation of the intended heterosexual identity that now is the identity that you have embraced. You marvel and praise God for each new facet that comes alive. You are irrevocably committed to feeding the new man and starving the old man to death. The alternative is never even considered anymore.

X. When you fall into temporarily embracing the fantasies of the old nature, your return is quick and with deep and true repentance.

In moments of discouragement, weakness, or carelessness, if you discover that an old fantasy has developed in your mind without being cast out, you use the opportunity of your imperfection to remember once again what Christ has done for you and return to Him with deep and true repentance. You use the opportunity of your failure to rejoice in the grace of God, to rejoice in your weakness and release anew God's mighty power to keep you pure. You keep short accounts—i.e., each failure, no matter how large or small, is quickly countered with true repentance. It is not allowed to continue and condemnation over the failing is not allowed to take hold. Instead, you run back into God's arms as quickly as possible knowing that He is waiting with open arms.

XI. Your focus continues to shift from self to serving others.

One major indication of growth and maturity is a shift from thinking of yourself first to thinking of others first; a shift from getting what's yours to giving what's yours; a change from selfishness to servanthood. In fact, one of the best things you can do during your healing process (and after) is to deliberately enter into selfless acts of service; to give things away to the point where you actually suffer from the loss. Tithing is a helpful tool to get you started. Then add offerings to it. Give away most of the clothes in your closet, especially the items you really like. Sell your car and go out on a mission trip. Truly store up for yourself treasures in heaven, as the Bible suggests. Remember, though, that such acts must be Spirit-led to be of value. To do them only to receive the praise of men will not cause you to grow at all.

XII. There is a growing larder of "eternal fruit" in your life.

Following on from the previous point, a healed person has learned the difference between acts that produce eternal fruit and those that do not. They have learned to wait on the leading of the Holy Spirit. They have also learned that they must do so from a predetermined decision to do whatever God may say to them. They await His leading, His opening of doors and His empowering before moving ahead. On the other hand, they have also learned to catch themselves when selfishness or laziness has caused them to begin playing the old "I'll pretend I'm not hearing God when it's something I don't want to do" game.

In short, to a significant extent, what they do for God is done for His glory alone, not theirs—at least, that is the sincere desire of their heart. They no longer serve Him in an attempt to earn His love or acceptance, or as a way to pay Him back for saving them. Their love for Him is such that they can't help themselves from serving His every wish. The focus of their life, both physical and spiritual, is no longer on them, but on Him and, as a result, eternal fruit is being produced.

XIII. Remnant behavior no longer misleads you into thinking something is wrong with you.

The healing process, in some ways, is really a reversal of the process that created the dysfunctional thoughts, feelings, and behavior. In the early stages of the development of homosexual neurosis, for example, it is purely an emotional problem. There is a search for completion or damage control, vis-a-vis one's gender identity. Unless the child's life has been prematurely sexualized through sexual abuse or exposure to pornography, the early stages are typified by feelings of needing to be near or accepted by certain same-gender people who symbolize or possess the completion that is lacking in the seeker. There is nothing sexual about it. So early behavior is more a turning of the head, a catching of the eye, a staring at certain people, a feeling of exhilaration when they brush by you or acknowledge you. Sometimes it's as weird as a need to be near something touched or used by your idol—a piece of clothing, even sitting where they have just sat. Such moments bring a feeling of satisfaction as though, in touching what they have touched, a part of their sufficiency has been transferred into you. This kind of behavior is the first to appear and is often the last to go. Many people are panicked at its reappearance after years of healing and fear it is a sign they haven't gotten anywhere. Actually, it is a sign they've traveled a great distance and, as they move on, it too will pass, at least as a controlling force.

XIV. A healed person has learned one thing so thoroughly that they operate in it without thinking—"Knowing why helps, but knowing Him heals."

The "disease of introspection" that Leanne Payne so often talks about has been healed.[2] The obsessive search for meaning in the whys and wherefores of the "old man's" path have been jettisoned. Fixing hope in the search process has been rejected for fixing hope in the goodness of God. A healed person no longer seeks to perform "steps" in order to achieve healing and right standing before God, but rather places hope and trust in the Creator and His righteousness imputed and infused into them.

As we have seen, the answer to the question "What Does it Look Like to Be Healed?" is a complex one. It does not mean the absence of temptation or the absence of a vulnerability to returning to old habits and patterns of living and thinking. No healing of the soul looks that way. In fact, our ongoing vulnerability to the old nature is one of the primary tools in God's hand to motivate and encourage us to stay under the shelter of His almighty wing.

But we can expect certain patterns to emerge and predominate in the life of someone who can reasonably consider himself healed and healthy. Let's be careful to keep this question in its proper context and then encourage one another with these things.

*　　*　　*　　*

Let's now move on to a discussion of the primary indicator of having grown in Christlikeness: our willingness to humbly use what we have learned to help others.

Part Four:

When God Invites You To Minister To Others

11

Why Some People Remain Trapped in Sin and Brokenness

One of the most frustrating times in ministry is when you pour your heart and wisdom into someone, to help them get free from a sin problem, and they fail to change. Such moments drag you through all kinds of thoughts and emotions—e.g., "Have I failed?" "Is what I'm teaching true?" "Is this person an exception?" "Am I being taken for a ride by someone who doesn't really want to be free?" It can really take the wind out of your sails to live with this kind of self-doubt and confusion.

As reluctant as we may be to draw such a conclusion, there may be no other but to recognize that the enemy is using our brother or sister to sap us of the faith and vision that God has for the overall call on our lives. That being the case, it is important to recognize as quickly as possible those cases where people are seeking freedom and transformation without being willing to do what it takes.

I used to be the "Floor Pastor" and trainer for the Los Angeles area counseling center of the "700 Club." One day we discovered that we had a serious problem. Our phone counseling was going on so long with some callers (sometimes an hour or more per call) that the entire CBN telephone ministry was threatened with bankruptcy. The obvious solution was to shorten the phone conversations. But how? Upon seeking the Lord for an answer, He gave me two questions to ask every caller in the early stages of the conversation:

1. "Are you willing to do whatever it takes to get healed, delivered, transformed, etc.?"

2. "What exactly would you like God to do for you right now?"

As we asked these two questions of each caller, the focus of the conversation shifted from the problem to the power, provision, and intention of the Lord to bring permanent healing and change. It increased our expectation that God was actually going to give us something concrete to respond to in the midst of our prayer. And sure enough, when we turned to God for answers with this newfound expectant faith, He gave them to us. In fact, it opened a virtual floodgate of words of wisdom and knowledge from the Lord on behalf of the callers.

The phone conversations shortened considerably. What happened was that those who were calling just to talk or get sympathy for their situation but who did not really want to change were suddenly confronted with having to take Spirit-led (and empowered) responsibility for changing things in their lives, and many realized that they didn't want to. They were getting too much affirmation and attention by remaining dysfunctional, and they weren't about to do anything that would jeopardize that. Within a very short time, such people stopped calling, and our phone time per caller dropped significantly. The ministry was saved, and it continues on to this day offering prayer and ministry to those who really need it and who want to change.

How often do you minister with someone who has a sin problem and are unable to do or say anything that will bring permanent change to their life? Let me suggest that what you probably have is a person who either doesn't know what to do to get free, or who is unwilling to do what it takes to get free. Those same two diagnostic questions that the Lord gave me at the "700 Club" may help you to get to the bottom of things with your counselee.

When people are unwilling to do what it takes to get free, they usually don't tell you that. You need to regularly ask God for discernment in this area. Many people who are unwilling to do what it takes aren't even aware of that fact. They really believe that they are willing and yet are self-deceived.

I regularly find areas in my life where I am fooling myself into believing that I want something godly, when I really don't. Layers of self-deception collect over the years, as we rationalize and deny our sin, until one day our mind is effectively veiled from seeing the darkness that is truly there. The heart is desperately wicked and deceitful above all things (Jeremiah 17:99). We must ask the Lord, who alone can read the heart, to show us if there be any wicked way in us (cf. Psalm 139:23).

The mind and heart of man has an amazing capacity for self-deception, which is why the second diagnostic question that God gave me for the "700 Club" prayer ministry can be so very helpful: "What exactly would you like God to do for you right now?" This question gives both you and the person you are trying to help a tangible way to test their true, inner will. It also enables you to see more clearly when God has answered a prayer because, if you have been specific in your request and the answer comes, then it is all the more obvious that God did it. He, then, receives the praise, instead of the "spirit of coincidence."

Since that time at CBN, I have done a considerable amount of one-on-one and group counseling through the ministry God has given me to sexually broken people, and I have learned that the reasons for people's failure to realize freedom from the sins that beset them are more numerous than those two diagnostic questions can account for. One day I was commiserating over my failure to succeed with a particular counselee, and I asked the Lord what the most common reasons were that explained why certain people did not get free. He gave me twelve of them.

1. Failure to make an across-the-board commitment to holiness.

Many of us want God to free us from one area of sin while we remain unwilling for Him to free us from another. For example, I can spend years crying out to God to deliver me from an addiction to pornography, yet if I am unwilling for Him to deliver me from lying, I have missed the point. Now God may choose to deliver me from one sin even while I continue in another, but that is His prerogative based on a lot of considerations of which I am totally ignorant. However, if I try to "selectively" live the Christian life, it should not surprise me if He does not respond to such prayers. The Kingdom of God is not a supermarket.

I believe that this is one of the biggest reasons why God does not deliver us from particular sins that are a concern to us. We remain unwilling to cooperate with Him in delivering us from other sins that He has already made known to us. God wants us to commit to holiness across-the-board. As the Holy Spirit brings them to our attention, no area of sin should remain untouched. Walking in the Spirit and in the power of the Kingdom of God requires a full commitment to holiness. We are not talking about performance here (i.e., sinless perfection) but, rather, the intention of the heart and the setting of the heart permanently toward the God of absolute holiness and power.

If we shy away in incredulity at such a prospect, it is because we somehow believe that it has to be our righteous effort that will carry it off, and we know that we are incapable of such a feat. However, the truth was and is and will remain that God offers to infuse us with His righteous power to "keep us from falling" (Jude 1, 24) and to make us "eager to do what is good" (Titus 2:14). We not only have salvation by grace, but sanctification by grace as well. Having already given us everything we need (2 Peter 1:3), it is God's purpose to empower us to walk holy "in this present age" (Titus 2:12).

Those we counsel, as well as the church at large, need to make this commitment to walk as holy people in every area of life. It is our call, our witness and the glory of God to make it so. Though we tend to shy away from committing to something we know we cannot do, once we have made the commitment, we will discover that God is faithful to empower the keeping of it. Our results waver only as our faith and resolve waver. But God remains constant.

2. Failure to believe in and act upon God's power to deliver and keep us.

Many people are ignorant or unbelieving when it comes to the knowledge of God's power as it relates to His will and purpose for our lives here on earth, as well as the extent of our authority and capability under His guiding and delivering hand. Most need reminding. Many good books have been published on this subject—most notably Neil Anderson's *The Bondage Breaker* and Tom Marshall's *Living in the Freedom of the Spirit*. Much of the counseling process for such people is a matter of educating them on who they are in Christ and what God has given them authority to do and be.

This is an area of "faith" that we must pursue and receive revelation on from the Father. In a very real sense, we need to receive for ourselves the "faith of God" (Mark 11:22), which is a gift from God (Ephesians 2:8). We need to have God's level of faith. We need to pursue God and wrestle with Him until He blesses us with great faith (Genesis 32:26). Part of this pursuit of faith is accomplished through practicing the presence of God (discussed under reason # 5), and part is accomplished through what I call, "truth therapy." "Truth therapy" involves regular meditation on the truths of Scripture—in this case, those that contradict what we are feeling and experiencing in our battle with sin.

The fact is, our natural thoughts and feelings lie to us constantly. Remember the story that I told in chapter four about the lady who abruptly stood up and walked out of the room during one of my lectures? I was immediately assaulted with thoughts and feelings of failure. I thought to myself: "What did I say to offend her? What an insensitive lout I am! I've got no business even teaching when I am so obviously deficient in basic interpersonal sensitivity!" On and on my mind went as I began to feel like and believe that I was a first class failure. In just a matter of seconds, right there in the middle of my lecture, I became depressed and defeated. She had only gone to the bathroom.

When I fail to become planted in the ground of my identity in Christ, His call on my life, and His empowerment of that call, I am a sitting duck for the lying thoughts and feelings that periodically invade my soul.

People who fail to embrace the truth of who they are and what they have in Christ are often people who are so enslaved to their feelings that they are incapable of believing anything else. Many are unaware that they can say "No" to feelings and emotions. They think it would be hypocritical or artificial to do so. They are sorely deceived and need to put Christ and His truth on the throne of their lives and learn how to deny and put down the tyranny of the god of emotion. Again, this is not to suggest they deny their feelings and emotions, but that they discern lying ones and put them away with the truth that comes from God and His Word.

"Truth therapy" also involves worshipping Christ with our focus on those very attributes of His that we need. Do we need purity of mind, heart, and action? Then we need to worship Him for His purity. We need to see Him "through the eyes of our heart" in His holiness. In Ephesians 1:18, Paul prays that: "...the eyes of your heart may be enlightened in order that you may know the hope to which He has called you, the riches of His glorious inheritance in the saints, and His incomparably great power for us who believe." It is through this very enlightenment that we receive the faith to believe and to appropriate the power over sin.

Do we feel powerless against sin? Has the omnipresence of the power of evil in our world tricked us into believing that evil is more powerful than good? If so, we need to repeatedly meditate on and worship the Lord for His power. As we feed these truths into our mind and spirit, they become more real to us. We begin to believe that they are available to us and that they can be built into us by God.

Faith is an indispensable conduit in the flow and outpouring of God's power and kingdom life. Without faith, as the scriptures say, "It is impossible to please God" (Hebrews 11:6). We need faith to fully believe in the power of God, in the goodness of God, in His unconditional love for us, in the grace that He extends toward us when we sin, in His concern for us, in the intention of His will to make us holy, in the truth of His Word, and in all of the other promises and statements about Him and about life.

3. Failure to undergo a transformation of the will through a belief in and embracing of God's unconditional love.

Once a person has become fully persuaded of the truth behind God's power and our authority in Him, then freedom from sin becomes a matter of the will. Many people simply are not willing to do what it takes, even with God providing all of the healing and delivering power. They love the sin too much—usually because they don't fully realize, deep within their spirit, that God loves them completely, no matter what they have done nor how many times, and that He can meet their need better than the sin can.

They need to know that despite continued sin and failure in their life, God's loving arms are still extended out to them with as much love and compassion as if they had been living in perfect victory from day one—as if they had never sinned! They need to truly understand that God's love for those who have put their faith in His Son Jesus is not now, nor ever will be, contingent upon their behavior. They must embrace the truth of His unconditional love, for it is from believing in this truth that they are empowered and motivated by love not to sin. Dudley Hall has written an excellent book on this called, *Grace Works*.

This message of the power of grace is most clearly given in Titus 2:12 where the Apostle Paul says, "It is the grace of God . . . that teaches us to say 'No' to ungodliness and worldly passions, and to live self-controlled, upright and godly lives." How does the grace of God do that?

In the first chapter of this book, I described the moment in my life when God transformed my heart in this area. As you will recall, I was busily engaged in a sin (probably for the 10,000th time), and the Holy Spirit spoke to me, saying, "David, if you will turn to Me right now, I will love you, forgive you, and embrace you." I can remember thinking at the time, "That's ridiculous! I'm in the middle of a sin here!" And I ignored the voice of God and continued on. When I had finished my sin, the Holy Spirit again spoke to me and said, "David, if you will turn to Me right now, I will love you, forgive you, and embrace you." It seemed like such an unreal thing to be hearing, that deep inside I knew it could only be God. I was so intrigued by the possibility that the voice might really be God that I turned to Him in my spirit to see if He would really have me back after I had refused to abort my sin at His first entreaty. When I turned to Him, to my utter surprise and amazement, He swamped me with a wave of love. It was clear to me that my sin was not His focus—that all He wanted, and all He had ever wanted, was for me to turn to Him and receive His love. It was an awesome moment as my heart was melted by His unconditional love and grace. I left the room completely changed. He had so taken my heart by His love that I now wanted to do what He wanted me to do. I no longer was suspicious that He was some control freak out to rob me of my freedom. I was now convinced that He was always and only concerned with one thing—loving me.

God changed my heart, simply by loving me unconditionally. He had broken the power of sin and had transformed my will through grace— taking me from rebellion to submission. I now wanted to do what He wanted. I now fully believed in His loving heart toward me. I was now ready to believe whatever He said and do whatever He suggested. Titus 2:14 had come true in my life in those brief moments as God revealed His unconditional heart of love and grace toward me.

How does the grace of God teach us to say "No" to ungodliness and to live a godly life? By breaking our heart with the relentlessly unconditional love that the Savior holds out to us in spite of our sin. As a result, we fall more and more in love with Him. Our desires change from wanting the impurity of the world to wanting whatever such a wonderful Savior wants. We come to admire Him, to love Him, to believe more deeply in Him, and to desire what He wants. Our hearts are changed from the inside out. Instead of operating out of the willful self-effort of performance, we now operate out of pure heartfelt desire and faith, knowing from the depths of our being that what God wants is, without a shred of doubt, what we want.

As far as those of us who have been changed in this way are concerned, God is imminently trustworthy and designs His commands around only one principle—what is best for us, His dearly beloved children. Meditating on the proof of His love—His sacrificial, agonizing death on the Cross—is always helpful in coming to believe these things. Satan will try to use the tragedies of life to persuade us differently about God, but meditating on the Cross has greater power to overcome Satan's lies. Jesus' demonstration of love through the Cross is inescapable and incomprehensible except that He did it out of love for mankind.

What we really have been talking about in this third area of counseling for someone in bondage, is how God's unconditional love results in a transformation of the will. As fallen men and women, we too often strive to correct our will through logic and independent self-effort, which eventually fails. God's way is to change our will through the irresistible power of unconditional love. He then will receive the glory for our eventual choice to do His will. "For it is God who is at work in us both to will and to do that which is according to His good purpose" (Philippians 2:13).

When our will has been transformed by the power of Almighty God, we find that we have also gained two crucial products of a sanctified will—persistence and obedience. We obey Him because we love Him (John 14:23-24). Our obedience is born out of being fully persuaded by love, not by duty or performance. We are persistent in our pursuit of Him for the same reason—we have been irresistibly drawn by the glory of His love. Without persistence, we cannot get very far in walking with God in holiness (ref. Jeremiah 29:13; Hebrews 11:6). Holiness is a promise from God for this life as well as the next—as it says in Galatians 5:16, "Live by the Spirit, and you will not gratify the desires of the flesh."

4. Failure to see healing as a process with a purpose.

Those who come for help are often spiritually naive and think that their sin problem will go away once you've cast out some demon or called to God for that special delivering anointing that will finally rid them of their temptation and sin.

The first counsel that must be given to such believers is that their healing will be a process—a process with a purpose. Even those of us (and I am one of them) who receive an initial, powerful deliverance from the power that certain sins have over us still have a long process of healing to look forward to—a process in which God shows us the root causes of our behavior, the root needs that we are trying to meet, and His more perfect provision to meet those needs. Most of us look at the idea of process with impatience and gloom. We want healing and perfection now! But God is wiser than that. He sees the benefits for us that can only be derived through process. For example, through this process of healing, we develop a relationship of love and dependence on God because we have need to turn to Him often for power over temptation. In the midst of turning to Him often for help, He becomes more real to us. His promises and His presence become practical, almost tangible. We get to know Him better. He goes from being one who theoretically loves and empowers us to one who engages in the deepest fabric of our lives, and that is what life is all about.

Yes, we are to be holy as He is holy, and that is a primary goal and directive. However, the greater goal of knowing Him intimately is what brings about the goal of holiness. This is clearly stated in 2 Peter 1:3: "His divine power has given us everything we need for life and godliness *through our knowledge of Him* who called us by His own glory and goodness" (italics mine). And so, it is from our "knowledge" (deep intimate knowing) of Him that everything we need for life and godliness is made manifest.

With the healing of our relationship with God comes the healing of our relationships with others. One flows naturally out of the other, for in our intimate moments with God, He reveals to us the roots of our broken relationships with people and empowers us toward resolution and healing. Bondage is essentially a problem of broken relationships—first with God, and second, with human beings. As these are made healthy, we are made healthy.

Another reason that healing must often be a process is that we are so very ignorant of the complex web of contributing sins that underlie our behavior. We need to learn what these sins are and be persuaded to respond accordingly to what God has shown us. As previously noted, many people who are entrapped in the sin of pornography are unaware that one of the foundational pillars to their surface sin is the very serious crime of "idolatry." If I am unaware that I am engaged in idolatry, then I am not going to confess and repent of that sin, am I? Consequently, no matter how much I plead with God to "deliver" me from the sin of pornography, He cannot, because the deeper sin that fuels the behavior remains.

And so, we see the immense benefit and undeniable necessity behind God's decision to make most of our deliverance from sin a process. It is a process of revelation, repentance, and transformation of the will through coming to know Him as He really is. And that brings us to the next reason why some people are not able to be free from their sin.

5. Failure to develop an intimate relationship with God the Father.

Many of us fear intimacy. It's where we got hurt. It's where we got shot down. It's where we are painfully vulnerable.

It amazes me how that when I teach on this topic, people kind of smile patiently while they wait for me to go on to something more "practical" for them. For most people, even most Christians, intimacy with the Father is just a sentimental notion. They don't see it as a real possibility. Nor do they have any idea how to achieve it or what it will look like when they get it. They're happy to be given "10 Steps to Holiness" that they can perform in the privacy of their own homes. Besides, intimacy means commitment and loss of independence.

It's almost as if Satan has put a veil over people's hearts so that they will not do the very thing that will result in their empowerment, freedom, and existential fulfillment. At the same time, he's trying to rob God of the thing that God wants most—intimacy with His children.

To answer the question of "What" intimacy is, we need only point to its appearance in certain human relations. It is two hearts becoming one, two minds thinking together in harmony, two bodies moving in service to each other. It is the deepest level of knowing, of loving, of feeling—producing the fruit of inner joy and completion.

How do we achieve such a state with the God no one sees? Foundationally, it has to do with our response of love to the sacrifice of Jesus on the Cross and the faith in God that that historic action elicits. This is nurtured through a lifestyle of worship—something sorely lacking in modern Christian experience. We worship on Sunday; yet, if the object of our worship is worthy at all, He is worthy of ongoing, daily worship. It is in that intimacy of worship that God reveals Himself to us in ways He does not show the common man. It is there that we come to recognize His voice, know His heart, His mind, experience His love, grace, and mercy in the deepest recesses of our hearts. It is there that the "image" is restored— where we receive the transformation of ourselves into the likeness of our Lord—and we emerge shining with the glow of His faith, wholeness, holiness, purity, and love (cf. 2 Corinthians 3:18).

Intimacy, then, is established through a lifestyle of worship and praise—singing love songs to our Lord and gazing upon His glory in the Spirit—and practicing His presence with the same persistence and regularity as we would anything else that is necessary for life. It is also created through knowing Him by scriptural revelation—again, a regular feeding on Him, this time through His written Word which He, from time to time, brings alive to our mind and heart. Intimacy is, thirdly, created through the communion of prayer—simply talking to Him, spilling our hearts before Him, and then listening for His response. In these and other ways, intimacy comes when being with Him is a greater priority than doing for Him.

Without a growing relationship of intimacy with God, we cannot receive the revelation (the faith and the security of knowing we are loved) that enables and empowers a walk of holiness. Without intimacy, permanent, ongoing holiness is impossible, because it is from the womb of intimacy with God that He brings forth the new life of holiness in us.

6. Failure to humble ourselves in absolute dependence on God.

The sixth reason why someone might remain in habitual sin and bondage is that they may have been living in the pride of self-sufficiency and independence from God and, consequently, have not yet learned that they are completely dependent on God's power and wisdom in order to live any kind of meaningful existence. In such a condition, they can neither receive nor use God's power and grace because they are unaware of their need for it. There are people, as well, who have some idea of their need for

God, but haven't yet understood the full scope of that need.

And finally, there are those who theoretically understand their need, but still practice a life of independence from God. To them, humility is a weakness to be avoided and life's problems are challenges that God expects them to deal with on their own.

Man alone, without a continual interaction of dependence on God, is like an infant left out in the middle of a freeway.

Even the wisdom we do have has come to us from God. We're like a word processing program on a computer. We are prestructured to have the capacity to perform certain functions, but without the continual input of an outside force, we are virtually useless. Even the pre-structuring comes from that outside force. In like fashion, part of the knowledge that the natural man (who does not know God) seems to have has been given to him by God and is good and useful—e.g., "$E = MC^2$." The rest of it is of his own design and is of limited value—e.g., "Darwinian evolutionary theory." As part of a finite creation, we are completely dependent on God to reveal to us what is true, as distinguished from what is a product of our own misunderstanding. We must continually approach the throne of grace, not only for forgiveness, but also for knowledge and wisdom. We are far more dependent in this area than we realize; we don't know anything, truly, until we have God's assurance that it is true.

The humility of knowing our limitations, as well as the depths to which we have fallen as a part of sinful humanity, is extremely valuable currency in the Kingdom of God. Take, for example, the teaching in Luke 7:47 when Jesus noted that a person who has been forgiven much will love much and the one who has been forgiven little will love little. If I live in such a state of pride and arrogance that I'm unaware of just how much a sinner I am, (the state of the Pharisee), then I am not going to love Jesus very much, if at all. In that frame of mind, I don't believe that there is much to forgive, and so, I have been forgiven very little. However, the closer I get to Him, the longer I sit at His feet and allow Him to uncover the depths of my sinful heart, the more I am going to grow in the humility of understanding the grace in which I stand, and I will love Him much more.

The same goes for power. Without Jesus, we can do nothing (John 15:5)! We cannot heal ourselves spiritually, mentally, or physically. We can do nothing unless God empowers and guides us. That holds true especially in the area of sin. Our first response to temptation must always be a heart of utter dependence turned toward God for power and wisdom. Then and only then can we effectively use the tools that He has given us to overcome the evil one.

7. Failure to learn and practice spiritual warfare.

That brings us to the seventh area in which we might want to counsel someone who appears hopelessly bound in sin. We need to train them in spiritual warfare—the core lessons for which we are discussing in the twelve points of this chapter. They are an indispensable foundation for victory in spiritual warfare. The weapons of our warfare are mighty to pull down strongholds, but only when employed in the ongoing reality of these foundational pillars of incarnational relationship and empowerment.

When we turn to the God with whom we have an ongoing, intimate relationship—our will fully persuaded in wanting what He wants, because our hearts have been changed by His loving grace; in great faith, because we have practiced His truth and chosen to believe it despite all appearances to the contrary; with a heart filled with the humility of knowing that we are utterly dependent on Him for wisdom and power, as well as life itself; with a heart that is fully turned and committed to holiness in every area of life—then when we go to pick up the weapons of our warfare, we will find that we already have them on. (Referring to truth, righteousness, readiness, faith, salvation, the Word of God—as listed in Ephesians 6:14-17.) And if we have been wearing our battle dress all along, then we'll have greater facility in using it when it is needed during those inevitable times of trial and temptation.

Spiritual warfare simply involves using the power of God, the wisdom of God, the discernment of God, the peace of God, the faith of God, and the love of God to proclaim the will of God at any given moment. It is in the midst of the honor that we have been given to proclaim the glory of God and His already accomplished victory (see Psalm 149:1,5), that those things that He already has willed come to pass. With the prayer and the praise of our heart, released in the full faith and confidence that results from an intimate knowing of Him, the forces of heaven are released to engage and to defeat the enemy.

8. Failure to truly repent.

There is a difference, biblically, between mentally agreeing with the truth of something and fully believing. In western thinking, to "believe" means to "give mental assent to" something. The biblical concept, however, is more than that. To "believe" according to the way biblical writers thought is to so agree with a matter that one's life naturally realigns itself to become consistent with that belief. Thus James could declare: "Faith without works is dead!" (James 2:17, 20, 22). In western thinking, a person believes with the *mind*. In biblical thinking, a person believes with his or her *life*.[1]

This difference has critical ramifications for what it means to truly repent. Though our western mind-set causes us to think so, many people weeping at Christian altars are not experiencing true repentance. They are often weeping for themselves—sorry that they've been caught and embarrassed by the public revelation of their deeds, or frustrated over being "messed up" and feeling quite sorry for themselves. Some are even trying to manipulate God and their loved ones into lightening up on them by acting out the role of a penitent, while inside they have no real intention of changing.

True repentance occurs when one is struck to the heart with grief and sorrow over the fact that their actions have hurt the One who died on a cross for them and grieved in their spirit that their behavior added to His sufferings. It is accompanied by a desire to change and a sincere amendment of the will to do so by God's grace.

If a person has not truly repented from the heart, he/she has not yet positioned his/herself to receive God's empowerment to live a holy life. All of the attempts at "being good" remain self-powered and, therefore, destined for failure.

9. Failure to forsake idolatry of the intellect.

Many people have sophisticated, hidden demands and expectations of God that have gone unmet and are sometimes unknown even to them. Deep inside, they are waiting for God to meet those demands, and until He does, they continue to withhold a piece of their heart from Him. In other words, until He gives them what they want, they refuse to fully commit their life and trust into His hands.

A very common hidden demand is a demand for information. We want God to explain something to us before we will trust Him fully.

In many cases, this intellectual demand concerns the matter of why He allows innocent children to suffer. God's withholding of that information kindles in us a doubt about His goodness, a doubt that He really loves us, a doubt that He can be trusted. And we don't want to rest in the arms of someone we can't trust.

What we often do not see is that our withholding of trust in God until He explains the matter more fully is extortion. It is rank manipulation. It is intellectual idolatry. We are placing the idol of the intellect before Him and demanding that He bow down to it. Since He cannot participate in idolatry, we are inadvertently preventing Him from giving us the very answer that we do desperately desire.

I remember the night when I was placing this very demand before the Lord and He unveiled to me the idolatry and manipulation behind my request. Further still, He pointed out to me that my request to know why He allowed suffering was actually a search to understand how He could love me and have allowed me to suffer. What I was really after was something on which to lay my hope and trust in His love.

While He didn't answer my intellectual question that night, He did point me to the place where the answer to my deepest question had already been provided. He told me to look at the Cross. If I needed to have proof that He loved me, I needed to look at the Cross. Then He said, "And when the Cross becomes enough for you, then you will find the peace that you are seeking."

That night I repented of my intellectual idolatry and decided to believe that God loved me based solely on the evidence of His sacrificial death on the Cross for my sins. Then, with my sin of idolatry absolved and forsaken, my healing progressed at a much faster clip.

10. Failure to work through an unresolved sense of justice.

Deep inside of each one of us, God has placed a desire for balance, for justice. We want to see good rewarded and evil punished. And when we look around us and see evil flourishing and good being suppressed, like the prophets of old, we get angry.[2] We want justice!

What we don't yet have is the perspective of eternity, and so our time-table for seeing justice meted out is not in sync with God's. Satan uses that to plant lies in our minds, to wit: that God is not just; that we need to take matters into our own hands; that God cannot be trusted. So because of our unbelieving hearts and our foreshortened perspective, we ignore God's promise of ultimate justice, such as is found in 2 Thessalonians 1:5-10[3].

Often, part of the problem is that well-intentioned friends have tried to force us to forgive certain offenders before we were ready. They have laid Bible verses on us in a fashion that seemed accusatory rather than liberating, and we have been left feeling like no one really cares about what we went through or understands how impossible it is for us to forgive such matters without further healing and help from God.

We want to know why God allowed it to happen in the first place. We want to know why He then places a burden of forgiveness on us when we were the victim! We want to know why all the demands for action are being heaped on the one who was hurt while the offender seems to escape all consequences for his or her actions. Our sense of justice is screaming for satisfaction.[4]

Earlier, I wrote about an incident in my life when something had gone wrong, and I began to complain to God. In the middle of my little temper tantrum, He said to me: "David, have you ever noticed that every time something goes wrong, your immediate response is to question Me and doubt Me?" He nailed me with that one! The second He said those words, I realized for the first time in my life just how habitual and pervasive my doubts about God really were. Despite the thousands of songs of faith and testimonies of love that I had proclaimed to Him by then, deep down inside, when the chips were down, I still fundamentally did not believe in His perfect goodness. In addition, I observed that my reaction to my unrequited expectation of God in that moment had been frighteningly automatic. So that day I determined to stop each time something went wrong and deliberately resist the temptation to blame or question God. It has made a world of difference in my inner beliefs about His goodness and in my capacity to truly trust Him.

Every person needs to enter into a close relationship with God, so that they can see for themselves that the thoughts and hidden inner beliefs that accuse Him are lies. They need time to receive direct assurances from God of His love and His concern for their plight. They need to learn how to receive power from Him to forgive. They need to develop trust in Him that He will indeed act justly and with perfect timing. When these things are finally worked through, a desire and an empowerment for holiness begins to rule one's life.

11. Failure to let go of a "victim" identity.

Our culture is so man-centered that a "victim" mentality has become an acceptable identity. We are entitled! We are taught to put ourselves first and to see every other relationship as having importance only in relation to that priority.

Secular therapies do not focus on repentance and humility, nor do they see man in light of God's supremacy. At best, God is a tool to serve the idol of man. So, when we become dysfunctional, God is used as a cosmic personal care physician, if He is acknowledged at all. Sinful behavior (such as unforgiveness) is often legitimized, particularly if it is found to be a coping mechanism for having been a victim. Instead of being renounced, it is prescribed "to protect one's boundaries," and to keep the divine man functioning with equilibrium.

With the authority figures of culture preaching and modeling the gospel of the divine man, legitimacy is given to remaining in the role of victim as a coping mechanism that no one is suppose to "judge."

Why, then, do the difficult healing work that can shift one's need-meeting to God? If you are already the center of the universe, why not opt for the easier, less taxing, amoral prescription that the world sees as healthy and normal? Why not throw off this preposterous notion of "dying to self," which must certainly be a dangerous throwback to superstitious ignorance and, thus, most unhealthy?

If we take the path of divine man, however, a stronghold will develop in us—an inner structure of beliefs that holds that we deserve something more from God, that we've been robbed, that God owes us something. It is a prescription for disaster. It is a demonic construction of thought and belief that leads one to continuously justify one's self and one's actions in the face of God's requests that we relent and repent.

Even though we may have been victimized, we still need to die to self. After spending some time working through our pain by the guidance of the Holy Spirit, we need to move on to renounce all of our excuses for our poor and sinful choices in life and throw ourselves on the mercy of God. We need to take on a new identity by seeing ourselves reflected in the eyes of God's loving gaze during regular moments of intimate oneness with Him. In the light of that, what others have done to us loses its power to perpetuate the victim personality.

Those who insist on holding on to their victimhood will at some point stop growing in Christ. The frustration of that arrested development will eventually generate anger at God and a consequent employment of interior rationalizations for returning to (or taking up) habitual sin.

This is such an insidious phenomenon that we will use the next chapter to examine it in detail.

12. Failure to utterly forsake the love of one's sin.

Our heart is exceptionally devious. It can believe and hold on to something in the subconscious long after we have sincerely believed that the issue has been resolved in God's favor. To be more specific, we can harbor love for a sin deep inside, that on the conscious level, we believe we have renounced and permanently rejected.

The best illustration of this phenomenon is the area of forgiveness. Many of us have experienced the stages that forgiving can go through before it is finally and completely effectuated. We can often see the difference between what we have desired, what we have declared, and what we still feel and believe on the inside.

In cases with besetting sins that do not respond to normal Christian therapeutic means, you often find this to be one of the underlying problems. We simply love the sin too much, or we believe that we deserve to commit it. Or we believe that we can't live without it.

One night I was complaining to God about a relatively small sin that I could not gain victory over. "You set me free from far more wicked strongholds of sin," I complained, "why won't you set me free from this one?" The answer was clear as a bell: "Because you still love it." At that point, I knew that deep inside, there was a part of my heart that still loved that sin, that still wanted it to stay, and I had to repent of that reality and renounce my love for it before any progress could be made.

On another occasion, I was crying and begging God to set me free from a sin that had beset me for thirty years. It wasn't the first time that tears had been streaming down my cheeks in prayer over this sin either. I could not, for the life of me, figure out why God had not set me free from a sin that, from all appearances, I was deeply grieved over and dying to be free from. That night, the power of God suddenly overshadowed me, and I was instantly set free. But rather than rejoicing, in that split second of realizing that after thirty years, I was permanently free and would never sin that sin again, from deep within my heart arose the words, "Oh, no!" In an instant, the layers of self-deception were removed, and I saw what was truly in my heart. Deep inside, despite all my begging and crying, I did not want to be free from that sin. In truth, I was terrified at the thought of living without it. And I went right back to it days later. It took another six months of prayer—asking God to remove from me my love of that sin and to instill in me faith that He could meet my need instead—before I was finally ready to be "set free indeed" (cf. John 8:36).[5]

We need to ask God to search our hearts so that we can know if there be any wicked way left within—even beyond our ability to see or feel (cf. Psalm 139:23-24).

So, it's easy to see how a process of change and growth is necessary for all of this to come about. And it all starts with step one. My guess is that those who live in the defeat of habitual sin are those who have not yet fully fallen in love with Jesus. They have not yet received the depth of revelation of His love and awesome beauty that transforms the heart and mind. Rather than spending copious hours psychoanalyzing these folks, why not take them afresh to the throne of the Almighty King of Kings—back to the simple, profound truth of His glory and grace. I speak not in theory, but as one who has been healed of numerous severe, lifelong sinful addictions and obsessions. This is the way of God's permanent deliverance and healing. For man, it seems too simple. But once again, God has chosen to make foolish the wisdom of man through the simple truths of His gospel.

In summary, then, what are the primary causes for a failure to find deliverance from on-going sin? They are:

1. Failure to make an across-the-board commitment to holiness.
2. Failure to believe in and act upon, God's power to deliver and keep us.
3. Failure to undergo a transformation of the will through faith in God's unconditional love.
4. Failure to see healing as a process with a purpose.
5. Failure to develop an intimate relationship with God the Father.
6. Failure to humble ourselves in absolute dependence on God.
7. Failure to learn and practice spiritual warfare.
8. Failure to truly repent.
9. Failure to forsake idolatry of the intellect.
10. Failure to work through an unresolved sense of justice.
11. Failure to let go of a "victim" identity.
12. Failure to utterly forsake the love of one's sin.[6]

*   *   *   *

Now let's take that promised, detailed look at the greater issues surrounding sin, psychology, and the crippling effect of an unhealed "victim" identity.

12

Victim Nation:
A Fallen World's Take On Sin

---

ave you noticed that nobody is "guilty" anymore?

"We're victims! We couldn't help it! Our genes made us do it! It was those evil parents that you, (God), gave us! It was the lack of money that made us rob that bank! It was my hormones that made me rape that girl! It was low self-esteem that made me kill my children!"

Lucky for us, we have science and psychology to give us the alibis we need to avoid taking the rap and that excuse our choice to continue in sin. Too bad for folks in bygone days who had to suffer consequences for their actions.

Have you noticed that the word "sin" isn't used in modern conversation anymore? When you use it, people actually blanch! You can see the wheels whirling in their heads, as they transfer you into the "fanatic" category (otherwise known as "one of those").

What's even worse is the subtle way that Christians use the grace and forgiveness of Jesus Christ as an excuse for refusing to renounce and forsake sin. Same game, different *modus operandi*. "We're going to heaven, so why obsess about our faults? Jesus loves us just the way we are! He was tempted just like me. Everyone makes mistakes. We're only human! Just sinners saved by grace!"

It all sounds very pious, doesn't it? And in the context of true repentance, most of it is true! Yet, we too often use such euphemisms to excuse ourselves from the high call of becoming more like Christ. We forsake our inheritance as mighty warriors in the Kingdom of God for the low calling of "victim." Like Esau, we trade in the glorious mandate given the people of God for immediate gratification, little realizing that the game we play of pretending "not to be able to help it" will be revealed as "the love of sin" that it really is when Jesus comes, and that we will, in fact, answer for the choices we have made in this life.

Intellectual Idolatry

You can trace a large part of the problem to the effects that Enlightenment "rationalism" has had on Christian thought. The philosophical underpinnings of rationalism assume that man can use reason alone to find his way to God without the need for special revelation such as Holy Scripture.[1]

In an attempt to prove that Christianity (and the Word of God) are supremely rational, the western Church has sometimes tried to win the world to Christ by force of reason alone. The mistake in making this our singular approach is that God is full of mystery. When we focus our attempts to persuade on reason alone, we come up looking unreasonable in areas that God has left unknowable, and we find ourselves consorting with a philosophy that exists to excuse sin and deny God.

Modern science and psychology are in headlong pursuit of rationalistic answers to life's problems. They are attempting to answer questions that involve body, soul, and spirit with thinking that addresses just body and soul. If the things of the spirit are acknowledged at all, it is from a post-modern worldview that humors those "who need such a crutch" or that regards it as merely some impersonal, amoral, universal force. Conse-quently, their answers are flawed, inaccurate and potentially far more damaging than the presenting problem. What finite creatures find reason-able is often a reflection of their own limited perspective, rather than truth. And what fallen finite creatures find reasonable sometimes isn't even on reality's chart. Without the divine revelation of truth, we are doomed to aim at a target we cannot even see, much less hit.

Because much of the western Church practices the "intellectual idolatry" of rationalism, we quite naturally fall victim to its ways, becoming fools while gorging on knowledge. We have God all figured out, with more infor-mation about Biblical theology, archaeology, and history than the world has ever known. Yet, like the Pharisees of old, it is fixed in our minds, unable to make the transition between head and heart.

By buying into the paradigm established by rationalism, our capacity to know the things of the Spirit has wasted away. We actually come to desire staying fixed in our heads so that we can remain in control and independ-ent of God. The things of the Spirit are unpredictable, uncontrollable and often force us to do things we'd rather not do. So we focus our lives around reasoning our way to health, performing steps, and putting our hope in our own personal selection of "experts." Nothing contributes more to this self-deception than the idea that being a victim frees us from responsibility for our actions.

The Tyranny of Our "Culture of Experts"

A serious consequence to our blindness is the modern tyranny of a "cul-ture of experts" who silently control modern thinking from a pool of knowledge that is woefully inadequate to the task. The field of psychology, for example, is still in its infancy, much like the medical field was 100 years ago, yet postures itself as though its knowledge was infinitely greater. Many of the "models" that today are the newest and most necessary means of therapy will tomorrow be recognized as the malpractice that they truly are. Consider the carelessness already exhibited in such therapies as "primal scream," "past-life and future-life regression," "hypnosis," the use of pornography to treat sex offenders and attempts within the American Psychological Association to deem it malpractice to counsel homosexuals to change. Even with such a universally embraced therapy as 12-Step groups, it's becoming clear that a mistake is often made in fixing on this helpful tool to such lengths that a life-long self-focus and "victim" identity is unwittingly sanctioned rather than healed.

Part of what it means to live as a victim is living one's life from an attitude of "I deserve!" Counseling lingo can be a co-conspirator in this process. It can suppress the impulse for true Biblical repentance. If I am an "addict," or if I have a "disease," then I have an excuse, a legitimate reason for doing what I am doing. Where, then, is the need to repent? If I am sinning because I have deserved an outlet for my rage over being victimized, then why weep and wail before God in sorrow for my actions? "I'm entitled to my actions! I've earned the right! The least God and man can do is to allow them, considering all I have gone through!"

Thus, we excuse ourselves, forgetting that God holds us to a higher standard. How can He? Because He has provided a way for us to walk according to that standard by the power of the Holy Spirit, as well as a means of cleansing through repentance when we fail. We are not suppose to live our lives in the hopeless bondage of Romans 7, but rather in the victory of a co-partnership with God's Holy Spirit, offered in Romans 8.

Archbishop Randolph Adler (primate of the Charismatic Episcopal Church) wrote:

> In a culture where the therapeutic attitude dominates, therapeutic categories displace moral categories to the point that moral thinking seems no longer possible. Health, disease, dysfunction and 'well-adjustedness' replace categories of good and evil, wise and foolish.[2]

He then quotes Alister McIntyre, from his book, *After Virtue*:

> . . . the concept of the therapeutic has been applied far beyond the sphere of psychological medicine and thereby, the truth has been displaced as a value and replaced by psychological effectiveness![3]

Adler then concludes:

> None of these critics are opposed to therapy as therapy; they are opposed to the kind of reductionism, whereby therapeutic categories replace moral ones.[4]

Thus, the problem lies not as much in what psychology is as in what it replaces.

How do therapeutic categories usurp God's throne? It begins with the "experts," who displace God as the voice of truth in culture. They gain a controlling influence in political and educational systems and intimidate opposition with the threat of regulation and punishment. They posture themselves as the only reliably informed reservoir of truth, erecting gates of "accreditation" and "licensing," keys held in an iron grip. By pretense, they assume the high moral ground of "benevolent caretaker," while dispensing prescriptions that further separate man from God. The longer their answers appear to work, the more man becomes deceived into thinking he isn't accountable to and doesn't need help from God. It is a very subtle process by which man is persuaded to seek after psychological answers as the hope of healing rather than fixing that hope in Jesus Christ. Thus, man as counselor supplants God as Counselor.

With the empowering of secular gods, even some Christians become convinced that there are certain people with certain backgrounds for whom the Word of God will not work, who must instead have therapy or drugs to get better. In truth, there *are* people who need such things to get better. However, it's not because the Word of God won't work for them. It is, rather, because they (and those who are helping them) refuse to believe in it. They place their faith in secular gods and dance to the lyric: "Did God really say?" Thus, even some Christian counselors forsake the powerful truths of Scripture for the intrigue of man's wisdom. While giving lip service to the Bible, in practice they chose to rely wholly on the world's systems, theories, steps, and programs, rather than building people up in the mighty Word of God.[5]

It's not that psychological models and theories are inherently evil. The problem lies in becoming so enamored with their newness and novelty that we unconsciously begin placing our hope and fixing our eyes on them, rather than on what has to be the central focus of any healing process—the development of an intimate relationship with God, coupled with embracing the promises of Scripture by faith.

Concomitant with that is another great danger—that of focusing on the details of the process to the point where we put our hope for change on performing "the program" rather than in our Father in heaven. As Loren Cunningham once wrote: "You never want to look at the need before you look at the greatness of God." The program may be helpful, but when it becomes the focus and the hope for change, whatever temporary benefit it may produce will ultimately fail to serve permanent, God-centered transformation.

We must bathe ourselves in the promises of God and the knowledge of His goodness and power. We must replace our old image of God the Father with a new one birthed in His presence during long hours of seeking after Him (Jeremiah 29:11-14). We must reconfigure our belief systems by rehearsing God's declarations and promises, so that our thoughts become one with the Word of God.

The lion's share of our healing process should involve practicing the truths of scripture—what I call "Truth Therapy"—so that every waking moment is moved and filled with knowledge sprung from a marriage of both head and heart. We need to know without a shadow of a doubt that:

- the weapons of our warfare have divine power to demolish strongholds and everything that sets itself up against the knowledge of God (2 Corinthians 10:4-5);

- that we wrestle not with flesh and blood but with principalities and powers and forces of evil in heavenly realms (Ephesians 12-12);

- that God has not given us a spirit of fear, but of power, love and a sound mind (2 Timothy 1:7);

- that we are to take every thought captive to make it obedient to Christ (2 Corinthians 10:5);

- that we can do all things through Christ who strengthens us (Philippians 4:13);

- that if we live by the Spirit, we will not carry out the desires of the flesh (Galatians 5:16);

- that God has given us everything we need for life and godliness through our knowledge (intimate relationship) of Him (2 Peter 1:3);

- that He is able to keep us from falling (Jude 1:24).

We need to be built up in our holy faith!

Unfortunately, such truths often take a back seat to man's wisdom when they should be center stage in the healing process.

Yes, it may take time to guide someone to the place of being willing to trust, believe, and stand on the goodness and power of Almighty God. But too often, we don't even try. Instead, we forsake the Bible way for man's way, and imprison our charges in performance orientation, self-obsession, and the pride of man.

Is There Anything of Value in Psychology?

Does this mean that there is nothing of value in science or psychology? Are we to let the misuse of the "abuse excuse" rob us of the benefits that do exist? Despite all the crazy therapies out there and the anti-christian worldview underlying much psychological theory, there is an enormous storehouse of data gathered from a century of observing human behavior that should not be discounted or jettisoned. It is neutral data that can be useful when enrobed in moral principle and a Biblical worldview. A careful contextualization is required under the guidance of the Holy Spirit. But if we can achieve that without becoming enamored with our growing knowledge and without becoming focused on it as the source of our hope in counseling, then we have something of value. To be fair, there are thousands of sound, committed, and healthy Christians out there attempting to do just that who need the support, guidance, prayers, and blessing of the Church.

Historically, the Church has gotten into trouble when it has failed to integrate legitimate discoveries into the Biblical worldview. Then, when we've realized our mistake, we've often gone too far in the opposite direction in order to make up for the error, trying to show ourselves reasonable again to a skeptical world. This recurring fear and obsession with what the world thinks about us creates an unhealthy focus on new discoveries that lures us away from the correct posture of fixing our eyes primarily on Jesus and our ears on the Holy Spirit.

Is the use of therapeutic language ever warranted then? The Bible indicates the affirmative. Consider Paul's "unknown God" apologetic on Mars Hill (Acts 17:22-32), or the Apostle John's use of "logos" terminology in his gospel (John 1:1). These were instances where Christian leaders used the language of culture in order to better communicate to that culture the truths of God.

A difference should be noted, however, in how these apostles used such language. They redefined and recontextualized it. Rather than settling for adopting entrenched definitions within entrenched world-views, they lifted common terms from those alien world-views and redefined them within the context of Biblical teaching, saying in effect: "This 'logos' idea of yours speaks of Christ." "Your 'unknown God' is YAHWEH."

One mistake that modern Christians make is to utilize secular concepts without redefining them according to a Biblical worldview. Instead, we adopt the fallen concept as a way of proving to the world, "We are educated, too!" We try to validate ourselves in their eyes by becoming like them in the misguided hope that if we prove to them that we are like them, they will then want to become Christians.

Has anyone noticed that this is not working? Has anyone noticed that the idea of attaining friendship with the world goes against everything Jesus prophesied Christians would face if they were truly His disciples?

Worse still, as though it were possible to separate secular from sacred, we sometimes adopt the world's misguided concepts in order to curry favor with fallen humanity (e.g., to get our school "accredited," to gain that coveted secular "licensing," to be nominated for that "chair" at the University, etc.). Such a focus is often fixed on self rather than the purposes and goals of God.

Christians should be defining the parameters of culture as we've done in the past (e.g., when we created the great universities, hospitals, sanctuaries for throwaway kids, etc.). We should be establishing licensing and accreditation standards for the world, not vice versa.

We must retake the offensive posture of taking ground for the kingdom of God rather than drowning in the defensive "victim" posture of always defending besieged territory. Pride, intellectual idolatry, and the siren song of a godless world have blinded us to our true call. The self-obsession of a world in therapy, this "victim nation," has diverted our eyes from the God who can heal and transform any brokenness to secular gods who can only create an appearance of rightness.

As we have seen, the Bible does give precedent for using the terminology of the world as a tool for helping people understand what is really true, but not for becoming a part of its system. Use the words "addiction" and "disease" if it will help bridge someone's understanding to the realities of the Kingdom of God. Be a light. Be one whom God can use to define the perception of reality for the world. But do not so adopt their labels as to become confused as one of them. Do not so benignly adopt their concepts and definitions of reality so as to curry favor or prove yourself to them.

It may be that psychology is necessary to the world in which we live. Today, we don't spend time talking to each other. In generations past, there was a stronger sense of community and linkage to the personal lives of others. The loss of intimacy in today's world has created a need for the contrived friendship of counselor-counselee. Since the world has already legitimized and normalized the use of fake things to meet our needs, (pornography, prostitutes, drugs, etc.), it no longer seems foreign to create temporary "pretend" friendships for counseling purposes.

An article in *Newsweek* magazine revealed some recent research on the simple benefits of talking out problems with someone else. Brain research has now shown that through "talk therapy," the unhealthy brain chemistry of patients suffering from depression or obsessive-compulsive disorders corrects itself in ways similar to the effects of antidepressant drugs.[6] In this disconnected world, where intimate friendships have become more and more scarce, psychotherapy has become the "paid" friend who can facilitate the need to talk out our problems and bring correction to physiological imbalances.

The problem is, most people will never visit a therapist, and even if they do, success is very unpredictable. They may get a therapist who fills them with destructive, ungodly ideas and concepts or one who uses them as a guinea pig to try out the latest therapeutic theory. They may get someone who unnecessarily exaggerates the need for therapy in order to increase their own wealth. (Lawyers and car mechanics are not the only ones with a reputation for doing so.)

Fortunately, a study some years ago at the University of London (the Eysenck study) indicated that people who talked out their problems with friends were more likely to get better than those who entered into psychotherapy.[7] The truth is, God has always provided a way for us to work through the emotional and psychological damage caused by life's traumas. In that sense, the emergence of psychotherapy, benefit or no, is a sad testimony to the rampant depersonalization that has overtaken this generation.

Blaming Mom and Dad

Many who are opposed to psychology view the search for childhood traumas and neglect as simply an attempt to find excuses for sin. If that were the reason, then, indeed, it would be wrong. However, from observing human behavior, we have discovered that some people use painful events in their past as "subconscious excuses" for justifying their rebellious behavior. This can include anger at God as well as the person who hurt them. By understanding why we do what we do, we sometimes are enabled to see that it is not a hopeless defect in us that keeps us in bondage, but rather, circumstances that we can learn to respond to in ways that release us from that bondage.[8]

Many see the taking of a family history by a counselor as an attempt to fix blame on mom and dad for the person's own sinful choices. The truth is, in any Christian-based model for therapy, the point is not to look back at the failings of parents and others as a means of fixing blame, but as a means of removing the blame that has already been fixed.

You see, when they hurt us, when they neglected us, we fixed blame then. Now, as we discover where we have harbored bitterness and unforgiveness from past events, we can chose to forgive and so remove the ground that Satan gained in our lives when we first committed such "sins of response."

In working through the memory of the sins of others against us, our "sins of response" (such as envy, idolatry, unforgiveness, vows, judging, hating, dishonoring parents, etc.) are exposed as the sins that they are—sins which have empowered Satan to keep us in bondage. As God releases a capacity in us to humble ourselves and forgive as God has forgiven us, we are set free.

The one caveat in such a search of one's past is that it be done by the guidance and direction of the Holy Spirit. If the counselor is using his/her past experience and expertise to merely guess at what may have created the problem and is not yielded and submitted to the leading of the Spirit, then the search can devolve into something self-centered and unredemptive. It may also develop into something whereby the hope for change is being fixed on the self-discovery rather than on the redemptive power released in an intimate relationship with God.

The goal of examining one's life is to examine causal factors without remaining fixed on them as fuel for blame and unforgiveness, or as the focus of hope for change. We must always remember that knowing why helps, but knowing Him heals.

Using others' faults to justify our own sinful decisions will not fly with God. Taking responsibility for our actions is critical for permanent transformation and for winning God's participation in the healing process. Ultimately, mom and dad will not be the cause of our failure to live godly, productive lives. We will be the cause.

Self-pity is foundational to "Victim Nation" but is highly destructive. It feeds narcissism and other destructive directions. So, balance and perspective are critical in this healing process.

We all have a predilection to sin, yet God requires holiness. He is fair and justified in doing so because He provides the way to overcome our victimization, handicaps, and fallenness. In fact, it is His glory to raise up the most victimized, the most handicapped, the most fallen and wretched of sinners to be faithful servants and trophies of His grace and power.

Sin, Addiction or Disease?

In the early part of this decade, buried in the back pages of the *Honolulu Advertiser* was a story reporting that there had been a failure to replicate the results of previous studies that had shown a genetic link to alcoholism.

Why was such a huge story buried in the back pages of the newspaper? It was because too much had been invested in the theory. Psychologists would look bad. People would lose confidence in their experts. It was safer to just ignore the matter and pretend the theory had still been conclusively proven.

The Bible stills calls it drunkenness, and whether someone has a physical predilection to fall victim to it or not is a moot point considering that the God of the universe, who created the heavens and the earth, has the power to keep us from falling, no matter what our defect of body or character.

Sin often cloaks itself as disease. The Bible tells us in Romans 1 that when a person gives himself to an idol rather than trying to find his healing, nurture, and completion in God, the Lord then gives him over to the power of that idol, and he becomes deceived. This is how "sin" takes on the characteristics of what modern psychologists call "addiction" or "disease."

The problem with these modern terms is that they imply innocence on the part of the addict. In such matters, however, it is a condition for which the person was the cause and for which he bears full responsibility, even though he may now be overtaken by the power of what he has given himself to.

The deep anger, distrust, and rebellion against God that fuels our fallen nature persuades us to use the trials, traumas, and neglects of life to justify our decision to seek solace in the creature rather than in God. God then gives us over to the power of the idol we have chosen, and we come under the demonic power that lurks within it. Thus, sin takes on the out-of-control nature of "addiction" or "disease," and we come to a place where we do things obsessively, compulsively, recklessly, and dangerously— things we don't even want to be doing.

Sinful decisions, actions, or neglect by others may have contributed to my brokenness, but usually, not as much as my own selfish responses to those people, events, and to God. The heart of the problem lies in my own self-centered demand to have my needs served regardless of the needs and conditions of those around me. The people or events of my life that have brought pain become my excuse, but the cause for the consequent disasters of my life is my own sinful heart.

That is not to say that God does not take into account the traumas and tragedies of our lives when judging our actions, but without our admission of ultimate guilt and true repentance there can be no deliverance from the bondage by God—only the specter of a lifetime of trying to maintain sobriety by our own finite wit and strength.

Despite the benefits of understanding how our traumas have encouraged us in one direction or another, it is most important that we remember that the reason we sin is because we have fallen hearts. Our personal history should never be made the scapegoat for our willful choices. We are in bondage to the things we love more than God. We are addicted to our idols—those things which we have chosen to turn to other than God for the assuaging of our pain. Though we may be out of control now, we are responsible for getting that way.

The ultimate answer is found in confessing our guilt, yielding ourselves as containers of Christ's righteous life, and walking by the power of the Spirit (Galatians 2:20). To the degree that our 12 steps and psychological models cause us to forget that, successful as they may be in keeping us from acting out, to that degree they are hurting us rather than helping. If we fail to put God first and depend on His deliverance and transformation, then we will live in bondage to maintenance programs, rather than obtaining the transformation program that God has for us.

We need to be turning to God first, rather than to man. We need to forsake the moniker of "victim" and repent before God for the choices we've made that may have ended in addiction or "disease." That is what will set us free.[9]

*   *   *   *

As you can see, the things one should consider as God is leading him/her to minister to others can be complex. Leadership in general is complicated and made even more so by the plethora of gurus who hawk their sure-fire methods for becoming a leader in the marketplace of worldly ideas.

In our final chapter, we are going to take a look at the elements that make for a godly minister/leader, which is really the end-game for our growth in holiness and Christlikeness, to one degree or another. We'll also look at some of the decisions that often need to be made by such servant leaders. With Jesus as our example, the conclusions that we'll draw will be different than the methods and models promoted by world. But isn't that how Christ said it would be?

13

The Making of A Minister

I. SELF-PREPARATION

Discerning God's "Call" and "Timing"
Am I Really Being Called to This?

One of the first matters that must be addressed as one is drawn toward ministry is: "Am I being called by God to do this, or is my impulse to minister in this area, and at this time, a manifestation of unhealed ego needs?" This is undoubtedly one of the reasons that Paul exhorts Timothy not to lay hands too quickly on anyone (1 Timothy 5:22). If, as a result of our own healing process, we have been eliminating numerous life-dominating props and masks (various people, places, things, and behaviors previously used as unhealthy coping mechanisms), it is not unlikely that we might unconsciously use the romantic notion of "being in the ministry" as a self-induced means of reestablishing an identity, a purpose for life, or as a new source of positive reinforcement.

So, a *perceived* call is not necessarily a *true* call, and the sense of *timing* for a call is not necessarily God's *true timing* for that call. I made both mistakes.

When I was first saved, I had a very strong desire to minister to prostitutes in Hollywood. I had been one, and I knew that I was an extremely rare candidate for such a ministry. Church leaders in Hollywood could have taken advantage of my misguided zeal to fill their ministry needs. Entering into that ministry would have made me feel highly valued and honored by them—thus meeting an internal need for attention and affirmation that had neurotically and powerfully driven my entire, massively dysfunctional life. Swearing love and devotion to Jesus all the way, I would have been doing it solely for my own glory and thus, frighteningly, in my own strength. It could very possibly have meant my downfall as well, since many of the issues that had drawn me to that sin had yet to be healed. I would have been a sitting duck for the enemy in such an arena so soon after being saved. As time went on, I realized how fleshly and self-wrought my desire for that ministry had been, and I was very glad that God had kept all doors closed to it.

Alternately, our impulse to minister may stem from an inner drive to *repay* God for His mercy, *earn* or *maintain* His love through performing agreeable services, or any number of other aberrant reasons. The drive to minister, in such cases, is driven by unhealed wounds and insecurities rather than a genuine call from God. We are trying to fix ourselves or atone for our past and are using ministry to achieve self-centered goals that can never be accomplished in such ways. Our focus on ministry, then, is not centered on love of God, or those to whom we minister, but on our selves and our insecurities.

The more prone we have been to magical thinking or escaping into fantasy as a coping mechanism, the more likely it is that such aberrant, interior motivations are present. The better we have been at masking or denying reality, the more likely this is to be a problem. We must ask God to unveil our hidden heart. While He is certainly capable of bringing good from the efforts of one who is ministering from the wrong heart, that is not the way He wants it to happen.

Timing is also a very critical factor. God often calls a person into the ministry years before actually commissioning and releasing him or her into the work of that call. If Moses had to wait forty years, if the Apostle Paul had to wait in the desert for years, if Jesus Himself had to wait thirty years before being released into the ministry for which He was born, so too will we have a season of preparation. We must be very careful not to manufacture a call from ego needs or run ahead of God's timing for using us in ministry. Neither should we procrastinate when God finally does open the doors and sends us out.

These observations beg three questions. 1. How then can a person know if he or she is being called into a particular ministry? 2. How can someone know when to proceed into that calling? 3. And what should one do in the interim?

Each answer will come as the person concentrates on developing an intimate relationship with God. When the focus finally becomes God Himself and not the "call," then the timing is often nigh for God to use them.

One of the first lessons that God teaches us in the school of His Presence is that He is the purpose of life—that everything we could ever want is found in Him. That includes our daily bread and our ego needs, our healing and our redemption, our purpose for living and our pleasure in life. When we become satisfied with Him and Him alone, then He can trust us to participate in His redemptive, healing acts in the lives of others.

You see, He doesn't need us to minister to anyone. He could cause the rocks to sprout arms and legs to do His bidding! To receive a call to minister to His flock is a gift, a blessing, and an honor. Ministry is a privilege that is bestowed on those whom He trusts because they have sat long in His Presence and had their interior drives and motivations transformed by the direct experience of His love. Their fallen motivations for achievement in life have been replaced by His very heart to the point that the impulse to minister now comes from the heart of God Himself. They are now more purely driven by an undying and unconditional love for Him, and they can't help but share that love with others. They have become a channel of His love, rather than an isolated spigot of their own resources.

Of course, God does not wait until this transformation is fully completed before sending a person into ministry. Transformation and renewal are a lifelong process. They begin with rudimentary steps of commitment— seeing through a glass darkly with the light we have been given—and finish in being transformed into His image, from glory to glory (2 Corinthians 3:18).

As we ground ourselves in the very Being of God through intimate moments spent in His Presence, we learn well the sound of His voice. We even come to know His thoughts without His having to utter them to us. Our hearts become knit—He in us and we in Him (John 17). Our perception of His will becomes a settled knowing, enveloped in a sea of peace.

Upon becoming convinced that God has called us to a particular ministry, the next step is to ask for confirmation(s) of that call. Sometimes it is appropriate to lay out a fleece before Him—a specifically arranged scenario by which He can bring confirmation (Judges 6). At other times, one senses that it is not appropriate to designate to the Lord how He should confirm the call. One simply requests confirmation. It often comes in multiple forms and in ways that speak not only the word of confirmation, but also a reaffirmation of just how deeply He knows the ways that will most perfectly speak to our heart. Every act of God is an act of love—even in the midst of providing us with practical direction.

In the interim, between the call and the commission, is a time of preparation wherein He may provide opportunities for brief forays into ministry without yet giving the full release and provision. He lets us get our feet wet, little by little, in proportion to our growth in maturity and understanding. Timing is everything, and the timing for our release into ministry has just as much to do with what will make for our optimal growth in holiness as it does any benefit that there may be for the people to whom we are sent to minister. The discovery of this fact alone creates a powerful reservoir of desire within us to be ever more faithful and obedient to the call and to the One who calls.

This life is as much a time for being trained in the school of God's Presence as it is a time to learn from any other school to which He might send us. We must learn well both the Scriptures and the heart of God so as to aptly represent and defend both Word and Lord. Some will need formal theological training. Others may have a call on their life that requires that their formal training be in some other discipline—such as nursing or counseling (though every calling requires a thorough examination and ongoing life of Scripture study, reflection, and meditation). In short, the training should be appropriate to the requirements of the call and provide ample preparation prior to the actual commissioning.

It is absolutely crucial that we learn from God what we are called to do and what we are not called to do. There are many worthy causes, many critical needs, but each of us was created to fill one specific set of "good deeds" during our life (Ephesians 2:10). One benefit of inestimable value that is obtained in the school of God's Presence is the desire and capacity to cleave singularly and faithfully to His purpose for our lives, so that when well-intentioned friends or well-financed ministry leaders try to persuade us to serve the purpose God has given them, we can stand firmly in the will of God and say a friendly "No thanks."

So the question remains: Are you going to spend your life on Ishmael or on Isaac?

This was a challenge that I faced. As I began to write my first book, *Sexual Healing*, my ego needs told me to build an elaborate ministry system, with ministry franchises around the world, to gather an entourage of traveling ministers, and to make my book into a new curriculum that would replicate the models already in use by Leanne Payne, Andy Comiskey, and others. The dominant ministry model was, and still is, support-group-based, so success seemed to demand that I follow that model. I was on staff with a first-class mission organization at the time, and was being offered a worldwide ministry if I would give them my seed and let them mold and nourish it. But the Lord said "No." He didn't want me to reinvent that wheel. He wanted me to do something new. He wanted me to create a reference manual that would delve beneath the surface of existing ministry approaches in order to reestablish the primacy of God's simple, yet powerful, provision for the healing of bound and broken people, *which is intimacy with God and reliance on the Holy Spirit as Counselor*. He also wanted me to establish the fact that His simple plan for healing would work for any kind of healing, whether the brokenness was homosexual, heterosexual, or of a kind completely unrelated to sex. He didn't want me to create entourages or group franchises or complex models for therapy. He simply wanted me to illuminate the foundational components for the healing of all brokenness and to show how they had worked in the worse case of brokenness that I had ever seen—my own! What good would it do to establish a competing ministry system to Leanne's or Andy's, except to prove to myself that I was just as talented and spiritual as they? No way was I going to drive down that neurotic trail. I decided then and there that my needs to be affirmed and to feel successful were going to be met God's way and by His direction. If I never received public affirmation, I was going to bless the heart of God with my life. *That's* when God began to use me.

Leadership

Almost everyone is a leader in some arena—having some degree of influence over people at some level. It may be the father leading his family, the mother leading the kids when dad is gone, a teacher and his or her students, a pastor and congregation, a web site chat room facilitator, a writer, or any number of other situations.

However, when someone is feeling a call into the full-time ministry, or is being regularly placed over a group of people in a situation that demands a high degree of responsibility, one of the things he or she often ask themselves is: "Do I have the qualities of leadership that will enable me to successfully lead the people that God will be placing me over?" It's a legitimate question and one that everyone struggles with—a struggle made worse by the plethora of inane leadership models that are being touted in the marketplace of ideas.

Everyone and their uncle, it seems, have become "leadership" strategists. Our positive American work ethic, entrepreneurial spirit, and lust for material success have hatched a cottage industry of gurus, each with their own "perfect formula" for the making of a leader. They come on our television sets or in workplace training seminars with pithy, smart-sounding lists for "How to be a leader and make ten million dollars before you are thirty," or some variation on that theme. By using the standard American positive but aggressive pitch (or hype), they project a picture of leadership that is cutthroat, obsessively driven, and fixed on wealth and position as the measure of success. We are taught that to be a successful leader, we must be proud, arrogant, and devious. "Beating the system" (often, meaning the law) is promoted as a legitimate and smart way to achieve wealth, happiness, beautiful buxom ladies, and the praise of Americans everywhere.

Christians have, of course, entered the fray and tried to produce redemptive models of leadership—those that incorporate Biblical virtues and values into the formula. More often than not, however, such models end up looking very much like their secular counterparts. They continue to hype American cultural indices for success, but add a coating of spiritual language. Some, however, do get close to a genuinely Biblical leadership model, particularly those that focus on the talents and character of a leader rather than whether the leader produces American-style results.

George Barna has taken a shot at this in his book, *The Second Coming of the Church*, with mixed results. His emphasis seems to be on the nature of the person rather than personal character, however. Here are his "Eight Signs of God's Call to Leadership," (some of which I agree with and some I don't) to which I have added my commentary:[1]

1. Leaders have an awareness of God's call. . . .

2. Leaders possess an inclination to lead. . . . or a nagging sense of the necessity to lead, . . .

3. Leaders perceive reality differently from non-leaders. . . .

My understanding of the ministry vision that God has given me is often so clear that I make the mistake of not sharing the detail of it with others. I assume that they see it just as clearly as I do. I have to take the time to carefully and repeatedly convey the vision to others who have probably not received it from God in all its glory or detail.

Another problem associated with a leader's perception of reality, and one that Barna did not seem to recognize, is the fact that God often gives only part of a vision to the leader, and fills in the details only as they are obedient to what He has already shown them. Many teachers on leadership seem to believe that a real leader has a strong, full, and certain vision and direction at all times. This just isn't so in my experience, though I see many people pretending to be that certain in order to get people to follow them.

Barna sees leaders as change agents, "willing to take risks if they are reasonable and if they can produce significant returns." While this is true to a certain extent, I have learned that much risk taking in leaders is ego driven and not of God. As the years in ministry have passed, some 21 now, I have, thankfully, lost what turned out to be a reckless need for excitement that never should have been a part of my actions, and I have learned more about how to properly assess the consequences and payoffs of an action for the Kingdom.

We mustn't confuse the need to obey God when He calls us to take actions that only He can make succeed (which is a hallmark of His ways) with its flesh-based counterpart, which is an ego-driven, adrenaline-addicted license and impulse to keep from being bored or boring, so as to attract the praise of others. Leaders learn this lesson quickly or fail miserably in bearing fruit for the Kingdom.

4. Leaders naturally influence people. . . .

Let me just disagree with the good Mr. Barna on this one. Not all competent leaders "naturally" influence people. Some have to work very hard at producing the stuff that influences. Some influence others, in spite of themselves, because an anointing from God comes upon their life to do so. That which influences is not necessarily natural to a person. It may be the result of a timely message that God has put on their heart, or the example of their life, or an anointing that God bestows. And it may come and go during the course of their life. Let us always remember, God's timing and His ways are not ours.

5. Leaders seek each other out as companions. . . .

True, but then everybody seems to seek out leaders as companions. It's natural that you would want to hang around people in the same kind of ministry as you—to pick up tips, bounce ideas around, see if anyone has an answer to a problem you can't seem to lick. This is not unique to the subset of leader and, thus, doesn't really seem to fit as a distinguishing mark of a leader.

6. Leaders receive external acclaim. . . .

Anyone in the public eye is going to receive external acclaim (and criticism), leader or not. Just by virtue of being on the TV or behind the podium or the mike, people will assume that you are praiseworthy for something. Otherwise, they assume, you wouldn't have been given that platform. When I was an actor in Hollywood, I was the farthest thing from a leader you could find; yet, I received acclaim simply by the implicit imprimatur placed on me for having starred in several movies, and because I was often surrounded by famous and powerful people.

God's definition of a leader is very different, however. God's leaders sometimes receive no external acclaim whatsoever.

7. Leaders possess internal strength. . . .

I can agree with this one as long as it is acknowledged that there are many people with internal strength who are not leaders.

One other slight correction is Barna's contention that an effective leader must have self-confidence. It should be recognized that the confidence that some leaders possess is not a confidence in themselves, but rather a confidence in the power and promise of God to do something wonderful through them. The inner strength within them is actually the release of the life of God in them in the midst of their own personal weakness. This is the inner strength that Paul rejoiced in—forsaking the manufactured facsimile that the world applauds.

8. Leaders derive joy from leading. . . .

Certainly, some do. I rather experience a good deal of discomfort from leading, since it is so unnatural to me. I do find joy in it, however. But it is the joy of pleasing God, rather than the joy of leading. If it will cause that joy in Him, then lead I will.

Being a leader in the Kingdom of God needs to have a more nuanced definition—one that accounts for the immutability of the Christian message as well as the qualities that are unique to a leader who is serving God. Jesus indicated that being a leader in the Kingdom of God should result in rejection from the world—that if it didn't, you were very likely failing to fulfill your call (John 15:18-20). Even in the church visible, which is often no different than the world, to be a leader sometimes means losing the support of large groups of people.

I think of Jesus saying the hard things—things that separated true disciples from those who were hanging on just for the thrill. In John 6, with His "eat My flesh and drink My blood" speech, for example, He lost a large number of followers, for it says: "From this time many of His disciples turned back and no longer followed Him" (John 6:66).

Much of what is taught about leadership today does not acknowledge this "true disciple" factor. In my line of work, it screams at me.

David Mains (of "Chapel of the Air") lists three goals of leading, particularly when one leads through teaching or preaching:[2]

1. **Communicating the subject clearly.**

2. **Communicating the response being called for clearly.**

3. **Communicating the way to achieve that response clearly.**

Mains also suggests that we need to teach discernment to our people—showing them how to evaluate their actions, the input that they are allowing into their life, as well as how to change or get rid of those things that fight against spiritual growth and life. These are all critical things to learn as one progresses in the skill of leading.

Dr. Sudduth Cummings has also suggested a list of the elements of spiritual leadership. I like his list the best (to which I have added my commentary).[3]

1. Spiritual Leadership is God-centered.

The very heart of our message to people should be that it is in intimacy with the Father that we become all that we are meant to be. It is in unity with Him, in being a vessel to communicate His heart to the world, that effective and eternally significant ministry is born. Knowing Him is the purpose of life from which all other purposes find their life and meaning. He is the One who loves us perfectly. He is the One who is unfailingly faithful and trustworthy. He is the Source of life. His is the Wisdom of life. He is the life.

One of the more difficult tasks in this regard is in persuading people to actually pursue God as a person—this ethereal, invisible, intangible God. Many have a history of trying and failing. Many others have deep-seated and unspoken expectations of God that haven't been met, and so they have little faith or expectation that He will be there this time. They may even be angry at Him. Thus, there is little impetus to pursue Him.

Others have some interest in Him, but no more than their interest in golf or football or romance novels. For some, He is a Santa Claus, a physician, or a butler, who is trotted out when needed but otherwise kept in the utility closet of their mind.

These levels of interest in God mock His glory and so darken even more the glass through which they see Him. Not understanding why, they remain satisfied with keeping the search at the level of the intellect, safely protected from any hint of commitment or true intimacy. That way, no demands are placed upon them, no changes are required, they can have the satisfaction of a certain level of knowledge without the inconvenience of real interaction.

Being a *leader* is to be one who takes the time to cast the vision of who God is in ways that even the most jaded and uninterested will find compelling. This is a challenge to the imaginative and intuitive faculties that western intellectualism has almost rendered inert. My experience has shown that the most effective way to do this is to carefully maintain one's own intimate life with God, so that the natural exuberance and excitement from that flows from your eyes and your voice, spilling out in full view of others. In other words, it is more caught than taught. A leader, therefore, is the fruit of what he proposes. Like Christ, he embodies and bears fruit to the testimony that he proclaims, and it is that fruit that commands attention. Another word for this is integrity.

The great challenge for a leader comes when he or she experiences a "dark night" and loses their fire for God. In just such a crisis of my own, I wrote:

> The demands of single-handedly running a ministry have robbed me of the lengthy and lingering luxuries of being with God that I previously enjoyed. I've passed through one serious dark night of the soul, which I now understand was meant to train my affections to seek His presence without felt reward. Yet, I feel as though I have learned nothing by it. I fear that if this goes on much longer, I will be rendered incapable of even discerning the loss and miss out on the "better part" of life. Every resolution to go back to my first love seems to vanish by daybreak. Wise voices teach me that this is the expected way of the Christian life, as one is given more responsibility, but I am not yet convinced. I have heard that you can not long teach something you no longer live before it will destroy you. Lord, I am dying inside. Yet, Lord, I choose to rejoice that I am dying and proclaim with You that I no longer live, but Christ lives in me.

After writing that, and when the frenzy of anger and frustration had finally subsided, God was able to show me that the intense despair that I had experienced over not having felt God's presence during that time had actually been a demonstration of the depth of my love for Him. Had I little love for Him, the loss would have not seemed so great. I was thus enabled to peer into the secrets of my own heart and rejoice over how deep my love for God had grown. I was also able to get my first glimpse of what it means to die daily, to rejoice in my weaknesses, and to share in the sufferings of Christ. For if we are to participate in the divine nature, as 2 Peter 1:4 tells us we are, we must also participate or share in the sufferings of Christ, as it tells us in 1 Peter 4:13 and Philippians 3:10.

Allow God to teach you how to turn everything in life into a kliege light aimed at heaven. Then teach those lessons to others. Be honest. Tell them about the dark nights as well as the brilliant days. Let your leadership be real, honest, and God-centered.

2. Spiritual Leadership is Need Sensitive.

This one is tricky because sometimes the meeting of people's needs comes in conflict with what is best for them. We live in a culture of adult adolescents, who fly from one episode of need gratification to the other, with little thought of sacrificing their life for the welfare of others. So one must be careful not to appear to sanction that kind of immaturity while meeting their needs. The meeting of legitimate needs must take its proper place in the list of matters that comprise life with God and with one another.

I ask the Holy Spirit to uncover those needs buried deep inside of people that have been placed there by God and exhort them to first seek fulfillment of those longings. Thus, for example, when I encounter a prostitute, I try to look beyond the obvious sin in her life to her need to be pleasing to and affirmed by her father, which she has been attempting to meet in unhealthy ways. I validate that legitimate need and then show her how God the Father intends for it to be fulfilled. Then I tell her about her destiny in Christ as an ambassador of the Kingdom of God, a soldier in God's army, a person with a unique purpose and plan created by God that perfectly matches her personality and talents. I speak to her of the Father's love, of her acceptability to Him because of Christ and of the joy and ful-fillment that she's always wanted actually being possible through living in relationship with Him. In that sense, I am seeking to point her in a direction where her true needs will be met.

I also try to remain cognizant of the fact that some people are going to fix their hope in me rather than in the God that I preach—particularly if I say something that God uses to set them free. They are going to sometimes see me as the source of that wisdom or miracle and place their hope in me rather than God. This is one of the more difficult things to correct. Timing and subtlety are required, as well as a deferential pause to rejoice in what God has done.

This brings up the matter of cultural expectations for the counseling ministry of a pastor/leader. The field of psychology has successfully implanted the suggestion in people's thoughts that a person with emotional/psychological brokenness must go through months or even years of one-on-one counseling in order to discover why they got messed up, and that it is in that discovery process that healing will come. People come for pastoral counseling with the same expectation.

I can vividly recall harboring that expectation years ago when I walked through the doors of my church one day and asked for counseling. Their response was that they did not do counseling but believed that if I became a part of a home fellowship group, that many of my "issues" would be healed in the interaction, the worship, and the Word that I would find there. Well—I was incensed. "How dare a church not offer people counseling who needed it! How insensitive! How backward!"—were some of my thoughts. But I yielded to their preposterous theory, began regularly attending their "Kinship" groups—and it worked!

Part of what I am finding difficult in being a leader is the inability or unwillingness in many broken people to recognize the bankruptcy of modern psychological theory as a mechanism for permanent healing and transformation. They want ten steps. They want five principles. They want a hermetically sealed package that they can pop into their mental microwaves and come our normal in two weeks or less. And they will sometimes resist with everything that is within them the call to intimate relationship with God, and the similar call to connectedness and intimate relationship with fellow believers. Instead, they want to see the results of relationship without all the work, commitment and dependence that is involved. And when you press them too hard, many of them will leave and find someone who will give them what they want.

Yes, spiritual leadership is need sensitive. But it is also sensitive to the dangers of indiscriminate need-meeting, as well as the dangers of focusing one's hope for fulfillment in the practice of some method or model. It knows how to prioritize the meeting of needs and how to disciple someone so that their needs are met God's way. It sees the deeper needs of the heart, and shows the person how to shift their focus from self to sacrifice so that God's eternal provision for those needs is released.

3. Spiritual Leadership is Bible-based.

God's Word is our operator's manual. Yet, it unveils its treasures only as we progressively move toward a deeper relationship and union with Him. It is the road map, the cook book, the repair manual, the very food of life. It is the verbal expression of the person of Christ and thus conveys life and transforming power. Anything that excuses, avoids, ignores, or compromises personal and intimate fealty to God and His Word is a prescription for disaster, no matter how wise and holy it sounds.

When the wisdom of man contradicts the revealed Word of God, there is never a contest as to which is to be followed. Even should we honestly misinterpret a passage, I believe that God will honor our faith provided it remains consistent with His will, so as not to damage our reliance on the Word. God loves to honor the faithful intention of His people to believe in and stand on His Holy Scriptures.

Jesus said: "I tell you the truth, until heaven and earth disappear, not the smallest letter, not the least stroke of a pen, will by any means disappear from the Law until everything is accomplished. Anyone who breaks one of the least of these commandments and teaches others to do the same will be called least in the kingdom of heaven." (Matthew 5:18-19a)

The Bible teaches that the wisdom of man is foolishness. Such is the state of those who are living independent of the counsel of Scripture. That is true whether they be inside or outside of the church.

4. Spiritual Leadership is Incarnational (sacramental).

In years past, I never saw the real presence of Christ in Holy Communion as a means of communicating healing virtue to people. I see it now. It started back in 1981 at the Urbana missions conference when the presence of Christ filled that grand arena during the distribution of the Lord's Supper. There is a special presence of our Lord when we share together what *He* called His body and His blood. If our call is to lead people to the healing presence of Christ, what better vehicle than the one He instituted in that Upper Room two thousand years ago.

Previously, I had never believed in the supernatural infusion of God's presence and power into water and oil at the blessing of a presbyter. I'd known that demons sometimes manifested when Leanne Payne slung holy water over crowds of bound and broken people, but had never thought of it as more than the power of suggestion before.

There were times when John Wimber, my pastor at the time, would walk by people, and demons would manifest in them with curses and shrieks because of the incarnational power and anointing that was in his life. Oh, yes. Our faith is incarnational. I've seen too much to pretend otherwise.

The use of affirming prayers, speaking of blessings, and the calling on the Holy Spirit to do immediate ministry are additional "incarnational" areas of ministry. I can tell folks 'til I'm blue in the face how much God loves them. But to so many of them, that's just my opinion—an opinion that often flies in the face of the tragedies and traumas of their lives. If they are to be permanently transformed, they need to see Jesus and hear from the Father Himself just how much He loves them. That is where the incarnational realities of sacramental worship shine, whether in the sacrament of His body and blood or in the sacrament of Christ in you, the hope of glory. In the Gospel of John, Philip declared, "Lord, show us the Father and that will be enough for us." Jesus' answered, "Anyone who has seen Me has seen the Father." (John 14:8-9) Later, in John 17:21-23a,26b, He takes it further, praying that they "may be one, Father, just as You are in Me and I am in You. May they also be in us so that the world may believe that You have sent Me. . . . that they may be one as we are one: I in them and You in Me. . . that the love You have for Me may be in them and that I Myself may be in them."

5. Spiritual Leadership is Personal (experience).

Some people in ministry are fiercely project oriented and have to work hard at seeing people as people rather than as tools to achieve "God's purposes." Folks like this would do well to regularly and specifically pray to be motivated by love for people as well as for God. We need to ask for and receive by faith the capacity to love.

The importance of this struck me while watching a pastor give a message at a recent conference. He wept as he spoke of his gratefulness to God for the sacrificial acts of the saints in taking up an offering to help him obtain a church building. I began weeping and noticed him noticing. Then the Lord spoke to me and said, "You see, David, when that man speaks, he sees individual people who have personal lives, needs, cares, and feelings. When you speak, you see life forms who are reacting positively or negatively to your speaking skills and the words of your message." Then I felt God offering to enable me to see people the way that pastor did. I believe it is going to make all the difference in the world in the amount of power God will be pouring through me to heal the broken ones who come to me. In fact, I've already noticed a difference.

Another aspect of the "personal" part of spiritual leadership is the experiential. People today will not stand for the arrogant posturing of sinless perfection that clerics have been known for in the past. They want leaders who are vulnerable, who admit their faults, who reveal their humanity in the pursuit of holiness. It is that kind of leader who has and will succeed in today's ministries and churches and in today's evangelistic thrusts.

6. Spiritual Leadership is Corporate.

A spiritual leader must lead people together in community, never forgetting the corporate "body life" of God's design for His Church. This is very much connected to the previous element—the personal. Actually, it is the natural fruit of the personal, rightly directed.

Dr. Larry Crabb's book, *Connecting*, has been an enormous help. What would happen, he suggests, if when someone confessed a sin in our home fellowship group or support group, rather than trying to teach them what to do to get right and stay clean (our typical first response), we instead reacted with words like, "Your desire to be holy is such an inspiration to me"?

Dr. Crabb suggests that we form groups within our churches whose sole purpose is to build one another up to worship and good deeds—finding what is good in each other and affirming that. He believes, and I concur, that affirming the good in a person is what ultimately enables them to rise above what is bad. It names them. It calls them into their new identity in a way that law and instructions on being holy can never do. It is, in fact, the way God helps us to grow.

Another benefit of this way of thinking is that it gives substance to the corporate nature of the Church. In our various church groups, rather than specializing in head knowledge, or fixing people, we need to emphasize more the togetherness and the corporate power of union with Christ and one another that God intends. We need to see each other and treat each other as the new creations that we are—seeing things that aren't as though they were (Romans 4:17d; Hebrews 11:1). I'm certain that the power of that still lies mostly untapped in the church today.

7. Spiritual Leadership is Intentional and Systematic.

This is an area that requires continuing vigilance. Especially those of us who are prone to sloth must construct ways and means that remind and inspire us to be intentional and systematic in the process of spiritual leadership.

It is that way in every area of Kingdom life. The great and precious promises of Scripture do not just happen to us. We must intentionally and systematically desire and pursue them. Then and only then will we treat them in a way that reflects their true value—the value of the blood of God's one and only Son.

Leadership is both a natural and an acquired gift. Certain people are born with a personality or physical stature that enables them to more easily move into positions of leadership. Others only become leaders by virtue of a call from God. In calling them, He imbues them with important gifts, as well as giving them favor with men. He also provides them with a mind that can learn leadership skills. Finally, He gives them both common sense and spiritual understanding, so that they will reject the typical American business leader model in favor of one grounded in the example of His Son, Jesus Christ.

Humility

"... in humility, consider others better than yourselves...taking the very nature of a servant . . ." (Philippians 2:3,7)

"Clothe yourselves with humility toward one another, because, 'God opposes the proud but gives grace to the humble.'" (1 Peter 5:5)

There is a "humility boot camp" for those who are to be greatly used by God. None of us possesses humility naturally, so the more we learn of this wonderful virtue, the more effective our ministry will be. Unfortunately, humility is wrought in the crucible of suffering. A person's willingness and capacity to suffer is what will make the difference in this area. There are brilliantly crafted counterfeits to humility in this world. But when it is genuine, there are few things more powerful in releasing God's life and power through us in ministry to others. Gabriel of St. Mary Magdalen has written of humility:[4]

Humility is the firm bedrock upon which every Christian should build the edifice of his spiritual life. . . .

Humility forms the foundation of charity by emptying the soul of pride, arrogance, disordered love of self and of one's own excellence, and by replacing them with the love of God and our neighbor.

The more humility empties the soul of the vain, proud pretenses of self, the more room there will be for God. . . .

. . . if we wish to glorify ourselves, we must glory, like St. Paul, solely in our infirmities. It is only in our weakness, humbly acknowledged, that grace and divine virtue work and triumph (cf. 2 Corinthians 12:9). . . . [those] who are relying too much on their own powers and personal initiative, . . . are taking the wrong road; . . . [God] stoops only to the humble; the more lowly He finds a soul, the closer He draws it to Himself. Humility deepens the soul's capacity to receive the fullness of divine gifts. . . .

Humility makes us realize that, in the sight of God, we are only His little creature, entirely dependent upon Him for our existence and for all our works. Having received life from God, we cannot subsist even one moment independently of Him. . . .

God does not introduce a soul to a higher spiritual life, nor admit it to deeper intimacy with Himself, as long as it is not completely despoiled of all confidence in itself. When a soul practically forgets its nothingness, and still relies on its own strength, knowledge, initiative, or virtues—be it ever so little—God leaves it to itself. . . .

Confidence in God increases in proportion to our mistrust of ourselves; it becomes total when the soul, having acquired a thorough comprehension of its nothingness, has lost all faith in its own resources. . . . All its confidence rests on the infinite merits of Jesus, on the merciful love of the heavenly Father and on the workings of grace; and this confidence makes it more courageous, more daring than ever, because it knows that with God it can do everything. . . .

. . . Many souls would like to be humble, but few desire humiliation; many ask God to make them humble and fervently pray for this, but very few want to be humiliated. Yet it is impossible to gain humility without humiliations; . . .

. . . It is not the humiliation itself which makes us humble, but the act of the will by which we accept it. . . .

. . . Jesus [said] . . . "Learn of Me, for I am meek and humble of heart" (Matthew 11:29). . . . The example He gave in the extraordinary humiliations which made Him "the reproach of men, and the outcast of the people" (Psalm 21:7) . . . He was "made sin" (2 Corinthians 5:21) and the bearer of all our iniquities, even to being "reputed with the wicked" (Mark 15:28), is certainly the strongest stimulus and the most urgent invitation to the practice of humility. . . .

The exterior attitude and the humility of our words are useless unless accompanied by lowliness of heart; many times they are but the mask of a refined—and therefore all the more dangerous—pride. . . .

since God never refuses necessary grace to anyone, we have only to turn to Him and ask Him with confidence and perseverance for humility of heart. . . .

The fruit of humility is interior peace, for Jesus has said: "Learn of Me, for I am meek and humble of heart, and you shall find rest to your souls" (Matthew 11:29).

Love

This is another of the crown jewels of God's Kingdom. (The others include faith, wisdom, humility, grace, and holiness of heart.) More than anything else, these are the things that we should be asking God to impart to us on a regular basis. The Scriptures teach us that God is love (1 John 4:16b)—that in some mystical way, love is a part of that which constitutes God. Other Scriptures further define love:

If anyone loves the world, the love of the Father is not in him. (1 John 2:15b)

This is love: . . . that He loved us and sent His Son as an atoning sacrifice for our sins. (1 John 4:10)

. . . if we love each other, God lives in us and His love is made complete in us. (1 John 4:12b)

This is love for God: to obey His commands. (1 John 5:3a)

There is apparently a divine ontological reality to love, such that where love is, you have God Himself. That means that the world that does not know Him has only replicas of its own imperfect and incomplete idea of love.

The real thing should get their attention, which creates an awesome opportunity for ministry. If we will but love those who are lost and hurting, the manifest presence of God Himself in our love will do the rest. And I'm not talking about feelings or emotions. I'm talking about true biblical love, which the Bible defines as commitment, sacrifice, and obedience to God.

My own life produced a great example of this. There used to be a Christian in the office where I worked who would show up every day with a new Bible verse to show me. And each day, I would mock and curse him to the point where he would leave the room. But the next day, he'd be back with a smile on his face, as if I was his best friend, showing me another Bible verse. This went on for weeks until finally, one day, I realized that he really loved me; that he really cared about me; that he had something that I had been looking for my entire life. So I finally yielded to his kind gestures and began asking him questions about God. You see, when I finally had an encounter with God Himself, through the unconditional love of that believer, I was hooked.

More than all our clever evangelistic schemes, more than all our psychological methods and models, more than anything else, love is what people want, and love is what we should be communicating to them first and foremost. They don't have real love in the world, and when they finally see it in you and me, the barriers will come down.

The great and powerful fruit of ministry is carried on the arms of love. Therefore, pursuing God to manifest His love in and through us beyond the superficial levels of sentiment and feeling is a critical part of the preparation for effective ministry. Since God is love, the level of love that we walk in is directly connected to the level of ongoing intimacy that we achieve in Him. When we are thus saturated with His Presence, supernatural levels of love naturally manifest and spill into the lives of those we touch.[5]

Grace

This cannot be communicated too often, so let me say it once again. Titus 2:11-12 tells us that "the grace of God . . . teaches us to say 'No' to ungodliness and worldly passions, and to live self-controlled, upright and godly lives in this present age." In other words, God's grace is actually what produces heartfelt obedience. It is what undermines and eventually destroys the rebellion in the heart of man. It is the pen that writes His law on our hearts, causing us to delight in His law and to be eager to do what is good. We must model this same grace in ministry to others lest we drive our charges into legalism, or back into rebellion.

It is a well-known phenomenon that those who have been set free from a reprobate life can sometimes become very legalistic and judgmental in their attempts to minister to others. Especially over time, they can forget the grace given them by God and begin acting as though they had achieved their level of holiness. We must all be alert to this tendency and ask God to give us the humility of heart that will neutralize such pride.

A sister phenomenon is one where a person who has taken giant steps in freedom from sin over the years interposes his current level of holiness as the standard by which newcomers to the faith must instantly submit. He forgets the grace that was given him in the early stages of his walk with God. He forgets the time it took him in coming to know God's ways and the breathing room that was given him to learn how to depend upon God's power to keep him from falling. This premature imposition of a mature level of holiness is a lack of grace, a manifestation of pride, and it often exasperates the spiritual children with whom that person ministers.

On the other hand, learning how to model and teach the difference between true grace (which is given unconditionally in the midst of repentance), and license (which is offered indiscriminately in the absence of repentance) is just as crucial, lest grace be used as an excuse to "sin all the more."

In general, the church today has been so compromised by postmodern relativism that it all too often has erred in the direction of dispensing grace where there is no true repentance, no acknowledgement of sin. The result is an antinomian or lawless generation, most of whom claim to be "born-again," but who commit adultery and divorce, feed on immoral films and Internet sites, and kill their unborn children at levels similar or above that of the godless culture around them. We are like children who have never been disciplined. As a consequence, we harbor an inner disrespect for the moral leaders whom God has made responsible for our spiritual formation, and we use sin as our revenge.

Grace is not license, but it is merciful and longsuffering toward the heart that keeps wanting God even in the midst of failure. Learn to discern the difference.

Learning to Listen

. . . let the wise listen and add to their learning . . . (Proverbs 1:5a)

Everyone should be quick to listen, slow to speak and slow to become angry . . . (James 1:19b)

Most of us do not listen to people. At best, we learn to wait patiently until they have finished talking so that we can say what we want them to hear. We make quick judgments of the other person from just a few of their words, broadly generalizing, categorizing and dismissing ideas along stereotypical lines. We stereotype because our elaborate lines of opinion and defense depend on it.

In truth, much of our conversation with people is subconsciously contrived so as to display our brilliance and, thus, elevate ourselves in their estimation. Though we convince ourselves that our words are for their benefit, they, in fact, usually serve the god of self.

A good listener really believes that the other person can teach them something, no matter who they are. A good listener is humble. And since God loves to bring wisdom from the mouths of babes, they inevitably become wise. Their practice of honoring the opinion of the other contrasts so profoundly with normal conversation that they gain the trust and good will of people more quickly than others. These are among the best counselors, for they wait long enough in conversation to hear important parts of a person's mind and heart—things divulged only after trust and respect have been earned. They are entrusted with information given to no one else, making their counsel more well-informed.

The art of listening is something that must be intentionally practiced and developed. It is essential to effective ministry.

Biblical Knowledge

Zeal that is not based on the knowledge of God, His ways, and His Word (Romans 10:2) is dangerous. Much of modern psychology has been birthed from such zeal—man without God, refusing to acknowledge Him, becoming foolish through his own wisdom. To counsel without a solid foundation and belief in the knowledge of God's Word is malpractice. It will inevitably lead the person to destruction, albeit in a more presentable fashion. As I have said, it is a factory for manufacturing human Titanics.

We must prepare ourselves for ministry by learning the Bible well. We must learn to extract Biblical principles and apply them to modern problems. We must learn the spiritual roots and foundations of sinful/dysfunctional behavior. We must learn them so well that the theories and models of psychology never surmount the teachings of Scripture, nor lessen its primacy and supremacy for revelation and knowledge.

Knowledge of The Subject at the Heart of the Ministry

It is quite possible for God to raise up someone who knows nothing about an issue of sin and bondage and use that person to lead an individual to freedom through Jesus Christ. He does that all the time. However, if your calling is to minister to people with a particular kind of sin or brokenness, God will expect you to take the time to learn as much as you can about the problem. Though He sometimes works through a person in spite of their lack of knowledge, His more constant practice is to use people whom He has led through a process of gaining wisdom and knowledge. Jesus Himself spent countless years learning deeply the subject matter related to His calling as rabbi.

Read the literature on the subject of your ministry—primarily what has come from the community of faith—so that the Biblical worldview is already present in what you are taught. Learn the arguments of the opposition, so that you may aptly refute their claims. Get to know many who struggle with that sin or brokenness, so that you can observe their hearts and minds first hand.

Knowledge of Resources

Become familiar with the ministries, the teaching resources and the counseling resources that already exist. Since you will not be able to minister to everyone who comes your way, learn when to refer and who to trust as a referral. In prayer, determine what kind of ministry God has called you to be a part of. Are you to be in a counseling ministry or a teaching ministry or both? If a counseling ministry, will you offer one-on-one counseling or support group ministry or both? Will you charge and if so, how much? Do you have the gifts of a counselor? If a teaching ministry, do people come to hear you teach, and are they transformed by it? Are you willing to take on the greater accountability before God that comes with teaching others? Can you properly prepare and deliver a message? Is there an anointing on you when you do? Will your audience be intellectuals, common folk, young people? Answering such questions will tell you what kinds of resources you need.

Your goal should be to become as proficient with the appropriate resources in your field as a tennis player is with his racquet, the differing tennis courts, tennis balls, instructors, competitors, rules of competition, sources of stamina, power, encouragement, direction, skill-development, etc. While such preparation should never replace dependence on God, it is a mistake to presume that God doesn't want us to make ourselves as prepared as we know how.

Focus and Direction

These are often unclear at the beginning of a call. In fact, for some people, God's purposes are served in *keeping* them unclear even as the ministry operates through the years. Everyone has been given a measure of faith, and God will match the information that He divulges in accordance with our measure of faith so as to maximize our growth and the needs of those He has given us to help. That having been said, it is important to seek God at length and continuously to hone your focus and direction so that you are positioned for maximum effectiveness for the Kingdom. Ultimately, we serve Him for one reason—to bring Him glory. Helping to rescue lives brings Him glory.

II. Methods and Models

Support Groups

Despite all the hoopla associated with "groups," most people with life-debilitating lifestyles will never attend one—and they don't necessarily have to. Groups are not the panacea of brokenness, although, in individual cases, they can be the very lifeline that God uses to rescue a person from self-destruction. In general, people who are more relational will benefit more from a group. Those who have a history of needing or depending on others may do best with a group. Those who know little about resisting temptation often are benefited by a group. Certain personality types do better in groups. Others do best without them.

The jury is still out on the question of what kind of group is most effective. Some groups degenerate into pity-parties, where folks come simply for the camaraderie of sharing their mutual hopelessness. Other groups make an admirable attempt to press into the relevant issues, but make the mistake of putting their hope in the group, the group method and the discovery process rather than in God. These become adept at providing a "maintenance program" that helps people refrain from sinful behavior but do nothing to bring about the inner transformation that God has made available to us through Jesus Christ.

Sin-specific groups often make the mistake of perpetually labeling attendees, (-e.g., "I am an alcoholic," "I am a sex addict," etc.), and unwittingly create a fatalistic identity with the broken behavior. The reason that 12-step models do this is twofold.

First, they want to break through the denial that is typical in an addict, who is forever trying to deny or minimize the seriousness of his or her behavior. The stark reality of having to call yourself an alcoholic, or a sex addict at every weekly meeting helps break through such denial.

The second reason for having clients name themselves according to their sin, is to drill into their thinking the instinct to remain vigilant concerning their vulnerability to their dysfunctional behavior. Many who find freedom from their addiction become convinced that they are no longer vulnerable and begin to put themselves in dangerous situations again. This helps combat that phenomenon.

These are two very real problems, and in the early stages of therapy, such self-labeling may indeed be an effective way to help get things going in the right direction. However, if practiced long-term, I believe such tactics become counterproductive, primarily because a very important part of "transformational healing" is realizing one's new identity in Christ. There is power in names. We become what we name ourselves. So it is important that the name we give ourselves accurately reflects the new reality of who we are in Christ. Practicing the presence of the old man runs counter to that objective. Once the denial has been broken through, other measures should be used to help the client maintain a humble awareness of their vulnerability to their besetting sin.

It is never beneficial to create a sin-targeted group in which the attendees always remain members. This teaches hopelessness, a victim mentality and a lack of faith in God's power, albeit unintentionally. If a sin-specific group is used as part of a person's healing process, it should always be designed with the eventual goal being to wean attendees into the regular fellowship groups of the church, where healthy identity and modeling can be nurtured.

Since most people who need help will never go to a support group (for whatever reason), we need to decide if our ministry is going to provide an avenue(s) for them as well.

The Internet

Because so many people lead disconnected lives, the Internet has become a white harvest field for ministry to broken people. Even here, however, there is a broad spectrum of services needed. Some people on the Internet will only let you provide teaching resources that they can read, listen to or view in the privacy of their own home. They will not communicate with you, but can and do find freedom in absorbing your teaching resources and following up directly with God. This population comprises the bulk of visitors to your ministry web site. They wish to remain anonymous, so configure your site to give them as much help as possible.

Others are there because they are looking for interaction with people. They want an email address so that they can contact you, receive your counsel, persuade you to pray for them, etc. They want follow-up "connectivity"—people and places that they can call or visit, to follow-up on what they have found on the web site.

Make certain that you are ready for this. If you do not have adequate help in the office to handle a flood of such people, make certain to create a site with minimal to no opportunities for further contact (i.e., no displaying of your ministry's phone numbers, email addresses, physical address, etc.). One way to help visitors get the connectivity that they crave is to provide an ample "Web Links" section on your site. You need to determine in prayer how much of a variety of resources you are going to be able to provide and fashion our presence on the Internet to communicate those parameters.

Therapy

Despite all the hoopla associated with "psycho-therapy," most people with life-debilitating lifestyles will never go see a therapist or attend regular counseling sessions of any nature (-e.g., pastoral, etc.)—and they don't necessarily have to. The Holy Spirit is quite capable of being the only regular counselor a person ever needs. Everyone, however, needs to be teachable—to be receptive to counsel and not averse to it when the Holy Spirit makes it a part of the healing process.

Counseling that is carried on by Christian counselors who have properly integrated "philosophy-neutral" observations of human behavior into their pool of knowledge can be used by God to great effect. What is necessary, though, is that there be just such an integration of behavioral observations into the Biblical worldview. Jesus did this. He studied human behavior and used what He observed to speak to people's felt needs—showing Himself to be the answer to what they were looking for. We need that same preeminent guidance of the Holy Spirit as Counselor, even as we avail ourselves of the raw data accumulated by psychologists over the last century. Data is neutral. It is when it gets interpreted by unbiblical world-views and when it is enshrined into therapeutic models that are elevated to the place of being the source or hope for change that things go wrong.

Several studies have shown that "psychotherapy" is no more successful than sharing your problems with a close friend. Studies have also shown that people are helped only if another person communicates true love and concern for them, whether it be a therapist or a friend.

Here are the findings from a study conducted by two secular psychologists, as cited by Dr. Larry Crabb:[6]

> psychologists C.H. Patterson and Suzanne Hidore admit that psychotherapy is in chaos.
>
> Their solution is worth a second look. Professional helping efforts, they suggest, should abandon all hope of identifying specific diagnosable disorders and coming up with specific technical treatment plans. They should instead focus on one simple yet profound idea—that the essence of all successful psychotherapy is love. . . . when therapists accomplish good results (and many do), it is because they are lovers, . . .
>
> Jerome Frank, a leading figure in the field of therapy research [says]: "success in therapy depends on the therapist's ability to convey to the patient that he cares, is competent to help, and has no ulterior motive.". . . The roots of psychological problems and personal battles have to do with one's relationship to God. . . .
>
> . . . Beneath everything from eating disorders and dissociative identity disorders, to feelings of irritability and occasional peeks at pornography, is a proud spirit of independence that is our foolish response to the terror of being alone. It is a bad spirit that only a good spirit can replace.

So, the common impression that it is in therapy where a person's hope lies is misguided. It is love that heals, and God is love.

Inner Healing

There is a great deal of controversy and debate over the issue of inner healing. In the early years of its emergence as a method of ministry, certain practitioners became spiritually careless and promoted models that, in the estimation of many, opened a door for demonic deception. Today, those early problems have, by and large, been corrected. Even so, among those who practice inner healing today, there remain sharp divisions on other levels between the methods and models that are recommended (-e.g., Does one talk to a demon to obtain information prior to casting him out?).[7]

A difference has recently emerged between two profoundly different philosophies of how inner healing occurs. One approach takes the client back to the traumatic events of their childhood and there calls upon the Holy Spirit to heal the damage that was done in those moments of trauma or neglect (God being outside of time is present to that event as well as the present.) The other approach takes the person back to childhood traumas and there asks the Holy Spirit to uncover the lies that were generated in the person's mind as a result of the traumas, and then asks the Holy Spirit to break the power of those lies by speaking the truth into the person's mind. The idea behind this second model is that the power in the person's life that has been driving them to sinful and self-destructive behaviors is there because they have believed and acted upon things that are not true—lies such as: "I'm no good; I'm damaged goods; No one will love me now; I'm a bad and unredeemable person," etc. Thus, it is not the trauma that is addressed and healed by this second approach. Rather, it is the results of the brokenness (the lies believed) that is addressed—the idea being that it is the belief system that drives behavior and empowers demonic strong-holds, not the brokenness.

The two sides are actually closer together than it might seem. Although the first approach (seen in ministries like John and Paula Sanford and Leanne Payne) speaks primarily to the "feeling" person and the second approach (with names like Theotherapy and Theophostic) speaks primari-ly to the "rational" person, they are two sides of the same coin. If I have suffered a trauma in childhood and through ministry have the feelings associated with my trauma soothed by a healing touch from God, then the beliefs that I take away from that fuller experience ("beliefs" about God and myself) will not be as charged with intense, mindless emotion, and will conform themselves more to the truth.

My recommendation is that you study the various models out there, (which also includes models by Neil Anderson, Andy Comiskey, Francis MacNutt, Steven Arterburn and others as well as my own *Sexual Healing* materials), and choose the model that God indicates in prayer is the best fit for your situation. My personal preference is to mix together various ele-ments from all of the models according to the situation. However, for many for whom this is a new endeavor, a prepackaged model may work the best. The supreme model is the Bible and the example of Jesus. Other models are useful only as they reflect and interpret what is found there for our modern context.

Demonic Elements

The ministry of Jesus clearly shows that demonic elements can be found in certain illnesses and sinful lifestyles. Consequently, we must always ask the Lord to expose any such element that may be at work in the person to whom we minister. It is not a good thing to go on a witch-hunt, however. Simply acknowledge the possibility, ask the Lord to reveal anything that may be there, and move on if He doesn't.

One associated phenomenon is the passing down of the sins of the fathers to the third and fourth generations (cf. Exodus 20:5 and Numbers 14:18). A literal propensity to commit certain kinds of sin can be passed down from generation to generation. Consequently, I recommend that you always do a family history with a client to see if there is such a link to the besetting problem. Realize, however, that family-line curses often skip generations before reemerging. So go back four generations if possible in taking the history. If there is such a connection, according to Ezekiel 18:14-20, have the client renounce the sinful behavior for their own life and declare the family-line curse broken in Jesus' name. Once the curse has been broken, pray for the institution of a thousand generations of the righteous (Deuteronomy 7:9).[8]

Finally, there is the matter of the ongoing activity of Satan in our lives. He is an accuser, a liar, and a tempter. And so, we need to learn his schemes and how to use the weapons of warfare that God has given us against him and his demonic forces. We need to teach our clients how to recognize demonic lies and how to counter them with faith in God's truth. We need to show them how to use the name of Jesus to resist demonic powers, how to cast Satan out, how to discern the difference between demon-borne temptation and that which comes from our own heart so as to properly match our response to the actual problem.

Too often the demonic element is ignored, so we must determine not to let that happen.

III. Ministering to the Homosexually Confused Person— A Model for Ministry

Remember—homosexual neurosis is not a sexual problem. It is a case of arrested emotional development. The source of the arresting needs to be uncovered and worked through. Then the client needs to learn how to turn to God the Father to receive those things which were missed and/or to heal those things that were damaged. In this way, God will restart and complete their emotional growth, and as they mature, their dormant heterosexual nature will slowly emerge. If they are simultaneously putting to death the old homosexual identity by removing what feeds it and undoing those things that gave it power (-e.g., unforgiveness, idolatry, envy, etc.), the two identities will switch places (over a period of years), and the heterosexual identity will become the dominant one and the homosexual identity will become a remnant of its former self. (See the chapter: What Does it Look Like to be Healed? for further discussion on this phenomenon.) During this process, the client needs to have all the elements of healing taught, modeled, and reinforced on a regular basis. The change must be organic, not forced or coerced.

Patience is required. This is not an easy transition to make. Additionally, you are dealing with a population of adults (mostly) who are still emotionally preadolescent (including temper-tantrums and all-or-nothing, black-

and-white, unrealistic, outrageous, self-centered, romantic thinking and behaving). Your propensity will be to project adult expectations on folks who will be unable to meet those expectations as quickly as a healthy adult might. Be prepared to humble yourself so as to treat these 25- to 65-year-old adolescents in ways that will connect and allow them to grow.

Assessment

A very important first step is the assessment process.

At what level of "willingness to change" is the person? Are they militantly obdurate, humbly repentant, or somewhere in between? With the militant, a focus on God's love and power is where you start.[9] You don't even bring up homosexuality at this stage. With the repentant person, you can begin leading them through the elements for which repentance is needed—e.g., rebellion, idolatry, self-pity, unforgiveness (including childhood vows, judgments and dishonoring of parents), pride, unrighteous anger, rejection of how God made them, etc., though always in the timing and in the order that God reveals.

How did they come to you? If they were dragged in, the "willingness to change" or even listen level will be very low. A good deal more time will need to be spent communicating your genuine love and concern for them and for what they may have gone through in life.

Even if the person has come willingly and appears to sincerely want help, are they really willing to do whatever it takes to be healed? It is often helpful to assess this by periodically assigning homework by which the client demonstrates a willingness (e.g., reading a book or watching a video and doing a report on it; going to someone and asking forgiveness and reporting on the result, etc.). In my experience, only half the people who come for help are really committed to doing what it takes to change. The others have come to get stroked, sympathy, attention, a relationship, or are naive about how easily or quickly their problems can be resolved.

Have they engaged in homosexual behavior yet? Someone who hasn't often has foundational character and belief-system elements already in place. The fact that they haven't been reinforcing their orientation with immoral sexual pleasure will also shorten their healing time.

If they have been homosexually active, how long and with how many people? Normally, the higher the numbers, the more difficult the case, all else being equal.

If active, how perverse has their behavior gotten? Again, the more perverse, the more issues will need to be addressed. Greater levels of participation in darker behaviors also increases the likelihood that a demonic stronghold(s) has developed that needs to be removed. Demons don't cause homosexual neurosis, but they do sometimes attach themselves to the sin and brokenness that surround it. They gain ground in us by virtue of our sinful actions.

Is self-hatred present? Have there been suicide thoughts or attempts?

Is the person enmeshed emotionally with someone else? Can he remove himself from that relationship?

Does the person have a history of being obsessively fixed on him/herself (narcissistic personality disorder)?[10] Does the world revolve around them and them alone? Note: You should expect some focus on self from anyone coming for help, because their problems will naturally produce such a need. What you're looking for here is a more chronic level—what Leanne Payne calls the "disease of introspection"—whereby the person obsessively examines him(her)self and then crucifies him(her)self with what they find.

What is their spiritual background? A former Christian may not need to be taught as much about how the Christian life and faith works as someone who has had no Christian instruction.

Has their exposure to Christianity been positive or negative? A former Christian with a very negative experience can actually take longer to work with than a nonbeliever because of all the resentment, bitterness, and misjudgments that need to be uncovered and overturned.

What is the level of addictive behavior? Multiple addictions or a constant history of addictive behavior bodes that a host of additional elements will need to be worked through in the healing process. It also points to deep, internalized self-hatred that may or may not be obvious to them.

What is their childhood story? What was the relationship with mom and dad like? Look for broken or diseased emotional relationships—e.g., abusive or emotionally or physically distant fathering, or an overbearing or incestuous emotional life with the mother. (Emotional incest can be very subtle, but its damage can be profound in the more sensitive temperament.) Was there sexual abuse or other situations that may have created a fear or hatred of the opposite sex? When did their childhood change from being happy to sad? What happened during that transition period? Were they ridiculed or abused by their peer group? Were they ever humiliated by the opposite sex?

What has their experience been of the Church and Christians? Were they raised in legalism? Was sex taught as something dirty and to be hidden? Have they been cruelly rejected by Christians? Abused by a pastor or priest? Taught acceptance of immoral lifestyles by their church?

What is their support structure like now? Is it Christian-based or does it consist of people who might be antagonistic to the client's healing process? Can it be changed to create the optimal environment for the healing process?

What environment do they live and work in? Is it supportive or an impediment to the healing process? Can it be changed?

If the person has a history of sexual relations with either sex (or animals), it is possible that a prayer to break the "soul-ties" that have formed as a result may be in order. This is a breaking of the "one flesh" union that was created during those sexual relations. The person renounces the ties and commits to the one sexual bond that God has for them in marriage.

Uncovering the Lies

A major part of the healing process is the uncovering of the lies that were believed in childhood as a result of various incidents or circumstances. Satan is the father of lies and his entire kingdom of rebellion is founded on lies. The Holy Spirit will, as we ask Him to, uncover for us the lies that have been believed and replace them with the truth. The client's willingness to embrace the truth and reject the lies (no matter how they feel) is critical to their transformation.

The greatest stronghold to overcome is the web of lies that have formed into belief systems that control thoughts and feelings. If the lies can be overturned and replaced by what is true, this will create an entirely new foundation from which new beliefs and behaviors can grow. The work of Dr. Ed Smith (Theophostic Counseling), Dr. Chris Thurman (The Lies We Believe) and Dr. Neil Anderson (The Bondage Breaker) is helpful in this matter.

Instruction

With arrested emotional development comes an immature understanding of life and how to live it in a mature fashion.

Do they know what love really is? Have they felt and received God's love and the love of Christians?

Have they been motivated from a performance-orientation or by grace?

Many basic things may need to be taught, such as: how to love; how to consider others before self; how to pray; how to worship; how to exercise faith; how to give; how to operate as a part of the body of Christ; how to properly read and interpret Scripture; how to resist temptation; how to love holiness; how to live by faith; how to let God live His righteousness through them; what it means to forgive and how to do it; how the will is transformed; how to live from the new man rather than the old; how to do spiritual warfare; how to renew and guard the mind; how to live a disciplined life; how to live by the Spirit so as not to carry out the deeds of the flesh; how to pursue God to receive what was never imparted in childhood; how to pursue God for a new mind and perspective on sexuality and other people; how to permanently end the habit of masturbation; how to live content and at peace while single; how to find healing for emotional dependency; how to interact with the same sex in a non-sexual way and how to interact with the opposite sex in a healthy way (including matters related to dating, marriage, etc.); how to parent in a way that doesn't contribute to sexual identity confusion in their children; and how to know how much, where and when to share their past with others.

Relationships

Acceptance and integration into the life of the church, especially their same-sex peer group is critical. Relationships need to be formed with healthy men and women in the church.

Specific teaching on how to hear the voice of God, how to pray, how to be intimate with Him, etc., are critical. Encouragement and supportive structures to help them maintain an intimate relationship with God are important (such as home fellowship groups, men's/women's groups, etc.)

It is important to be careful in how these integrations are carried out. Some men's groups in churches, for example, are insufferable macho clubs that will only exacerbate the sense of differentness and rejection in a healing homosexual struggler. Check out such a group before sending someone into them to make sure that they will contribute to the healing process rather than damage it. Timing is likewise very important.

Another common problem that the healing struggler faces in church settings is pressure to "prove" one's healing by dating and marrying prematurely. It is never overtly imposed, but is rather heaped onto the person little by little over time. Before long, however, and in various ways, the message is given: "We can only be truly comfortable with you if you demonstrate that you are healed by getting married and having children." The pressure is found among heterosexual peers in church singles groups, to pair up and find one's future mate. There is also an incessant inquiring from well-intentioned ladies, (almost always, it's the ladies), who want to know: "So, have you found a girl yet (or a guy)?"—and sometimes the even more direct question: "So when are you getting married?" Warn the client about this impending pressure and give them tools to handle it.

IV. A MODEL FOR THE CHURCH

The Leadership

Model and communicate both truth and grace to strugglers through what you say from the pulpit or the dais. In every way, create an atmosphere of unconditional love. People who hate, condemn, mock, or look down on sinners of any kind should not be allowed a voice in the church. Parishioners should never hear the words "sodomite," "fag," or "queer" from church leadership, and those who say such words on church grounds should be rebuked. People trapped in homosexual neurosis should be able to tell from listening to sermons and Sunday School lessons that your church is a safe place for them to come and examine the claims of Scripture, a safe place to share their struggle and a prepared place to receive healing for their bondage.

Same-Sex Fellowship

Men coming out of homosexuality should be enthusiastically welcomed into all the appropriate fellowships of the church, especially the men's fellowship. One of their greatest needs is to be accepted by straight men. They should not be forced to participate but always invited. If sporting events take place, care should be taken that such events be played for fun and fellowship. The macho, "win at all costs," "showboat your athletic prowess by demolishing the opposition" kind of play can be very destructive for the sensitive male (gay or not). It would also be good if certain "ever-straight" men took it as a calling to befriend and build up someone coming out of homosexuality.

Women coming out of lesbianism need mentors also to show them how to be feminine without getting emotionally enmeshed. They need to be built up in their personal sense of being female and learning how good it is that God made them that way. They need a friend(s) to help them grieve their childhood sexual abuse.

General Fellowships

One mistake that is often made is to sequester people who struggle with homosexual temptation in a sin-specific group. In some cases, this can actually perpetuate their sense of being rejected and ostracized by the fellowship of other men.

A sin-specific group can be helpful in the early stages of healing for certain people, however. It can be a place where they can see that they are not alone and learn from the struggles of those who have gone before them.

Ultimately, however, the goal should be to wean these men and women into regular home or similar fellowship groups, where they can gain the acceptance they crave and the modeling they need from relatively healthy members of their gender group.

My recommendation is to have an entry-level group where people of all kinds focus on developing intimacy with God. After at least three months of "learning by doing" in such a group, they should hopefully be ready to move into an arena where the more specific details of their besetting bondage are addressed more directly.

If you put them in a sin-specific group *before* showing them how to be intimate with God, they may end up obsessively focused on their problems rather than the One who can transform their problems into blessings.

In one church that I attended, I started a generic "Men's Healing Group" which purposely lacked a "designated sin" so that men would feel free to come without fear of being publicly known for having a specific sin. We started the group by working through a book on anger (a relatively non-threatening sin) and within six weeks, we were so bonded as a group that we were able to take up sexual sin as our next topic without losing a single person. The theory behind having such a generic group is that the men are able to take it into whatever direction most concerns them for their personal lives. It also protects them from acquiring a public sin label. And finally, it recognizes that all sin has common roots and that it is those roots that must be addressed rather than the surface behavior. This group turned out to be the most successful group that I have ever tried.

Resources

Every church should be equipped with multiple resources for sexually broken people. There should be a set of videotapes, a set of audiotapes and many books in the pastor's or church counselor's library for loaning to people who are in the process of healing. If the church is large enough, seminars and conferences should be hosted on various related topics, groups should be encouraged to form, even outreaches should be developed to those in the community who struggle with such issues. Resources should also be available to help parents, spouses, and friends of people who struggle with homosexual confusion. Additionally, resources should be available for issues that can accompany homosexual neurosis, such as sexual addiction, pornography, masturbation, child sexual abuse, transgender confusion, etc. Feel free to contact Mastering Life Ministries in Jacksonville, Fl. for such resources and for suggestions for additional help.

Epilogue

Fr. George Rutler of St. Agnes Church in New York, in a monologue on his television program, *Grace & Truth*, said: "Christ lives in us (Galatians 2:20), but so does Adam. Therefore, the *Adam* in us must be conquered by the *Christ* in us."

Leanne Payne has written of the schism between head and heart, whereby we retain intellectual knowledge of something without our hearts and, thus, of our lives, being moved to change accordingly. It's essentially the difference between talking about something and actually experiencing the reality of it. What caused this rift to develop in modern man? Payne writes:

> The reason was that the central truth of God's forgiveness of sin, along with all the great spiritual realities of the Kingdom of God, had been largely relegated to the abstract. . . .

> . . . Kierkegaard cried out that we have forgotten how to exist, to be, and that we can only *think about* being.[1]

> In listening to the words that come from God, we become all we were created to be. . . .

> When God is centered in us and we in Him, we have a *home* within, a true self or center out of which to live. We cannot live from that center and at the same time be bent idolatrously toward the creature. . . .

> . . . The Tempter of our souls . . . says to us: "I want you to see yourself walking alongside yourself; . . . I want you to gain a dramatic view of yourself as the center of all things, and then to pity yourself when you are not.". . .

> . . . To fail to be centered is to "walk alongside ourselves," a stance whereby we live out of an activism separated from *being* and therefore from *meaning*. A person split in this way can never live in the present moment. He can only live for a future that never quite arrives, one that he is perhaps feverishly trying to control in order to avoid the pain of his past. . . .thus caught in a ceaseless *doing* and can only *think* about life, but never experience it.[2]

There we have the two great problems upon which lies much of our impotence as believers and as ministers. First, we have not yet understood nor practiced the remedy for the battle that goes on within us between the old man and the new man, or the "true self," and we have not adequately addressed this reality with those with whom we minister.

Secondly, we have erected an intellectual barrier between us and God that provides us with a sense of diminished responsibility and accountability and which protects us from a God we have not yet become willing to know at an intimate level. We have convinced ourselves that intellectual faith is good enough because to go any deeper would incur levels of responsibility and accountability that are too demanding or inconvenient. The so-called rift between head and heart is at its heart a refusal to love. It is a manifestation of the heart of self-centered, independence-steeped man. We are like the religious of Jesus' day who were certain that their version of religion was accurate, yet of whom Jesus said: "How often I have longed to gather your children together, as a hen gathers her chicks under her wings, but you were not willing!" (Luke 13:34b).

Jean-Nicholas Grou once wrote: "You ask me what this voice of the heart is. It is love which is the voice of the heart. Love God and you will always be speaking to Him."[3]

Satan has implanted in our minds an image of God that is a lie and that keeps us from wanting to get close to Him, and we've allowed him to do so, because we are either careless in matters of spiritual warfare, or it is simply convenient. We have become masterfully adept at creating deflections from the responsibility that we have as members of Christ's body. We have deceived ourselves into thinking that our watered-down version of the life Christ died to give us is praiseworthy or praise-giving to God.

Others hide within the lie that tells them that a life of empowered oneness with God is not possible. Of course, I cannot guess at all of the motives of all of the compromised hearts out there, but I can at least attest to those of which I have been guilty.

We do not need another method or model for living the Christian life and for leading people into the healing of their broken condition. Instead, we need to acknowledge and address our refusal to give our lives totally to Christ. We need to make deliberate daily choices to get into the presence of God so that He can show us our true heart, so that He can heal and transform us, and so that He can direct and empower a life of service for Him and others. We need to embrace sacrifice. We need to embrace our cross, for the sake of His Cross.

The real problems of our Christian culture are not the surface sins and brokenness that blanket the landscape. The problems are far broader, deeper and fundamental. We have suffered damage to the very foundations and superstructure of our way of faith. The answer to the epidemic of sexual immorality among our clergy and laity is not another 12-step program. The answer to the problem of the body of Christ being just as steeped in materialism, divorce, abortion, and pornography as the nonbelieving world is not another book on ten ways to keep our eyes from straying. The answer is a heroic honesty, a willingness to be humbled, and an enduring commitment to lay our lives down fully for Christ our Savior.

The "Catch-22" that the enemy has created, is that this solution galls the spirit of the person trapped by the problem. If the problem is a spirit of rationalism, sophistication, compromise, independence, and worldliness, then the answer—to return to the simple basics of the Christian message —is patently offensive. A proud and intellectually arrogant spirit deplores simplicity. It seeks complexity and self-made efforts to bring glory to itself. Sacrifice and humility are nonstarters for such a person.

Therein are the fractures that currently cripple our way of "living the Christian life," fractures that have been carefully painted over with centuries of Christian verbiage and sentiment so that we no longer notice that they are there.

The problem is not the problem—it is the structure; it is the materials with which we have been building our houses, and the ground upon which we have been building them.

Like the Ephesian church, we must return to our first love (Revelation 2:1-7). Like the Churches in Pergamum and Thyatira, we must repent of our immoralities and of our fraternity with with those who teach and practice immorality (Revelation 2:12-29). Like the Church in Sardis, we must truly wake up and complete our faith (Revelation 3:1-6). And like the Church in Laodicea, we must realize the deception that our wealth has engendered, acknowledge once again our neediness and, in His presence, acquire the fire to burn as a living, loving sacrifice for God (Revelation 3:14-22).

The implications of this message for our practice of ministry are revolutionary. In our church services and our conferences, it would be good if we stopped all the razzle-dazzle, hype, and entertainment and called our people to prayer and fasting, to love and commitment, and to sacrifice of life. It would be good if we became honest and straightforward with our people about their lives and the life to which God has called them, even if it means losing some of them to the lukewarm, compromised church down the street.

Simultaneous to such a radical call to authentic Christian living, however, must be a careful laying of a foundation upon which a willingness to say "Yes" to such a call is birthed. That foundation is love of God—not the vapid form of love that is built on the variance of emotion and sentiment, but real love, birthed in His presence and constructed with a lifestyle of sacrifice, commitment, and abject dependence on His Spirit.

Where do people go to find an example of such love? In His presence. That's the only place where it is found. He is both method and model. As we soak in His presence, the life and power of His love invades our being and eventually begins to exude from our own thoughts and actions.

We need to get the Randy Clarks and the Mike Bickles and the Tommy

Tenneys of this world into our churches so that we can see what simple, God-centered love is all about.

This summer, I will be starting a home fellowship group that will have one goal and one goal alone—fixing our eyes on Jesus and ministering to Him. We will not socialize. We will not have a teaching about how to be better Christians. We will not even pray for one another. Opportunities for these things are already being provided in massive quantities. The thing that is not being provided, however, is a time where we can focus on God alone, with no agenda to serve self whatsoever. We will sing to Him. We will pray to Him. We will listen to Him.

When the idea to do this first came to me, I remember thinking that it would never work. Why? Because the only model offered by the modern church is a self-focused one. Man-centered worship so saturates the entire consciousness of the body that doing anything outside of that form is bound to seem offensive and even sinful to many.

We must take such risks anyway!

We must change the way we minister to broken people as well. The typical reaction to sin and brokenness found in the church today is to quickly send them off to a group or counselor who specializes in their area of need, where they then enter into a detailed search for why they got so bound and broken. The focus is on them, the gory details of their sin or brokenness, and the sufficiency of the method or model being used to set them right. Even more, the focus of the counselor is more often than not on their own education and expertise. Thus, the obsession with self gets perpetuated on both ends—counselor and counselee. No one intends for this to happen. It just does, because the priorities and focus of modern ministry are set in the rationalism of our age.

It is not that such a search is useless. The problem is where the focus and the hope for change ever so subtly gets placed. The primary and initial setting of focus must be on God—His sufficiency, His power, His wisdom, His love, and His grace. When the counselee becomes immersed in these divine revelations first and foremost, counseling is often unnecessary, because the perfect Counselor, the Holy Spirit, often leads them through whatever details of examination are necessary and with a precision of timing and understanding that a human counselor cannot match. It is at this point that a trained counselor sometimes becomes valuable to God, provided the counselor understands that it remains the job of the Holy Spirit to direct the healing process and to empower the results. God will often bring a friend, a counselor, a preacher, a teacher, or even a stranger into the life of the person at just the right moment, with just the right example of life or counsel.

Of course, there will always be exceptions—particularly for those hurting ones whose hatred or fear of God is so great that they will simply be unwilling to pursue intimacy with Him until other matters have been cleared up first. God is gracious and will accede to their feelings provided they are genuinely heartfelt and flow from true ignorance of the truth. He has provided many helpful groups, counselors, and even live-in programs for them.

By and large, however, we must radically transform the way we do church and the way we do counseling, so that pursuing God truly becomes the priority. Our mistake is that we have let the accommodation for the exception become the norm. We must instead create structures that facilitate the proper focus for change, such as the "divine intimacy" groups or the "men's healing groups" that I have already recommended. We must alter worship and ministry structures to maximize a focus on God and create environments where experiencing the manifest presence of God and ministering unto God are the goal.

We need to insist on greater healing and education for those who minister whenever possible and create structures that facilitate the same. We must be more aggressive to insist on adherence to God's Word as the standard for faith and practice. We must alter the endless dependency on itself fostered by the parachurch structure and create ways that bring about a gradual integration of parachurch work into the regular body and governance of the church.

It is imperative that greater attention be devoted to creating means for such changes and for thinking through the various ways that such changes can be accommodated according to the peculiarities of the modern age.

We need to address the tyranny of experts and the entrenchment of rationalism in our Christian culture and ecclesiastical structures. Finding ways to persuade those who hold positions of power and who do not yet see the problem is also crucial.

I believe that if we are to come into our identity as Christ's very body, we must yield to this shift of priority and focus. Only as He is acknowledged as Head, both in word and in deed, will the incredible and precious promises of Scripture be unleashed—transforming us into His likeness. We must become truly cognizant of our weakness, and embrace it. We must forsake pride and self-centeredness. We must let go of our brilliant schemes for helping people and learn to truly listen to God's even more brilliant schemes. We must forsake our materialism, our sloth, our selfishness, and our iron grip on independence and, like Mary, come to the place of praying, "Be it done to me according to Your word" (Luke 1:38b, NASB).

It was Augustine who said that prayer is something Christ has provided in order to confer upon us the dignity of becoming causes. Let us then wake up from the "dream" of self-sufficiency and enter into a "real life" of prayer, sacrifice, intimacy, and love, so that God can entrust us with the power and wisdom to do "even greater things" (John 14:12) .

𝔑otes

Part One - The Problems

Chapter 1: The Purpose of Life

1. George Barna, *The Second Coming of the Church* (Nashville, Tn.: Word Publishing, 1998), 2-4, 7.

2. Ibid., 5.

3. Ibid., 8.

4. Ibid., 18-20.

5. Ibid., 60-61.

6. Ibid., 20

7. Ibid., 23.

8. Ibid., 23-24.

9. Which brings to mind the prayer of St. Francis of Assisi quoted in *Leanne Payne Newsletter*, (Wheaton, Il.: Pastoral Care Ministries, Spring 2000):

Christ be with me, Christ within me,
Christ behind me, Christ before me,
Christ beside me, Christ to win me,
Christ to comfort and restore me,
Christ beneath me, Christ above me,
Christ in quiet, Christ in danger,
Christ in hearts of all that love me,
Christ in mouth of friend and stranger. (1)

10. The difference between perfectionism and a fervent pursuit of being made perfect, is that perfectionists are performance-oriented people who seek to establish their worth and value through what they achieve, whereas someone seeking holiness understands how to let God do it for them.

11. Keith Green, "The Calling," read by Melody Green, *First Love: Vol. 1*, (Monument, Co.: Reel Productions, 1998), video cassette.

12. Keith Green, "Born Again," *First Love*, (Newbury Park, Ca.: Newport Records, 1998), audio CD

Chapter 2: Love is Not Love

1. I have a brief outline of Biblical passages on the definition of love in my book, *Sexual Healing: God's Plan for the Sanctification of Broken Lives* (Jacksonville, Fl.: Mastering Life Ministries, 2001):

> d. In the world, love is an earned commodity.
> "Give me what I want in this relationship, and I will love you."
> love = sex
> love = romantic feelings
> e. The Old Testament pictures Israel as God's unfaithful spouse.
> f. God's definition of love = commitment & sacrifice.
> "This is how we know what love is: Jesus Christ laid down His life for us." (1 John 3:16)
> Love = sacrifice
> "This is love...that God sent His Son as an atoning sacrifice for our sins." (1 John 4:10)
> Love = sacrifice
> "... love not with words, but with actions and in truth." (1 John 3:18)
> Love = actions
> "God is love." (1 John 4:16b)
> Love = God Himself
> (38)

2. A statement that plays off of a similar statement attributed to St. Francis of Assisi: "Love is not loved." Benedict J. Groeschel refers to the St. Francis statement in *Spiritual Passages: The Psychology of Spiritual Development* (New York, N.Y.: The Crossroad Publishing Company, 1983):

> St. Francis . . . in tears, . . went banging on the doors of Assisi, rousing the sleeping townsfolk with his cry: "Love is not loved." Little do most people in the illuminative way realize that in the very experience of

seeing their lack of love in the light of divine love, they are beginning to prepare for the searching trial of the Dark Night. (83)

3. 1 John 4:8.

4. 1 John 4:7.

5. It is not surprising that even leaders from the gay community agree with me. Self-avowed gay, Larry Kramer wrote the following in a leading gay publication. He is quoted by Ron Highley, "Gay Author Blasts Gay Culture," *Words of Life* 45 (July 1997): 3.

After reading Gabriel Rotello's new book, *Sexual Ecology: AIDS and the Destiny of Gay Men*, the gay author and activist, Larry Kramer, (co-founder of Gay Men's Health Crisis and Act Up) wrote an article deploring the sexual nature of gay culture and the grim results. Here is an excerpt: "Gabriel's book also makes the airtight case—still considered controversial, unfortunately, rather than undeniable —that we brought AIDS upon ourselves by a way of living that welcomed it. . . .

. . . we have made a culture out of our sexuality, and that culture has killed us. . . . We endlessly blame the government for its hideous response to AIDS. But we speak not one syllable about how we can repair the damage we have caused that brought about so much death in the first place. We do not even admit that we walked down the wrong path. We do not admit that we made a mistake. Only crybabies, petulant children and immature adults never admit when they've made a mistake.

We've all been partners in our destruction. AIDS has killed us, and while we certainly did not invite it in, we certainly did invite it in. We still invite it in. We certainly do not do everything we can to keep it out. We have been the cause of our own victimization. I know these are grotesquely politically incorrect things to say. So be it. We knew we were playing with fire, and we continued to play with fire, and the fire consumed monstrously large numbers of us and singed the rest of us, all of us, whether we notice our burn marks or not. And we still play with fire." (Larry Kramer, "Sex and Sensibility," *The Advocate*, 27 May 1997).

It seems to us that this blunt and unpopular honesty makes an unusual opportunity for Christians to show love and compassion while telling of God's love and His total ability to save and set free all who come to Him. May God help us all to learn to love and give the true counsel that liberates the captives!

6. Center for Disease Control.

7. E.L. Goldman, "Psychological Factors Generate HIV Resurgence in Young Gay Men," *Clinical Psychiatry News*, (October 1994): 5, quoted in Jeffrey Satinover, *Homosexuality and the Politics of Truth* (Grand Rapids, Mi.: Baker Books, Hamewith Books, 1996), 17.

8. Jeffrey Satinover, *Homosexuality and the Politics of Truth* (Grand Rapids, Mi.: Baker Books, Hamewith Books, 1996), 16.

9. C.W. Socarides, "Sexual Politics and Scientific Logic: The Issue of Homosexuality," *The Journal of Psychohistory* 10, no. 3 (1992): 308, quoted in Jeffrey Satinover, *Homosexuality and the Politics of Truth* (Grand Rapids, Mi.: Baker Books, Hamewith Books, 1996), 32.

10. Satinover, *Homosexuality*, 32.

11. R. Bayer, *Homosexuality and American Psychiatry: The Politics of Diagnosis* (New York: Basic Books, 1981): 102, quoted in Satinover, *Homosexuality*, 32.

12. E. Pollard, "Time to Give Up Fascist Tactics," *Washington Blade* (31 January 1992): 39, quoted in quoted in Satinover, *Homosexuality*, 38.

13. Satinover, *Homosexuality*, 34.

14. Satinover, *Homosexuality*, 34-35.

15. R. Bayer, *Homosexuality and American Psychiatry: The Politics of Diagnosis* (New York: Basic Books, 1981): 3-4, quoted in Satinover, *Homosexuality*, 35.

16. Satinover, *Homosexuality*, 35-36.

17. Ibid., 36.

18. Ibid., 37-38.

19. Associated Press report, "Gonorrhea Cases Among Gay Men Skyrocketing," *Tennessean*, 1998.

20. Thomas H. Maugh II, "New HIV Infections in S.F. Increase Sharply," *New York Times*, 1 July 2000, sec. A, 11.

21. Satinover, *Homosexuality*, 49, 51.

22. W. Odets, in a report to the American Association of Physicians for Human Rights. Cited in E.L. Goldman, "Psychological Factors Generate HIV Resurgence in Young Gay Men," *Clinical Psychiatry News*, (October 1994): 5, quoted in Satinover, *Homosexuality*, 57.

23. Gabriel Rotello, *Sexual Ecology: AIDS and the Destiny of Gay Men* (New York: Penguin USA, 1998); quoted in Bob Davies, "Half of Gay Men Will Get HIV, Author Says," *Inner Circle* (Sept-Dec 1997): 16.

24. Robert H. Knight, "Life Expect," *Culture Facts* (August 3, 1999), an Internet journal of The Family Research Council in Washington, D.C., which says:

Q: We've heard about Paul Cameron's 1998 study in *Psychological Reports* (Volume 83) titled "Does Homosexual Activity Shorten Life," in which he shows that the median age of death for homosexuals is 50 years. Are there any other studies that confirm this?

A: Scholarly journals and researchers appear reluctant to address the issue of the negative effects of the homosexual lifestyle. However, a 1997 study in the *International Journal of Epidemiology* (Volume 26) confirms Cameron's conclusions. "Modeling the Impact of HIV Disease on Mortality in Gay and Bisexual Men" summarizes a study of homosexual men in Vancouver, British Columbia, which concludes that "life expectancy at age 20 years for gay and bisexual men is 8 to 20 years less than for all men." The authors estimate that "nearly half of gay and bisexual men currently aged 20 years will not reach their 65th birthday."

By comparison, *The New England Journal of Medicine* has reported that smokers face a reduced life expectancy of "7.3 years for men and 6.0 years for women" (February 12, 1998).

Our society is expending tremendous efforts to educate people against the dangers of smoking and to prevent young people from taking up this unhealthy habit. Yet homosexual advocates are pushing their agenda openly in schools while their supporters remain silent about a health threat of a far greater magnitude to individuals.

25. Nancy Sutton, "Domestic Violence and Domestic Partners: Two Sides of the Same Coin," and Linda P. Harvey, "Lesbians As Violent Partners," *Mission: America* (Fall 1998): 4-6.

26. Marshall K. Kirk and Erastes Pill, "Waging Peace: A Gay Battle Plan to Persuade Straight America," *Christopher Street* 95 (December 1984): 38.

27. In this regard, he further mentions that "the National Gay Task Force has had to cultivate quiet back room liaisons with broadcast companies and newsrooms in order to make sure that issues important to the gay community receive some coverage"
Ibid., 37-39.

28. Ibid., 37-39. This magazine article is no longer available, but most of what was said in it was later repeated in M. Kirk and H. Madsen, *After the Ball: How America Will Conquer Its Fear and Hatred of Gays in the 90's* (New York: Doubleday, 1989).

29. Congregation for the Doctrine of the Faith, *Letter to the Bishops of the Catholic Church on the Pastoral Care of Homosexual Persons* (1 October 1986) by Joseph Cardinal Ratzinger, Prefect, 1-7 (Rome, 1986), letter.

30. I cover the major studies and related questions in my book, *Sexual Healing*, with multiple quotes from David Gelman, "Born or Bred?" *Newsweek*, 24 February 1992, 46-47:

   b. Even if homosexuality was discovered to have a physiological component, the point is moot for several other reasons:

      (1) Even though alcoholism is believed to have a genetic link, (although the early studies on that are currently being questioned), God still calls us to live sober lives. He clearly labels drunkenness a sin worthy of eternal damnation (Galatians 5:19-21). His power is available to us in the areas where we fall short, whether the problem is physiological, emotional or psychological and so the, "I couldn't help it," defense can never be used for sin of any kind.

      (2) Everyone is born with an inherited propensity to sin. The formative code of the entire human race has this same inbred mutation. We sin as a natural course of being. Yet God expects us to take advantage of His provision to overcome that predilection so as to live holy lives instead of sinful. This is as true of the homosexual inclination as it is of the basic inclination to sin.

      (3) Even if one cannot accept the first two propositions, it could still be properly argued that genetics and hormones could never force (without recourse) a behavior that God condemns man for acting out. If they could, God would be unjust for condemning mankind for a behavior that could not be helped.

   c. Scientific studies continue to bear out God's intention that we operate heterosexually.

      (1) A number of years ago, *"fetal brain androgen" studies* were said to indicate a physiological component to some sexual identity confusion. However, the studies were few and highly speculative, creating a great deal of unscientific, biased speculation by pro-gay propagandists.

      In an article, "Born or Bred?" the February 24, 1992 issue of *Newsweek* magazine reported more recent studies using the size of the hypothalamus gland as "proof" that homosexuals were born that way. Another study of identical twins supposedly "proved" the same thesis according to pro-gay groups. Fortunately, the *Newsweek* article fairly reported the insurmountable evidence against these "political" conclusions. Here are some reasons why:

      (2) Regarding the *twin experiment*—"Instead of proving the genetic argument, it only confirms the obvious: that twins are apt to have the same sort of shaping influences. 'In order for such a study to be at all meaningful, you'd have to look at twins raised apart,' says *Anne Fausto Sterling, a developmental biologist at Brown University*. 'It's such badly interpreted genetics.'"

      Newsweek quotes the response of *the dean of American sexologists, John Money (of Johns Hopkins University)* to the "discovery" that there are brain differences involved in sexual orientation as: "Of course it is in the brain. The real question is, when did it get there? Was it prenatal, neonatal, during childhood, puberty?"

"Many scientists (says *Newsweek*) say it's naive to think a single gene could account for so complex a behavior as homosexuality."

(3) Even the man who conducted *the study on the hypothalamus glands of AIDS infected cadavers* admits, "We can't say on the basis of that (the size difference of the gland in some homosexuals) what makes people gay or straight." In fact, *Newsweek* points out, "One of the major criticisms of the study was that AIDS could have affected the brain structure of the homosexual subjects."

Newsweek goes on to say, "The trickier question is whether things might work the otherway around: could sexual orientation affect brain structure? *Kenneth Klivington, an assistant to the president of the Salk Institute,* points to a body of evidence showing that the brain's neural networks reconfigure themselves in response to certain experiences. One fascinating NIH study found that in people reading Braille after becoming blind, the area of the brain controlling the reading finger grew larger. There are also intriguing conundrums in animal brains. In male songbirds, for example, the brain area associated with mating is not only larger than in the female but varies according to the season.

Says Klivington: 'From the study of animals, we know that circulating sex hormones in the mother can have a profound effect on the organization of the brain of the fetus. Once the individual is born, the story gets more complex because of the interplay between the brain and experience. It's a feedback loop: the brain influences behavior, behavior shapes experience, experience effects the organization of the brain, and so forth.'"

Newsweek quotes *the researcher of the hypothalamus study* as admitting he knew "regrettably little" about the sex histories, or the presumed orientation of his subjects. "That's a distinct shortcoming of my study," he said. In the article, he also confesses to going into the experiment with the intention to prove that homosexuality is genetically caused.

Of *the study on identical twins, Newsweek* reports that it had its own "dramatic" shortcomings. Some of the identical twins had one homosexual and one heterosexual. "Many critics have wondered about these discordant twins. How could two individuals with identical genetic traits and upbringing wind up with totally different sexual orientation (if sexual orientation is genetically determined)?" Even the researchers admitted, "There must be something in the environment to yield the discordant twins," reports *Newsweek*.

Newsweek also reveals, "Even within the enlightened ranks of the American Psychoanalytic Association there is still some reluctance to let homosexual analysts practice. As arrested cases themselves, the argument goes, they are ill-equipped to deal with developmental problems. The belief that homosexuality can and should be cured persists in some quarters of the profession."

New York City analyst Charles Socarides says, according to *Newsweek*, that the only biological evidence is "that we're anatomically made to go in male-female pairs." "Some psychiatrists still see the removal of homosexuality from the official list of emotional disorders as a mistake. It was instead innocuously identified as 'sexual orientation disturbance.'"

E.L. Pattullo, former director of Harvard's Center for Behavioral Sciences, recently pointed out in *Commentary* magazine that the scientific evidence does not support the claim that sexual orientation is biologically fated and thus entirely impervious to environmental influence." (from Chas Krauthammer commentary in the *Honolulu Advertiser* (April 1993)—columnist for the *New Republic* and *Time*)

(4) *The 1993 Hamer et al. "Genetic Link" study,* touted by the press as "proof" that homosexuality is genetically caused, did not prove any such thing. This was an investigation of 40 pairs of homosexual brothers, whose X chromosomes were studied to see if they shared inherited genetic peculiarities that could be attributed to sexual orientation.

In their research article in the July 16, 1993 issue of *Science* magazine, the researchers admitted that seven of the 40 pairs of homosexual brothers did not co-inherit the variation in the genetic region that supposedly was the locus for the "homosexual gene" found in the other pairs, and that these discordant pairs might be the result of "non-genetic sources of variation in sexual orientation." Neither did they have any control data indicating the presence or absence of the genetic variant in non-homosexual men. At the end of their report, the researchers admitted: ". . . a single genetic locus does not account for all of the observed variability," and that the sibling pairs that did not fit their conclusions might exist because there could be "environmental, experiential and cultural factors that influence the development of male sexual orientation." Hardly "proof" of a genetic cause for homosexuality.

In an accompanying article in the same issue of *Science*, Robert Pool commented: "The field of behavioral genetics is littered with apparent discoveries that were later called into question or retracted. Over the past few years, several groups of researchers have reported locating genes for various mental illnesses—manic depression, schizophrenia, alcoholism—only to see their evidence evaporate after they assembled more evidence or reanalyzed the original data. 'There's almost no finding that would be convincing by itself in this field,' notes *Elliot Gershon, chief of the clinical neurogenetics branch of the National Institute of Mental Health.*"

Pool goes on to note: "(Researcher) Hamer warns, however, that this one site cannot explain all male homosexuality."

In a letter to the editor in the September 3, 1993 issue of *Science* magazine, *Evan Balaban of Harvard University and Anne Fausto-Sterling of Brown University* criticize the weaknesses of the Hamer et al. study, noting the lack of an adequate control group and a logical misassumption of the study: "We wish to emphasize that…correlation does not necessarily indicate causation. A gene affecting sexual orientation in some segment of the male population might do so very indirectly. For instance, any gene that might increase the tendency of brothers to psychologically identify with one another might influence their similarity in such matters as sexual orientation and would be picked up in the present study." In other words, the data collected by the study doesn't even begin to prove the hypothesis that it purports to prove.

Finally, the researchers themselves admit, in a letter of response: "We agree that genetic studies can never, in and of themselves, determine the mechanism by which a locus influences a trait." You certainly didn't hear them saying that before being publicly challenged with the erroneous conclusions that had been publicized about the study.

Richard Dawkins, a geneticist at Oxford University says that homosexuality is *not genetic—that genes do not affect behavior.* (111-116)

31. This explains why NAMBLA (a pro-pedophilia group) has been allowed to march in many gay and lesbian parades over the years and why during ten years in the gay lifestyle, I never saw anyone even bat an eye when someone brought an under-aged person to a gay party. To the contrary, their "finds" (usually a runaway kid) became such objects of lust and jealousy that they were never allowed out of the sight of the one who brought them. These were average gatherings that I witnessed throughout the country and at almost every level of the gay culture.

The largest and most experienced organization for helping those who suffer from homosexual neurosis, Exodus International, has observed in its 25 years of experience that over 90% of all gay men who've gone through Exodus programs were introduced to homosexual sex by an older man.

A study published in the November 5, 1990 *Insight* by WF Skinner, *Jenny et al study* showed that 22% of child sex abuse cases were same-sex abuse. With 2% of the population being homosexually oriented, this tells us that taking into account their small percentage of the whole, it is 10 times more likely that any given person struggling with homosexual neurosis will also be struggling with the desire to be sexual with children or teenagers (more likely teenagers). Reported by the Family Research Institute, "Gay Rights Trumps Pediatric Science," *Family Research Report*, January-February 1995, 1, 3-5. So, although most child molesters are heterosexual (because most people are heterosexual), taken on a per capita basis, homosexually oriented people have a much higher incidence of pedophilia and pederasty than do heterosexuals. (Having noted that fact, it is important to understand once again that the majority of homosexually oriented people do not have a problem with pedophilia).

Why is this incidence of pedophilia and pederasty so much higher in the homosexual population? It is because of the profound identity confusion, lack of emotional stability, the idolatrous worship of youth and beauty and the need to recapture a childhood lost to sexual abuse and neglect that runs rampant in homosexual neurosis.

32. Exodus International, P.O. Box 77652, Seattle, Wa. 98177 • (888) 264-0877 • www.exodusnorthamerica.org / Courage (for Catholics), 210 West 31st St, New York, NY 10001 • (212) 268-1010 • http://CourageRC.org/ / Homosexuals Anonymous, PO Box 7881, Reading, Pa. 19603 • (800) 288-4237 • http://members.aol.com/hawebpage

33. NARTH, 16633 Ventura Blvd., # 1340, Encino, Ca. 91436 • (818) 789-4440 • www.narth.com

Chapter 3: Dark Night of the Soul

1. Ignatius of Loyola wrote about this loss of consolations, in Richard J. Foster and James Bryan Smith, eds., *Devotional Classics: Selected Readings for Individuals and Groups* (San Francisco: HarperSanFrancisco, 1993):

> I call it *consolation* when the soul is aroused by an interior movement which causes it to be inflamed with love of its Creator and Lord and consequently can love no created thing in this world for its own sake, but only in the Creator of all things. It is likewise consolation when one sheds tears inspired by love of the Lord, whether it be sorrow for sins or because of the Passion of Christ our Lord, or for any other reason that is directly connected to His service and praise. Finally, I call consolation any increase of faith, hope, and charity and any interior joy that calls and attracts to heavenly things, and to the salvation of one's soul, inspiring it with peace and quiet in Christ our Lord.
>
> . . . It is also desolation when a soul finds itself completely apathetic, tepid, sad, and separated as it were, from its Creator and Lord. . . . In time of desolation one should never make a change, but stand firm and constant in the resolution and decision which guided him the day before the desolation, or to the decision which he observed in the preceding consolation. . . .
>
> . . . One who is in desolation must strive to persevere in patience which is contrary to the vexations that have come upon him. . . .
>
> There are three reasons why we are in desolation. The first is because we have been tepid, slothful, or negligent in our Spiritual Exercises, . . .
>
> The second is that God may try to test our worth, and the progress that we have made in His service and praise when we are without such generous rewards of consolation and special graces.
>
> The third is that He may wish to give us a true knowledge and understanding so that we may truly perceive that it is not within our power to acquire or retain great devotion, ardent love, tears, or any other spiritual consolation, but that all of this is a gift and a grace of God our Lord. . . .
>
> A person who is in consolation ought to think of how he will conduct himself during a future desolation and thus build up a new strength for that time.
>
> A person who is in consolation should also take care to humble and abase himself as much as possible. . . .

On the other hand, a person who is in desolation should recall that he can do much to withstand all of his enemies by using the sufficient grace that he has and taking strength in his Creator and Lord. (225-226)

2. Gregory of Nyssa, as quoted in Foster, *Devotional Classics*, 157.

3. Another treatise on this topic can be found in Fr. Gabriel of St. Mary Magdalen, O.C.D., *Divine Intimacy: Meditations on the Interior Life for Every Day of the Liturgical Year* (Rockford, Il.: Tan Books and Publishers, Inc., 1996), including a quote by St. Teresa Margaret from her letters:

> In order to enter the fullness of the hidden life, it is not enough to hide one-self from the attention of others; we must also hide from ourselves, that is, forget ourselves, avoiding all excessive concern about ourselves. We can be preoccupied with self not only from amaterial point of view, but also from a spiritual point of view. To be overly concerned about one's spiritual progress, about the consolations which God gives or does not give,about the state of aridity in which one may be - all this is often the sign of a subtle spiritual ego-ism, a sign that the soul is more occupied with itself than with God. We must learn to forget ourselves, to hide from ourselves, by refusing to examine too minutely what is happening within our soul, and by not attaching too much importance to it, renouncing even the satisfaction of wanting to know the exact condition of our own spiritual life. It is well to understand that God often permits painful, obscure states just because He wants the soul to live hidden from itself. . . . the *negative* exercise of not thinking of itself must accompany the *positive* exercise of fixing its *center* in Christ, of "burying in Christ" every thought, every preoccupation with self, even in the spiritual order. No one can succeed inturning away from himself unless he concen-trates all his attention on the object of his love. . . .

> A soul entirely oblivious of self is also completely disinterested. It no longer serves God in a mercenary spirit, with more regard for the reward which it may receive than for His glory, but it is "at His service," according to St. Teresa's beautiful expression, "*gratuitously*, as great lords serve their king" (L). . . .

> This total purity of intention makes the soul act for God alone and never for personal interest, even of a spiritual nature. God will certainly reward our good works, but concern about this is wholly abandoned to Him as long as the soul is intent only on giving Him pleasure. The hidden life thus finds its culminating point in a complete disinterestedness, not only concerning human rewards and praises, but also in regard to spiritual consolations; our soul seeks God alone and God alone is sufficient for us. Even if, apparently unaware of our love and our services, He leaves us in aridity and abandon-ment, we do not worry nor stop on this account, since the one motive which actuates us is to please God alone. . . .

> . . . O Lord, . . . I understand that if You lead me by an obscure and arid road, if You often permit the darkness to deepen around me, it is only because You want to teach me to serve You with a pure intention, seeking nothing but

Your satisfaction, not my own. If You allow me to continue to practice the interior life and virtue without seeing any results, if You veil my eyes to my slight progress, it is to establish my soul in humility. If I had more light, or if the workings of Your grace were more evident to me, perhaps I would glorify myself and halt my progress toward You, the one object of my affection. (338-340)

4. Foster, *Devotional Classics*, 33-36.

5. In referring to a related problem having to do with the jealousy we sometimes feel in seeing God pour fruitful gifts into the lives of others, Francois Fenelon wrote: "Why would we prefer to see the gifts of God in ourselves rather than in others, if this is not attachment to self?" Quoted in Foster, *Devotional Classics*, 49.

6. Foster, *Devotional Classics*, 62.

Chapter 4: Living by Grace Rather Than Performance

1. Except men like Dudley Hall, who has written one of the best books on the subject: Dudley Hall, *Grace Works: Letting God Rescue You From Empty Religion* (Ann Arbor, Mi.: Servant Publications, Vine Books, 1992).

2. Ibid., 21. Hall also suggests that there are four characteristics of the flesh:

Aspect #1 - The Natural As Opposed to the Spiritual

Aspect #2 - Outward Conformity As Opposed to Inward Transformation

Aspect #3 - Human Zeal As Opposed to Divine Passion

Aspect #4 - Self-Righteousness As Opposed to Faith Righteousness

(56-57)

3. Rick Joyner, *There Were Two Trees in the Garden* (Charlotte, NC: Morning Star Publications, 1992), 9-10.

4. Hall, 87.

5. An interesting parallel can be drawn between this point and the one Paul was making in Rom 2:28, where he said:

A man is not a Jew if he is only one outwardly; nor is circumcision merely outward and physical. No, a man is a Jew if he is one inwardly; and circumcision is circumcision of the heart, by the Spirit, not by the written code. Such a man's praise is not from men, but from God.

In the same way, a Christian is only a Christian if he is one inwardly, not simply by dint of any outward profession or show, though as James pointed out, a true Christian will exhibit the fruit of righteousness (James 2:14-24). God judges by what He reads in a man's heart -e.g., 1 Chronicles 28:9; Psalm 44:21; Jeremiah 17:10; Acts 15:8; Romans 8:27.

6. When you're a sex addict, your world is full of lies, because you are always trying to make excuses for your behavior and hide what you are doing. You deny it and minimize it before others, covering yourself all the time. But when you commit to never lying, you have lost a necessary support system for the sexual behavior. You don't want people to know what you've been doing. It's too embarrassing, too humiliating. And now that you are a man of truth, you're going to have to be known for who you are. This change goes a long way toward getting you set free from the sexual addiction. It really does.

7. To reckon means to accept as a fact for yourself and in your own experience.

8. A helpful tool in faith talking is Neil T. Anderson, *Victory Over the Darkness: Realizing the Power of Your Identity in Christ* (Ventura, Ca.: Gospel Light, Regal Books, 1990). A second great tool, this one for group study, is Neil T. Anderson, *Breaking Through to Spiritual Maturity* (Ventura, Ca.: Gospel Light, 1992).

9. A very strong theme, found in John 5:19-20, 30; 7:16; 8:26-29, 38; 12:49-50; 14:10, 24, 31; 15:15; 17:8. Said also of the Holy Spirit in John 16:13-15.

10. Anne Ortlund, *Fix Your Eyes On Jesus* (Nashville, Tn.: Word Publishing, 1991), 17.

11. When we are immersed in performance and goal achievement, not only do we tend to manipulate and use people, we do the same to God without even realizing it.

12. This was Jesus' first message. Note Matthew 4:17 and Luke 13:3-5.

13. Hall, 29.

14. This chapter was inspired by the "Study Section" outline found in David Kyle Foster, *Sexual Healing: God's Plan for the Sanctification of Broken Lives* (Jacksonville, Fl.: Mastering Life Ministries, 2001), 37-46.

Chapter 6: The Problem With Holiness:
How To Make it Work in the Real World

1. A great treatment on this theme can be found by Dudley Hall in, *Grace Works: Letting God Rescue You From Empty Religion* (Ann Arbor, Mi.: Servant Publications, Vine Books, 1992).

2. A phrase taken from Titus 2:12c, which clearly states that we are to "live self-controlled, upright and godly lives in this present age."

3. Her book that most directly addresses this need is Leanne Payne, *Listening Prayer: Learning to Hear God's Voice and Keep a Prayer Journal* (Grand Rapids, Mi.: Baker Books, Hamewith Books, 1994).

4. Fr. Gabriel of St. Mary Magdalen, O.C.D., *Divine Intimacy: Meditations on the Interior Life for Every Day of the Liturgical Year* (Rockford, Il.: Tan Books and Publishers, Inc., 1996), 266, including quotes from St. Teresa of Jesus, *Way of Perfection*, 28, St. Teresa Margaret of the Heart of Jesus, *Spirituality of St. Teresa Margaret of the Heart of Jesus*, and St. Thomas Aquinas, *Commentary on St. Matthew*.

5. Ibid., 292-293, including quotes from St. Thomas Aquinas, IIa IIae, q. 184, a. 3, St. John of the Cross, *Ascent of Mt. Carmel*, II, 5,7, and St. Teresa of Jesus, *Life*, II.

6. The First Epistle of John was written to answer the question posed by some in his day who were not quite sure if they were authentic believers. They had proclaimed Jesus with their lips but perhaps weren't demonstrating the holiness of life that true faith produces. The Apostle John writes in 5:13: "I write these things to you who believe in the name of the Son of God so that you may know that you have eternal life."
What were the criteria upon which believers could know this?
(1) The Test of Humility - They are repentant on an ongoing basis. When they sinned, they confessed their sin, were forgiven and purified from all unrighteousness (1:9).
(2) The Test of Obedience - A true believer obeys God's commands on a consistent basis out of love for God and thus overcomes the world. "We know that we have come to know Him if we obey His commands. . . . This is how we know we are in Him: Whoever claims to live in Him must walk as Jesus did" (2:3-6). (cf. also 3:24; 5:3-5)
(3) The Test of Love - A true believer loves his brother. "Anyone who claims to be in the light but hates his brother is still in the darkness. Whoever loves his brother lives in the light, and there is nothing in him to make him stumble" (2:9-10). (cf. also 3:10,14; 4:7-8,16, 20-21; 5:2)

Love is defined in 1st John as: "This is how we know what love is: Jesus Christ laid down His life for us. And we ought to lay down our lives for our brothers. . . . not . . . with words or tongue, but with actions and in truth. This then is how we know that we belong to the truth, and how we set our hearts at rest in His presence whenever our hearts condemn us" (3:16-20a). (See also 4:10, where love is equated with sacrifice).

(4) <u>The Test of the Heart's Affections</u> - A true believer no longer loves the world. "If anyone loves the world, the love of the Father is not in him" (2:15b).

(5) <u>The Test of Doctrine</u> - A true believer acknowledges that Jesus is the Messiah sent from the Father. "Who is the liar? It is the man who denies that Jesus is the Christ. . . . No one who denies the Son has the Father; whoever acknowledges the Son has the Father also" (2:22-23). (cf. also 5:1,12) In 4:2b, John adds: "Every spirit that acknowledges that Jesus Christ has come in the flesh is from God, . . ." This is reminiscent of Jesus' statement to the Jews in Jn 8:24, that they would die in their sins if they refused to believe that He was the One He claimed to be. Finally: "If anyone acknowledges that Jesus is the Son of God, God lives in him and he in God" (4:15).

(6) <u>The Test of Paternity</u> - A true believer lives the righteous kind of life that is consistent with his true parentage. "If you know that He is righteous, you know that everyone who does what is right has been born of Him" (2:29). (cf. also 3:7-10)

Dogs act like dogs. They bark. They can't help it - they just do. Sons of God have a natural drive within them to act like the Son of God, because His nature has been implanted into the very fabric of their being. When they act contrary to that nature, they bring great discomfort upon themselves. There's an inner knowledge that something is not right - that they have gone against their very nature. It's like stuffing a bale of grass in your mouth and pretending to enjoy eating it. You know better. You know that if you continue, something very destructive to the integrity and peace of your being is going to take place. Because of your ignorance or willfulness you may try it a time or two, but ultimately you realize that what you are doing is going against your very nature. The love of God and of yourself will unite to bring a change of behavior.

(7) <u>The Test of the Merging of the Human Will with God's Will</u> - In a true believer, habitual, willful sin progressively fades from their life. "No one who lives in Him keeps on sinning. No one who continues to sin has either seen Him or known Him" (3:6). (cf. also 5:18a: "We know that anyone born of God does not continue to sin; . . .")

The sense of the verb tense in the original Greek text points to the fact that what John is talking about is a consistent walk toward the goal of sinlessness, (that Paul elsewhere calls pressing toward the mark of the higher calling in Christ Jesus - Philippians 3:12-14), rather than an instant and perfect achievement of it. (Remember that earlier in 1st John 1:10 John said that if we claim to have no sin we make God out to be a liar.) That is why an ongoing provision for cleansing has been provided for us (see 1:9). Our body has been cleansed - it is just our feet (that which touches and is polluted by this world) that continues to need periodic cleansing (cf. John 13:9-10).

(8) <u>The Test of Confirmation by God's Spirit</u> - In a true believer, there is the witness of the Holy Spirit. "And this is how we know that He lives in us: We know it by the Spirit He gave us" (3:24b). (cf. also 4:13) This is similar to the message in Romans 8:16-17 - "The Spirit Himself testifies with our spirit that we are God's children. . . . and co-heirs with Christ, if indeed we share in His sufferings . . . ")

(9) <u>The Test of Opposition from the World</u> - There is another test of a true believer provided by John in his Gospel, when Jesus proclaimed: "If you belonged to the world, it would love you as its own. As it is, you do not belong to the world, but I have chosen you out of the world. That is why the world hates you" (15:19).

7. Martin Luther, in his *Theologia Germanica*, wrote about this problem of moving our knowledge and experience of God from the outer to the inner person, edited by Richard J. Foster and James Bryan Smith in their *Devotional Classics: Selected Readings for Individuals and Groups* (San Francisco: Harper SanFrancisco, 1993):

> Four kinds of people deal with order, command, and rule in four different ways.
>
> Some lead an ordered life neither for God's sake nor out of a particular personal desire, but simply because they are compelled. They do the least possible and it all turns sour and burdensome for them.
>
> A second group observes laws and rules for the sake of reward. . . .
>
> The third kind . . . think of themselves as perfect . . . They think that they do not need any rules and laws . . .
>
> Fourth, we have those who . . . do what they do in the ordered life out of love. . . . they also know that their salvation and happiness are not dependent on the observance of rules. Therefore they are not as anxious as others. . . .
>
> . . . a lover of God is better and more pleasing to God than a hundred thousand hirelings. (148-149)

8. Leanne Payne, preface to *Restoring the Christian Soul Through Healing Prayer: Overcoming the Three Great Barriers to Personal and Spiritual Completion in Christ* (Grand Rapids, Mi.: Baker Books, Hamewith Books, 1991), xiv.

9. cf. Matthew 7:6.

10. This sentiment is most powerfully taught by Jesus in John 17:20-23:

> My prayer is not for them alone. I pray also for those who will believe in Me through their message, that all of them may be one, Father, just as You are in Me and I am in You. May they also be in Us so that the world may believe that You have sent Me. I have given them the glory that You gave Me, that they may be one as We are One: I in them and You in Me. May they be brought to complete unity to let the world know that You have sent Me and have loved them even as You have loved Me.

11. John R.W. Stott, *The Cross of Christ* (Downers Grove, Il.: InterVarsity Press, 1986), 160.

12. Referring to the lion (Christ) character in C.S. Lewis' children's book series, *The Chronicles of Narnia*.

13. cf. Ephesians 1:13-14 and 4:30.

14. Historical accounts of people literally experiencing this "river of living water" are more prevalent than one might imagine. One can find references to direct experience of it in writings by Christian leaders such as D.L. Moody and Charles Finney.

15. Mike Bickle, "Developing Passion For God in Your Congregation," *Ministries Today*, (January/February 1998): 44-45.

16. Leanne Payne, *Restoring the Christian Soul Through Healing Prayer: Overcoming the Three Great Barriers to Personal and Spiritual Completion in Christ* (Grand Rapids, Mi.: Baker Books, Hamewith Books, 1991), 53.

17. Ibid., xiii. Borrowed from: ". . . the three great barriers to personal and spiritual wholeness in Christ. They are 1) the failure to gain the great Christian virtue of self-acceptance, 2) the failure to forgive others, and 3) the failure to receive forgiveness for oneself."

18. Ibid., 32.

19. Ibid., xiv.

20. Ibid., 24.

21. Ibid., 50-51.

22. Ibid., 52.

23. Ibid., 26.

24. Ibid., 27.

25. Ibid., 38-40.

26. An excellent tool for guiding us in this endeavor is Neil Anderson, *Victory Over the Darkness: Realizing the Power of Your Identity in Christ* (Ventura, Ca.: Gospel Light, Regal Books, 1990).

27. Romano Guardini, "The Acceptance of Oneself," *Die Annahme seiner selbst*, 5th ed. (Wurzburg: Werkbandverlag, 1969), 14,16; quoted in Payne, *Restoring the Christian Soul*, 31; quoted in Walter Trobisch, *Love Yourself: Self Acceptance and Depression* (Downers Grove, Il.: InterVarsity Press, 1976), 9.

28. Payne, *Restoring the Christian Soul*, 42.

29. An example of such a prayer can be found in Payne, *Restoring the Christian Soul*, 23.

30. C.S. Lewis, *Mere Christianity* (New York: Macmillan, 1960), 190; quoted in Payne, *Restoring the Christian Soul*, 32.

31. C.S. Lewis, *Experiment in Criticism* (Cambridge: Cambridge University Press, 1969), 138; quoted in Payne, *Restoring the Christian Soul*, 32.

32. Payne, *Restoring the Christian Soul*, 32-33.

33. Ibid., 28.

34. Ibid., 45.

35. Ibid., 48.

36. Ibid., 46.

37. Dr. Larry Crabb, *Connecting: A Radical New Vision* (Nashville, Tn.: Word Publishing, 1997), 10-11.

38. Ibid., 13-15.

39. Ibid., 11,18, 21.

40. Ibid., 11,18, 20.

41. Richard Foster reflects on this rift between head and heart in response to the writing of Soren Kierkegaard in Richard J. Foster and James Bryan Smith, ed. *Devotional Classics: Selected Readings for Individuals and Groups* (San Francisco: HarperSanFrancisco, 1993):

> It is a wonderful thing to see a first-rate philosopher at prayer. Tough-minded thinking and tenderhearted reverence are friends, not enemies. We have for too long separated the head from the heart, and we are the lesser for it.
>
> We love God with the mind and we love God with the heart. In reality, we are descending with the mind into the heart and there standing before God in ceaseless wonder and endless praise. As the mind and the heart work in concert, a kind of "loving rationality" pervades all we say and do. This brings unity to us and glory to God. (111)

42. Payne, *Restoring the Christian Soul*, 145.

43. In some communions, the pastor or priest will actually say words of absolution over those who have confessed their sins, thus aiding them in a conscious embrace of God's forgiveness. They believe that God has commanded His ministers to stand in for Christ in such a way, based on the passage in Matthew 18:15-20.

44. Payne, *Restoring the Christian Soul*, 146.

45. St. John of the Cross, *Dark Night of the Soul*, trans. and ed. E. Allison Peers (New York: Doubleday, Image Books, 1990).

46. Payne, *Restoring the Christian Soul*, 146.

47. Ibid., 149-150.

48. Mike Bickle, *Passion for Jesus: Perfecting Extravagant Love for God* (Orlando, Fl.: Creation House, 1993), 109.

49. Fr. Gabriel of St. Mary Magdalen, O.C.D., *Divine Intimacy: Meditations on the Interior Life for Every Day of the Liturgical Year* (Rockford, Il.: Tan Books and Publishers, Inc., 1996), 324-325.

50. Fr. Gabriel, *Divine Intimacy*, 326-328, including quotes from St. Thomas Aquinas, IIa IIae, q. 161, a.6.

51. George Butron, "One Holy Passion," *Vineyard Psalms*, (Anaheim, Ca.: Vineyard Ministries International, 1992), audio CD.

Part Two - The Corrective Vision

Chapter 7: Sacred Mystery: The Heavenly Marriage

1. The text from which I derive such a claim is Ephesians 5:29-32. It is built on three observations: first, the logical conclusion that what is true of the whole can legitimately be seen as true for the parts of that whole; second, in the Ephesians 5 passage, Paul uses Genesis 2:24 as his proof text, which uses the idiom "two becoming one flesh" for which *The MacArthur Study Bible* footnote reads: "One flesh speaks of a complete unity of parts making a whole, e.g., one cluster, many grapes (Numbers 13:23), . . . This also implies their sexual completeness. One man and one woman constitute the pair to reproduce"; and third, it is common to find multiple levels of meaning in Biblical texts, especially metaphorical ones.

There has been a tradition throughout the Christian era, especially in the Catholic and Orthodox traditions, of seeing an individual "mystical marriage" as part of the greater corporate marriage between God and man. This is not the primary, surface interpretation of that passage, however. Nor is it the reigning interpretation in modern evangelical scholarship, and indeed it can be problematic if taken too far. I am not suggesting, as pagan religions have done, that we are to unite sexually with God. God is a spirit and the realms of heaven transcend earthly sexual need or behavior. What I am suggesting is that the metaphor of Christ marrying the Church can be taken individually by believers as well as the more common understanding of it being a corporate union.

Modern evangelical commentary on this metaphor mostly limits the comparison to a simple mystical union between the corporate body of Christ (represented by Eve in Genesis 2:24) and Christ Himself (represented by Adam in Genesis 2:24). My suggestion is that what is true of the whole body of Christ (we are His bride) is also true of the individuals that make up that body - that we can individually experience a oneness with Him that is only dimly prefigured in human sexuality and which transcends it.

Dr. Scott Hahn writes in his book *The Lamb's Supper*: "The earliest Christians taught that the sacred text operates on four levels, and all of those levels, all at once, teach God's one truth—like a symphony." Thus, in order to find scholarly support for extending the metaphor to the individual parts of the whole, one has to look to early Christian commentaries and mystic writings (Teresa of Avila, St. John of the Cross, etc.) or modern Anglican, Roman Catholic or Orthodox commentary (Leanne Payne, Dr. Scott Hahn, Fr. Isaiah Chronopoulos, etc.). Let's see what one of those modern scholars has to say—from Dr. Scott Hahn, *A Father Who Keeps His Promises* (Ann Arbor, Mi.: Servant Publications, 1998), pp. 255-256 (my underlining):

When the two become one in marriage, the bridegroom gives the bride his flesh and blood; the bride receives him, his flesh and blood. (The Greek word *haima*, usually translated "blood," can refer to other bodily fluids, including the man's "seed." See John 1:13.) When he gives and she receives, they bring new life into the world. When does Christ, the Bridegroom, unite himself with his Bride? When does he give his flesh and blood in order to bring new life? In the Eucharist. The Eucharist is the sacrament of the consummation of the marriage between Christ and his Church. In the Eucharist he renews the New Covenant, which is his marriage covenant with her. It is much more than a banquet. It is a wedding feast. We the Bride receive our Bridegroom's Body in the Eucharist.

The marital imagery of Christ's love for his Church becomes a powerful symbol for the sacrament of marriage. Or is marriage a powerful symbol of Christ's love for his Church—for each of us?

We may need to execute a sort of Copernican revolution in our understanding of love. Just as God's Fatherhood is the perfect reality that human fatherhood portrayed, though imperfectly, so the marriage of Christ and the Church is the perfect reality portrayed by human marriage. Our vision for marital love and sexual intimacy should reflect this reality.

This challenges believers, especially married ones, to make marriage and family life a sign of Christ's intimate union with his bride. This makes sex more than 'four bare legs in a bed,' as CS Lewis said. Every marital act becomes a sign and a renewal of the New Covenant, a reaffirmation of the intense love Jesus has for each of us. . . .

. . . God has placed in us these natural [sexual] desires, which reflect supernatural desires fulfilled only in him. . . .

. . . We desire intimacy, sexual union. We find it in other persons. But that desire points to a deeper desire, which only union with God can meet; and union with God proves to be deep intimacy, unimaginable ecstasy, infinite fulfillment of the desire to love and be loved, to give and receive totally, to become one with the other.

This is a truth that only the mystic can really understand; but then, mystics are lovers. And God wants us all to be lovers.

There is legitimate concern among evangelical scholars that when the church opens itself to the multileveled, type-filled hermeneutic that reigned during the early centuries of the church that a certain certainty of faith can be lost amidst the cacophony of purported meanings. It is a concern that we must continue to hold on to should we delve into such waters.

2. "The Mystery of Columbine High," *Doxa: A Quarterly Review* (Transfiguration/Dormition 1999): 1.

3. This, of course, is not an exegetically correct representation of John 13:3-12, but rather artistic license on my part—drawing together the image of Christ kneeling before man and a husband kneeling before his bride-to-be.

4. One of the problems in supporting certain "mysteries" of the faith is that they can't survive the rigorous exegetical demands that we might like to place on them (-e.g., the "mystery of godliness" has but one Scripture cited most obscurely; the mystery of the Trinity hasn't a single clear statement but can only be inferred from logic and the juxtaposition of the three persons of God in a single phrase). It is one of the things that makes them mysteries - left obscure by God intentionally until a time when they will be revealed either corporately to the Church or individually to those who intensely pursue God for deeper understanding (as the mystics have done throughout the centuries).

One might ask, why modern evangelical scholars have such an aversion to the reigning hermeneutical method amongst the early church fathers. Why do we have to go to ancient sources or modern Catholic, Anglican or Orthodox sources to find anything? As Alister McGrath explains it, the insinuation of eighteenth and nineteenth century rationalism into modern evangelical method might be one of the problems.

Alister McGrath, in his book, *A Passion for Truth: The Intellectual Coherence of Evangelicalism* (Downers Grove, Il.: InterVarsity Press, 1996), suggests the following (my underlining):

> . . . *rationalism* . . . is an exclusive reliance upon human reason alone, and a refusal to allow any weight to be given to divine revelation. . . .

> . . . By the middle of the seventeenth century, . . . a new attitude began to develop. . . . Christianity was . . . *reduced* to those ideas which could be proven by reason. . . . reason was understood to take priority over Christianity. . . without needing any assistance from revelation. . . .

> . . . Evangelicals have always been prone to read Scripture as if they were the first to do so. We need to be reminded that others have been there before us, and have read it before us. This process of receiving the scriptural revelation is 'tradition' —not a source of revelation in addition to Scripture, but a particular way of understanding Scripture which the Christian church has recognized as responsible and reliable. Scripture and tradition are thus not to be seen as two alternative sources of revelation; rather they are *coinherent*. . . .

> . . . For in part, the authority of Scripture rests in the universal acceptance of that authority within the Christian church. . . .

> . . . Throughout its history, evangelicalism has shown itself to be prone to lapse into a form of rationalism . . . [laying] too much emphasis upon the notion of a purely propositional biblical revelation. . . .

> . . . Revelation concerns the *oracles* of God, the *acts* of God, and the *person* and *presence* of God. To reduce revelation to principles or concepts is to suppress the element of mystery, holiness and wonder to God's self-disclosure. . . .

> . . . Curiously, . . . evangelicalism has been deeply influenced by the rationalism of the Enlightenment. . . .

. . . the Enlightenment worldview, . . . came to be dominant in those areas in which evangelicalism expanded as a consequence of the revivals and renewals of the eighteenth century, and in which it had to defend itself in the nineteenth. . . . As a result, <u>a number of foundational Enlightenment assumptions appear to have been absorbed uncritically into the movement at these formative stages.</u> . . .

. . . the evangelical fervor of the 'Great Awakening' was tempered by forms of Enlightenment moralism and rationalism, especially at Princeton. . . . Princeton was to be the crucible in which the great nineteenth-century evangelical theories of biblical inspirationand authority were forged. The result? The theories of writers such as Charles Hodge are deeply influenced by Enlightenment preconceptions. . . .

. . . The strongly rationalistic tone of this philosophy is particularly evident from the works of Benjamin B. Warfield, . . . The danger of this approach . . . reduces Scripture to 'a code book of theological ordinances'; . . . [and makes] the truth of divine revelation dependent on the judgments of fallen human reason. . . .

. . . Writing in the third century, Tertullian pointed out the danger of grounding or judging the gospel in what passed for human wisdom. . . .

. . . If divine revelation appears to be logically inconsistent on occasion (as it undoubtedly does: witness the doctrine of the two natures of Christ), this cannot be taken to mean that the doctrine in question is wrong, or that the doctrine is not divine revelation on account of its 'illogical' character. Rather, this merely illustrates the fact that fallen human reason cannot fully comprehend the majesty of God. This point was made regularly by Christian writers as diverse as Thomas Aquinas and John Calvin. (91-97, 106-107, 167-171)

There are other passages of Scripture that allude (albeit obliquely) to the idea that God's intimate union with His Church is at once both corporate and individual (my underlining):

Now you are the body of Christ, <u>and individually members of it</u>. (1 Corinthians 12:27, NASB)

. . . Father, just as You are in Me and I am in You. May they also be in us . . . I in them and You in Me. (John 17:21b, 23)

This passage speaks of a profound intimacy that goes beyond what the natural mind can immediately grasp. It speaks to the issue of a level of intimacy between God and man that we are only beginning to understand.

Song of Songs is a book filled with imagery about the love between God and believers. Also in Isaiah 62:5b:

. . . as a bridegroom rejoices over his bride, so will your God rejoice over you.

See also Isaiah 54:5, Hosea 2:19, and Matthew 22:2.

In a survey of Christian leaders who minister to sexually broken people taken by Mastering Life Ministries, 98% agreed with the statement: "God intended sexual activity as a symbolic enactment of the relationship between Christ and the Church. Therefore it must be monogamous, heterosexual and expressed only within the bonds of the covenant of marriage." Those who took the survey ranged from Nazarene, Baptist, Episcopalian, and Roman Catholic to Assemblies of God, from seminary trained doctors and professors to degreed psychologists.

Here are a sampling of Christian writings that have also shown agreement. From the *Ancient Christian Commentary on Scripture, Old Testament, Volume I - Genesis I-II* (Downers Grove, IL: InterVarsity Press, 2001), 67-72 [my underlining]:

> The union of man and woman implies a return to their origin (Ephrem). It also symbolizes the spiritual marriage of human beings with the church (Augustine) and their union with Christ (Ambrose).

Referring to the two uniting and becoming one flesh, Augustine goes on to say:

> This is what generally happens in the human race. There is no other way to view its plain, historic sense.

Chrysostom makes it clear that sexual activity is the subject in Genesis 2:24, commenting:

> Whence, after all, did he come to know that there would be intercourse between man and woman?

The commentary by Dr. Charles Ryrie in *The Ryrie Study Bible* on Ephesians 5:32 is:

> The relationship between believing husbands and wives illustrates that which exists between Christ (the bridegroom) and the church (His bride).

What relational aspect was Paul pointing to?—the uniting to become one flesh—a clear reference to individual, personal, and intimate interaction.

Editor Colin Brown, from his *Dictionary of New Testament Theology, Vol 2*, commenting on the word "one" says:

> There is a unity of believers with their Lord. There is also a unity of man and woman which comes about through sexual intercourse. . . . The believer's union with Christ is not a physical one but a spiritual one: "But he who is united with the Lord becomes one spirit with him" (1 Corinthians 6:17) (722)

Colin Brown *(Vol 2)* commenting on the word "marriage" says:

> Paul also saw marriage as a picture of man's relationship to God. (581)

In the *International Standard Bible Encyclopedia, Vol 3*, p. 265 on the symbolism of marriage:

> An equally important interpretive approach is viewing the intimate relationship between God and His people (God and Israel, Christ and His Church) as a paradigm or christological analogy of the husband-wife relationship in its earthly existence.

Covenantal and Church-bride imagery suggest that certain qualities are essential to marriage from a biblical perspective. Marriages should be characterized by (a) intentions of a permanent relationship (Hosea 2:19; Matthew 19:6), (b) overriding, sacrificial love of the husband for the wife (Hosea 2:19; Ephesians 5:25), and (c) <u>a unity by which the two becomes one</u>, physically and spiritually. (265)

In the *International Standard Bible Encyclopedia, Vol 1,* on the "bride of Christ":

> <u>An image for the Church which emphasizes the ideas of purity, subjection, faithfulness,</u> and intimate communion with Christ her bridegroom-husband; one constituent feature of alarger complex of nuptial imagery symbolizing the relationship between Christ and the Church. (546)

In the *International Standard Bible Encyclopedia, Vol 1,* on the "bride of Christ":

> In another allusion to Genesis 2:24 Paul tells the Corinthian congregation that <u>he who joins himself to a prostitute</u> becomes one body with her, "but <u>he who is united to the Lord becomes one spirit with him</u>" (1 Corinthians 6:15-17). (547)

> This is a clear application of the metaphor to individual cases.

From Francois Fenelon, *Meditations on the Heart of God* (Brewster, Ma.: Paraclete Press, 1997), 119-120:

> <u>Jesus Christ wants only to unite Himself with us and join with us in body and in spirit.</u> Why? So He can live deep within our hearts. He must be manifested in our mortal bodies; He must radiate from us, since He and we have become one flesh. I live, yet "it is no longer I who live, but Christ who lives in me."

From Brent Curtis & John Eldredge, *The Sacred Romance* (Nashville, Tn.: Thomas Nelson, 1997), 97:

> Lady Julian of Norwich was given a series of revelations into the sufferings of Christ and the glory of the gospel. She was taken into the heart of God and upon her return she concluded quite simply, "<u>We are his lovers.</u>" The bridal imagery often fails to capture a man's heart, but consider: God is neither male nor female. Both genders together are needed to reflect his image and he transcends them both.

From Dr. Scott Hahn, *The Lamb's Supper: The Mass as Heaven on Earth* (New York, NY: Doubleday, 1999), 73:

> <u>The earliest Christians taught that the sacred text operates on four levels, and all of those levels, all at once, teach God's one truth—like a symphony.</u>

In that passage, he is supporting a multileveled interpretation of the woman clothed with the sun in Revelation, but the principle remains the same. It has always been a legitimate exegetical consideration to see multiple levels of teachings and meaning in certain biblical statements provided they don't contravene the known revelation and provided they receive support from authoritative voices in the Church. Certainly the "mysteries" in Scripture are the primest of candidates for this. <u>It is significant</u> that this multileveled interpretive approach was a common and accepted way of interpretation among those who lived closest to the Apostles.

The *Catechism of the Catholic Church, Second Edition* (Vatican: Libreria Editrice Vaticana, 1997) is a <u>masterpiece</u> of theological exposition. Let me share some applicable quotes:

> Sacred Scripture begins with the creation of man and woman in the image and likeness of God and concludes with a vision of "the wedding-feast of the Lamb." Scripture speaks throughout of marriage and its "mystery," its institution and the meaning God has given it . . . (1602, p. 400)

> <u>Since God created him man and woman, their mutual love becomes an image of the absolute and unfailing love with which God loves man</u>. It is good, very good, in the Creator's eyes. (1604, p. 401)

> The nuptial covenant between God and his people Israel had prepared the way for the new and everlasting covenant in which <u>the Son of God</u>, by becoming incarnate and giving his life, <u>has united to himself in a certain way all mankind saved by him, thus preparing for "the wedding-feast of the Lamb."</u> (1612, p. 403)

Some of the mystics of the Church who wrote on intimacy with the divine (Therese of Liseux, Teresa of Avila, St. John of the Cross, etc.) were also Doctors of the Church—which as you know is a rare (given to only 33 people in all of history) acknowledgment from the Magisterium of their profound contribution to the <u>teaching</u> of the Church. Teresa of Avila was probably the foremost proponent of individual intimate union with God as in a marriage. Her book, *The Interior Castle* is filled with direct images of individual marriage to God.

From Bernard McGinn, *The Doctors of the Church* (New York, NY: The Crossroad Publishing Company, 1999), 140-141:

> *The Interior Castle* is one of the most sustained and profound accounts of mystical transformation in the history of Christian theology. . . .

> . . . The longest part . . . deals with . . . the stage of betrothal [with God] and the union of rapture. . . . the seventh dwelling place, [in her metaphorical castle is] the state of mystical marriage. In this stage the mystic attains a deep union in the Trinity achieved through Christ.

From *The Spiritual Canticle* by St. John of the Cross, Kieran Kavanaugh, OCD, and Otilio Rodriguez, OCD provide commentary on their Internet site:

> 1. These stanzas begin with a person's initial steps in the service of God and continue until <u>the ultimate state of perfection</u> is reached, which is <u>spiritual marriage</u>. They refer, consequently, to the three states or ways of spiritual exercise (purgative, illuminative, and unitive) through which a person passes

in advancing to this state, and they describe some of the characteristics and effects of these ways.

2. The initial stanzas treat of the state of beginners, that of the purgative way. The subsequent ones deal with the state of proficients, in which the spiritual betrothal is effected, that is, the illuminative way.

The stanzas following these refer to the unitive way, that of the perfect, where spiritual marriage takes place. This unitive way of the perfect follows the illuminative way of the proficients.

The final stanzas speak of the beatific state, that sole aspiration of a person who has reached perfection.

The beginning of the commentary on the love songs between the bride and Christ, the Bridegroom.

From *What the Church Fathers Say About*, ed., George Grube (Minneapolis, Mn.: Light and Life Publishing, 1996), 75-76 regarding marriage:

God created Adam and Eve that there might be great love between them, reflecting the mystery of the Divine unity. (St. Theophilus of Antioch - c. 180)

What God is going to give them is not something He has made; He is going to give them Himself, Who made all things. Toil then, to lay hold of God; yearn long for what youare going to possess forever. (St. Augustine - 430)

From Christopher A. Hall, *Reading Scripture With the Church Fathers* (Downers Grove, Il.: InterVarsity Press, 1998), 107-108 he writes of early church hermeneutics:

Ambrose's interest in discerning a mystical or allegorical meaning in the biblical text is surely the aspect of his hermeneutics that many modern interpreters will find most troubling. The lack of hermeneutical control in allegorical interpretation seems to lay the biblical text wide open for subjective whimsy. . . .

. . . Ambrose would insist it was perfectly legitimate to read Scripture through the lens of its overarching narrative. After all, Jesus himself had taught that the law and the prophets spoke of him (cf. Luke 24:25-27). . . . Ambrose, like many fathers in the Alexandrian tradition, believed that behind the literal shell of a biblical text lay enclosed a deeper meaning, a message to be discerned through the Holy Spirit and in line with the central biblical narrative centered on God's work in Christ. Why, Ambrose would ask, should we find it surprising to find Ezekiel speaking in a veiled way of Mary if he is speaking prophetically through the Spirit? . . .

. . . Ambrose trusted that the biblical narrative itself supplied a brake on interpretive fancy. Consider his exegesis of the creation accounts and birth narratives of Genesis 2 and 4. Eve is created from Adam's rib and in turn becomes the mother of Cain and Abel. Ambrose reads these texts in light of Christ's incarnation and redemptive work, and also sees them as relevant for understanding the nature of Christ's body, the church. . . .

. . . This type of christological/ecclesiological interpretation occurs frequently among the fathers, precisely because they read the entire biblical narrative in light of its fulfillment in Christ.

From Fr. Isaiah Chronopoulos, *Orthodox Monasticism, Word Magazine* September 1983,14 - 17 :

> . . . from the beginning of man on this planet to the establishment of Christianity, an evolution has taken place in the institution of marriage with Judaism and Christianity. Beginning with Adam, we read in Genesis that from his own body came the first woman. God blessed this first union which was between man and himself, so to speak. In essence, it was the union of the male and the female counterparts in the human person which had become two entities. . . . For the spiritual relationships established by the Church are of a higher nature than the physical. The highest state of monogamous marriage between a husband and wife is when the two look upon their spiritual union as being on a higher level than is the physical union.
>
> On the basis that marriage is a union between two entities, male and female, we can say that chastity establishes a union between a monk or a nun and God, the man or woman representing the Church (Bride) and Christ being the Head of the Church (Bridegroom). The successful discipline of chastity brings one to the highest form of union or marriage between God and man and that is what monasticism calls spiritual virginity. This state can be described as the equivalent state of grace and innocence which our first parents, Adam and Eve, experienced before they fell from God's grace and found themselves to be naked. Through this brief description of marriage, we can see how mankind, in conjunction with the process of procreation, can return, individually, to the original state of union with God and the preservation of that state forever. The pursuit of this state by monastics is supported by our Lord's words in speaking of the resurrection when He says that "in the resurrection they neither marry nor are given in marriage, but arelike the angels of God in heaven" (Matthew 22:30). It could very well be that monasticism is called the angelic life because of these words of our Lord.
>
> From this outline of the evolution of marriage in its physical and its spiritual sense, it is obvious that the institution of marriage is not in any way demeaned. God uses it to bring man back to his original state of grace and more. God Himself blessed the institution of marriage and our Lord Himself with the coming of the fullness of His Kingdom calls Himself the Bridegroom and the people, the Church, He calls the Bride.

5. Again, this is not meant to be a theologically precise representation of what the words "I accept Jesus as my Savior" mean, but rather artistic license on my part. If there were theological words that could constitute a marriage vow, it would be these, provided the full understanding and change of life that they imply is enacted in the life of the one who says them.

6. Christopher West, *Good News About Sex & Marriage: Answers to Your Honest Questions About Catholic Teaching* (Ann Arbor, Mi.: Servant

Publications, Charis Books, 2000), 18-28

7. Ibid., 62-63.

8. A story that I heard from Bishop Chuck Jones of Selma, Alabama.

Chapter 8: Spiritual Passages

1. St. Bernard of Clairvaux quoted in Benedict J. Groeschel, *Spiritual Passages: The Psychology of Spiritual Development* (New York, N.Y.: The Crossroad Publishing Company, 1983), xii.

2. Dr. J.I. Packer, *Knowing God* (Downers Grove, Il.: InterVarsity Press, 1973), 17-22.

3. Ibid., 23-26.

4. Ibid., 27.

5. Ibid., 33-34.

6. Ibid., 36-42.

7. Groeschel, 6-7.

8. Groeschel, 8, quoting *The Life of St. Thomas Aquinas*, ed. Kenelm Foster (London: Longmans, Green, 1959), 46.

9. Groeschel, 8.

10. Ibid., 8-9.

11. Groeschel, 10, quoting Augustine, *Confessions*, trans. F. Sheed (New York: Sheed & Ward, 1965), X, vi and xxvii.

12. Groeschel, 10.

13. Groeschel, 10-11.

14. Ibid., 18.

15. Groeschel, 67-70, including a quote from J.H. Newman, *Essays Critical and Historical* (London: Longmans, Green, 1901), 33.

16. Groeschel, 70-71.

17. Ibid., 79-81.

18. Ibid., 82-84.

19. Ibid., 84-85.

20. Ibid., 86-87, including a quote from Augustine, *Confessions*.

21. Fr. Gabriel of St. Mary Magdalen, O.C.D., *Divine Intimacy: Meditations on the Interior Life for Every Day of the Liturgical Year* (Rockford, Il.: Tan Books and Publishers, Inc., 1996), 338-341, including a quote by St. Teresa Margaret from her letters.

Part Three - Walking It Out Practically

Chapter 9: Taming the Wild Horses Within

1. *Webster's New Collegiate Dictionary* (1980), s.v. "destroy."

2. John R.W. Stott, *The Letters of John: Tyndale New Testament Commentaries* (Grand Rapids, Mi.: William B. Eerdmans Publishing Company, 1988), 129.

3. A great Christian therapy program that takes full advantage of this knowledge of the roots of satanic lies in personal strongholds is Edward M. Smith, *Genuine Recovery: Recoverer's Guide to True Inner Healing and Renewal of the Mind* (Campbellsville, Ky.: Alathia, Inc., 1997), also called *Beyond Tolerable Recovery: Theophostic Ministry*. Available as a video course. Visit their web site at www.theophostic.com.

4. P.T. Forsythe, *Justification of God*, 32, quoted in John R.W. Stott, *The Cross of Christ* (Downers Grove, Il.: InterVarsity Press, 1986), 336.

5. Philippians 3:12,14.

6. John Stott has written an interesting treatise on the battle of the two selves in John R.W. Stott, *The Cross of Christ* (Downers Grove, Il.: InterVarsity Press, 1986), 282-283:

> Our "self" is not a simple entity that is either wholly good or wholly evil, and therefore to be either totally valued or totally denied. Instead, our "self" is a complex entity of good and evil, glory and shame, which on that account requires that we develop more subtle attitudes to ourselves.

What we are (our self or personal identity) is partly the result of the creation (the image of God) and partly the result of the Fall (the image defaced). The self we are to deny, disown and crucify is our fallen self, everything within us that is incompatible with Jesus Christ (hence His commands"let him deny *himself*" and then "let him follow *Me*"). The self we are to affirm and value is our created self, everything within us that is compatible with Jesus Christ (hence His statement that if we lose ourselves by self-denial we shall find ourselves). True self-denial (the denial of our false, fallen self) is not the road to self-destruction but the road to self-discovery.

So then, whatever we are by creation we must affirm: our rationality, . . . sexuality . . . creativity [etc.] . . . True, it has been tainted and twisted by sin. Yet Christ came to redeem it, not to destroy it. . . .

Whatever we are by the Fall, however, we must deny or repudiate: our irrationality, . . . moral perversity . . . lack of sexual self-control . . . selfishness . . . proud autonomy [etc.] . . . Christ came not to redeem this but to destroy it. . . .

. . . Our new self has been created to be like God in true righteousness . . . Becoming a Christian is a transforming experience. By changing us, it also changes our self-image. We now have much more to affirm, not boastfully but gratefully.

7. Francis A. Schaeffer, *True Spirituality* (Wheaton, Il.: Tyndale House Publishers, 1971), 18.

8. Ibid., 16-17.

9. Larry Crabb, *The Safest Place on Earth: Where People Connect and are Forever Changed* (Nashville, Tn.: Word Publishing, 1999), 16-24.

10. Ibid., 26-27.

11. Ibid., 115.

12. Ibid., 130.

13. Ibid., 147-148.

14. A similar list that boils down the fundamentals necessary for transformation can be found in David Kyle Foster, *Sexual Healing: God's Plan for the Sanctification of Broken Lives* (Jacksonville, Fl.: Mastering Life Ministries, 2001), 134:

The most important factors for change—all of which increase as you seek greater intimacy and revelation of the Lord are:

a. The intensity of your desire for change.

    b. The degree of faith with which you hold on to God's promises.

    c. The depth of your love and commitment to Jesus Christ above all others.

    d. The degree of your willingness to be faithful to God's will and direction.

    e. The degree to which you can keep the perspective that it is God's working in you that brings permanent transformation.

    f. The amount of time you spend seeking God in prayer and crying out to Him for help.

15. I learned this tidbit one night when I was commanding some demons to go to the lake of fire and to the outermost darkness. As I was so engaged, the Lord spoke to my heart, saying, "David, you do not have the authority to send fallen angels or demons to those locations. Reread the Scriptures and you'll see that they will be cast to such places at an appointed time, and by My angels. When you command those entities to go to such places, because you have no authority to do so, you are sending them nowhere." I then asked the Lord where instead I should be sending them. He said, "Tell them to go where Jesus sends them." So I did, and the difference has been quite dramatic. I don't know where Jesus sends them, but wherever it is, they definitely do not want to go there!

16. Larry Crabb, *Finding God* (Grand Rapids, Mi.: Zondervan Publishing House, 1993), 96-97.

17. Ibid., 168-170.

18. Ibid., 180-181.

19. Ibid., 196.

20. Years ago John Wimber was my pastor. He was an awesome man of God with a great anointing on him. He would often say that his favorite prayer was this: "Help! O God, O God, O God - Help!"

Chapter 10: What Does It Look Like To Be Healed?

1. Two excellent books on this topic: Timothy M. Warner, *Spiritual Warfare: Victory Over the Powers of This Dark World* (Wheaton, Il.: Crossway Books, 1991), and Neil T. Anderson and Timothy M. Warner, *The Beginners Guide to Spiritual Warfare* (Servant Publications, Vine Books, 2000).

2. The "disease of introspection" is an obsessive and destructive, mental self-examination. Leanne Payne writes extensively about it in books such as *The Broken Image: Restoring Personal Wholeness Through Healing Prayer* (Grand Rapids, Mi.: Baker Books, Hamewith Books, 1981), and *The Healing*

Presence: How God's Grace Can Work in You to Bring Healing in Your Broken Places and the Joy of Living in His Love (Grand Rapids, Mi.: Baker Books, Hamewith Books, 1989).

Part Four: When God Invites You To Minister To Others

Chapter 11: Why Some Remain Trapped in Sin

1. Alister McGrath describes the differences in, *Christian Theology: An Introduction*, 2nd ed. (Oxford, U.K..: Blackwell Publishers, 1997):

> 1. *Faith is not simply historical knowledge.* Luther argues that a faith which is content to believe in the historical reliability of the gospels is not a saving faith. Sinners are perfectly capable of trusting in the historical details of the gospels; but these facts of themselves are not adequate for true Christian faith. Saving faith concerns believing and trusting that Christ was born for us personally, and has accomplished for us the work of salvation.
>
> 2. *Faith includes an element of trust (fiducia).* . . . Faith is not merely believing that something is true; it is being prepared to act upon that belief, and relying upon it. To use Luther's analogy: Faith is not simply about believing that a ship exists - it is about stepping into it, and entrusting ourselves to it. . . .
>
> 3 *Faith unites the believer to Christ.* . . . (it) then, is not assent to an abstract set of doctrines. Rather, it is a "wedding ring," pointing to mutual commitment and union between Christ and the believer. It is the response of the whole person of the believer to God, which leads in turn to the real and personal presence of Christ in the believer.(155-157)

2. cf. Job 12:6, Psalm 37; 73; Jeremiah 12; Habakkuk; et al.

3. All this is evidence that God's judgment is right, and as a result you will be counted worthy of the kingdom of God, for which you are suffering. God is just: He will pay back trouble to those who trouble you and give relief to you who are troubled, and to us as well. This will happen when the Lord Jesus is revealed from heaven in blazing fire with his powerful angels. He will punish those who do not know God and do not obey the gospel of our Lord Jesus. They will be punished with everlasting destruction and shut out from the presence of the Lord and from the majesty of His power on the day He comes to be glorified in His holy people and to be marveled at among all those who have believed. This includes you, because you believed our testimony to you.

4. For a more detailed discussion of the possible reasons, consult *Sexual Healing, 170-177.*

5. St. Augustine wrote about this problem of the duplicity of the heart, as edited by Richard J. Foster and James Bryan Smith in their *Devotional Classics: Selected Readings for Individuals and Groups* (San Francisco: HarperSanFrancisco, 1993):

Why does this happen? The mind orders itself to make an act of will, and it would not give this order unless it willed to do so; yet it does not carry out its own command. But it does not fully will to do this thing and therefore its orders are not fully given. It gives the order only in so far as it wills, and in so far as it does not will, the order is not carried out.

For the will commands that an act of will should be made, and it gives this command to itself, not to some other will. The reason, then, why the command is not obeyed is that it is not given with the full will. For if the will were full, it would not command itself to be full, since it would be so already.

It is therefore no strange phenomenon partly to will to do something and partly not to will to do it. It is a disease of the mind which does not wholly rise to the heights where it is lifted by the truth, because it is weighed down by habit. So there are two wills in us, because neither by itself is the whole will, and each possesses what the other lacks. . . .

. . . The same is true when the higher part of our nature aspires after eternal bliss while our lower self is held back by the love of temporal pleasure. It is the same soul that wills both, but it wills neither of them with the full force of the will. So it is wrenched in two and suffers great trials because while truth teaches it to prefer one course, habit prevents it from relinquishing the other. . . .

. . . My lower instincts, which had taken hold of me, were stronger than the higher, which were untried. . . .

. . . Habit was too strong for me when it asked, "Do you think you can live without these things?". . .

. . . I read . . . "arm yourselves with the Lord Jesus Christ; spend no more thought on nature and nature's appetites" (Romans 13:13, 14, editor's trans.). . . .

. . . You converted me to yourself, so that I no longer placed any hope in this world but stood firmly upon the rule of faith. (53-55)

6. This is an expanded version of the chapter of the same name from David Kyle Foster, *Sexual Healing: God's Plan for the Sanctification of Broken Lives* (Jacksonville, Fl.: Mastering Life Ministries, 2001), 265-283.

Chapter 12: Victim Nation

1. A great summary of the problems associated with philosophical presuppositions and faith, past and present, is Alister McGrath, Chapters 4 & 5 in *A Passion for Truth: The Intellectual Coherence of Evangelicalism* (Downers Grove, Il.: InterVarsity Press, 1996).

2. Randolph Adler, "On Therapeutic Language," *Sursum Corda* 5, no. 5 (1998): 12.

3. Alister McIntyre, *After Virtue* (Notre Dame, In.: Notre Dame Press).

4. Adler, *Therapeutic Language*, 12.

5. A good, albeit somewhat biased, treatment on the integration of psychiatry and Christianity is found in Dan Blazer, *Freud vs. God: How Psychiatry Lost Its Soul & Christianity Lost Its Mind* (Downers Grove, Il.: InterVarsity Press, 1998) and a good, albeit somewhat biased, treatment on the integration of psychology and Christianity is found in Mark R. McMinn, *Psychology, Theology, and Spirituality in Christian Counseling* (Wheaton, Il.: Tyndale House Publishers, Inc., 1996).

6. John Leland and Claudia Kalb, "Herr Doktor, What Does It All Mean?," *Newsweek*, 12 October 1998, 60-61.

7. "When the Eysenck study was released at the University of London, there was a furor. Eysenck's study simply showed that among neurotics divided 50/50, those that underwent psychoanalysis had no better recovery rate than those who just lived life and saved the massive therapy fees. The recovery was the same, plus or minus a .02 percent statistical error factor. In other words, psychoanalysis did nothing. Eysenck drove home the fact that psychoanalysis was anything but scientifically proven. All it could do was hide behind its terminology and verify itself by its own closed definitions of reality" Tal Brooke, *When the World Will Be as One* (Eugene, Or.: Harvest House Publishers, 1989), 82.

8. A good argument for integrating the perspectives of psychology and ministry is advanced by Mark R. McMinn in his *Psychology, Theology, and Spirituality in Christian Counseling* (Wheaton, Il.: Tyndale House Publishers, Inc., 1996):

> When we view people as sick, we assume that they had little or no control over their current state: . . . This is called an *external* attribution. A frequent response to external attributions is to feel sympathy for the victim.
>
> A number of psychologists have provided evidence that our attributional style affects mental health. Depressed people, for example, are more likely than others to attribute bad events to their own internal flaws and good events to external causes, such as luck or random choice. Those who resist depression most effectively see bad events as resulting from external or unstable factors, such as a lack of effort or bad luck, and good events as resulting from internal, stable qualities such as good ability and dedicated effort.
>
> Thus, based on attributional theory, it is reasonable to assume that those who attribute bad events to personal sin are more likely to be depressed and angry than those who see themselves as sick or as victims of unfortunate circumstances. Not surprisingly then, the prevailing model of mental health found in psychology is to view people as sick, an external attribution, rather than as

sinners, an internal attribution. In order to break through dysfunctional cycles of shame and overwhelming feelings of guilt, counselors often help their clients externalize their attributions for failures in life. . . . Producing guilt and shame appears to drive people further into a state of addiction. . . .

In our Christian domain, we believe that sin is a willful rebellion against God and that it often carries painful consequences for oneself or others. . . . In our counseling domain, we are sometimes told that emotional problems result from things beyond a person's control: addictions, diseases, bad parenting, unfortunate circumstances, chemical imbalances. One system tells us that people are sinners; the other tells us that people are sick. . . . To reconcile these two seemingly distinct perspectives, we need to consider the contributions of Christian theology and spirituality.

. . . In the world of Christian theology, . . . sin and sickness are inextricably connected, . . . sin and sickness are intertwined and inseparable. Sin can be a matter of act or thought, as is generally assumed, but sin is also an inner disposition, a part of our character that resembles a chronic sickness. . . . In Scripture and theology sin is a conditionthat goes to the root of our being for it has to do with our relationship to our origin and to God. Christian theology includes both a personal and an original concept of sin. Too often counselors who are not Christians understand only the personal concept of sin and thereby misrepresent Christianity.

. . . Some Christians assume . . . that sin is only personal and that Christian piety is best defined by controlling specific behaviors. This is known as the heresy of Pelagianism: sin is just a set of bad habits that we need to eliminate. When we view sin as limited to personal behaviors or thoughts, we fall prey to a sin-management mentality and become vulnerable to legalism and asceticism and to excessive guilt reactions. . . .

Sin is more than a set of personal behaviors, and managing sin requires more than keeping a checklist of dos and don'ts. Sin is an original part of our character, a pervasive element of the human condition. Sin is our sickness. . . .

Christians who understand sin properly view themselves as part of a universal community of sinners. If sin is a sickness, something that affects all people and interferes constantly with our capacity to make good choices, then our attributions no longer need tobe internal and shame producing. We are all pilgrims together, struggling with common temptations and burdens. Those who understand sin most accurately are able to make both internal (personal) and external (universal) attributions for the causes of their problems. . . .

. . . Those who understand both the personal and original nature of sin are able to adjust to the nagging ache of fallen existence without succumbing to the excessive self-condemnation and guilt that psychologists have often associated with religion. The best response to sin is not to sink further into self-absorption and self-abasement but to recognize our need and look for healing in relationship with God.

Entering deeply into the spiritual life requires us to abandon sin-management and to seek inner transformation through the work of the Holy Spirit. . . .

. . . There are no rugged individualists living a victorious Christian life, only those who lean on God. (130-137)

9. This appeared in abridged form as David Kyle Foster, "Whatever Happened to Sin?" *Charisma & Christian Life*, April 1999, 100-107.

Chapter 13: The Making of a Minister

1. George Barna, *The Second Coming of the Church* (Nashville, Tn.: Word Publishing, 1998), 108-110.

2. David Mains, "Three Goals in Leading," (lecture given in the "Spiritual Leadership" class for the D-Min program at Trinity Episcopal School for Ministry, Ambridge, Pa., 23 June 1999).

3. Dr. Sudduth Cummings, "Elements of Spiritual Leadership," (lecture given in the "Spiritual Leadership" class for the D-Min program at Trinity Episcopal School for Ministry, Ambridge, Pa., 25 June 1999).

4. Fr. Gabriel of St. Mary Magdalen, O.C.D., *Divine Intimacy: Meditations on the Interior Life for Every Day of the Liturgical Year* (Rockford, Il.: Tan Books and Publishers, Inc., 1996), 312-328.

5. I recommend a set of books written by Tommy Tenney for those who need to reestablish themselves in the pursuit of God. He has written *The God Chasers: My Soul Follows Hard After Thee* (Shippensburg, Pa.: Destiny Image Publishers, 1998). Also available from Tommy Tenney is *The God Catchers: Experiencing the Manifest Presence of God, The Heart of a God Chaser* and *God's Favorite House.*

6. The findings from a study conducted by two secular psychologists is commented on by Dr. Larry Crabb in his *The Safest Place on Earth: Where People Connect and are Forever Changed* (Nashville, Tn.: Word Publishing, 1999), 48-49, quoting C.H. Patterson and Suzanne Hidore, *Successful Psychotherapy: A Caring, Loving Relationship* (Northvale, NJ: Jason Aranson, 1997), see chapter 1.

7. A fairly sharp contrast in opinion can be found by comparing Charles H. Kraft, *Deep Wounds, Deep Healing: Discovering the Vital Link Between Spiritual Warfare and Inner Healing* (Ann Arbor, Mi.: Servant Publications, Vine Books, 1993) who believes that talking to demons prior to casting them out can be a legitimate way to obtain information that will be helpful to the client, and John and Mark Sandford, *A Comprehensive Guide to Deliverance and Inner Healing* (Grand Rapids, Mi.: Baker Books, Chosen Books, 1992)

who believe that one should never talk to a demon, since they are liars and it is unnecessary anyway.

8. An excellent ministry in this regard is Craig Hill's "Family Foundations International" in Littleton, Co. He has a "From Curse to Blessing" and other video and live seminars that can aid in bringing significant breakthroughs and blessings to any congregation or ministry. They can be contacted through their web site at www.familyfi.org.

9. Generally, people who are living an addictive, obsessive or reckless life, are people who are angry at God. They may not have a conscious awareness of this cause, but it is the fuel that drives their rebellious life. If they can be made to see that God is not guilty of the charges that their heart has made against Him, their sinful lifestyle becomes unnecessary and even undesirable to them. Their lifestyle has, at its deepest roots, been an expression of their anger at God. It is the result of a faulty view of God. In the face of childhood traumas or neglect, they have drawn conclusions about God that are erroneous. Once that is corrected, (and it is corrected most effectively by the person getting into the presence of God and experiencing Him directly), then their inner rationalizations for sin vanish and they become amenable to His ways.

10. This is prevalent among people who struggle with sexual addiction and those who struggle with homosexual neurosis.

Epilogue

1. Leanne Payne, *Restoring the Christian Soul Through Healing Prayer: Overcoming the Three Great Barriers to Personal and Spiritual Completion in Christ* (Grand Rapids, Mi.: Baker Books, Hamewith Books, 1991), 68, 115.

2. Leanne Payne, *The Healing Presence: How God's Grace Can Work in You to Bring Healing in Your Broken Places and the Joy of Living in His Love* (Grand Rapids, Mi.: Baker Books, Hamewith Books, 1989), 53, 55, 62, 160.

3. Jean-Nicholas Grou, "How to Pray," *Devotional Classics: Selected Readings for Individuals and Groups*, ed. Richard J. Foster and James Bryan Smith (San Francisco: HarperSanFrancisco, 1993), 140.

Selected Bibliography

Books on Restoring Personal Wholeness

Anderson, Neil T. *The Bondage Breaker: Overcoming Negative Thoughts, Irrational Feelings, Habitual Sins*. Eugene, Or.: Harvest House Publishers, 1990.

Anderson, Neil T. *Breaking Through to Spiritual Maturity*. Ventura, Ca.: Gospel Light, 1992.

Anderson, Neil T. *Victory Over the Darkness: Realizing the Power of Your Identity in Christ*. Ventura, Ca.: Gospel Light, Regal Books, 1990.

Crabb, Dr. Larry. *Connecting: A Radical New Vision*. Nashville, Tn.: Word Publishing, 1997.

Crabb, Dr. Larry. *Inside Out*. Colorado Springs, Co.: NavPress, 1988.

Crabb, Dr. Larry. *The Safest Place on Earth: Where People Connect and are Forever Changed*. Nashville, Tn.: Word Publishing, 1999.

Dalby, Gordon. *Healing the Masculine Soul*. Nashville, Tn.: Word Publishing, 1988.

Friesen, James G., E. James Wilder, Anne M. Bierling, Rick Koepcke, and Maribeth Poole. *Living From the Heart Jesus Gave You: The Essentials of Christian Living*. Van Nuys, Ca.: Shepherd's House, Inc., 2000.

Kraft, Charles H. *Deep Wounds, Deep Healing: Discovering the Vital Link Between Spiritual Warfare and Inner Healing*. Ann Arbor, Mi.: Servant Publications, Vine Books, 1993.

Nouwen, Henri J.M. *The Wounded Healer*. New York, N.Y.: Doubleday, Image Books, 1972.

Payne, Leanne. *The Healing Presence: How God's Grace Can Work in You to Bring Healing in Your Broken Places and the Joy of Living in His Love*. Grand Rapids, Mi.: Baker Books, Hamewith Books, 1989.

Payne, Leanne. *Real Presence: The Glory of Christ With Us and Within Us*. Grand Rapids, Mi.: Baker Books, Hamewith Books, 1995.

Payne, Leanne. *Restoring the Christian Soul Through Healing Prayer: Overcoming the Three Great Barriers to Personal and Spiritual Completion in Christ*. Grand Rapids, Mi.: Baker Books, Hamewith Books, 1991.

Pearson, Mark A. *Christian Healing: A Practical and Comprehensive Guide*, 2nd ed. Grand Rapids, Mi.: Baker Books, Chosen Books, 1995.

Sandford, John, and Mark Sandford. *A Comprehensive Guide to Deliverance and Inner Healing*. Grand Rapids, Mi.: Baker Books, Fleming H. Revell, Chosen Books, 1992.

Seamands, David A. *Healing for Damaged Emotions*. Wheaton, Il.: SP Publications, Inc., Victor Books, 1981.

Seamands, David A. *Healing Your Heart of Painful Emotions*. New York, N.Y.: Budget Book Service, Inc., Inspirational Press, 1993.

A compilation of four of Seamands' books.

Smith, Edward M. *Genuine Recovery: Recoverer's Guide to True Inner Healing and Renewal of the Mind*. Campbellsville, Ky.: Alathia, Inc., 1997.

Thurman, Dr. Chris. *The Lies We Believe Workbook: Your 12-Week Interactive Plan for Finding Emotional and Spiritual Freedom*. Nashville, Tn.: Thomas Nelson Publishers, 1995.

Warner, Timothy M. *Spiritual Warfare: Victory Over the Powers of This Dark World*. Wheaton, Il.: Good News Publishers, Crossway Books, 1991.

Wilson, Dr. Sandra D. *Released From Shame: Recovery for Adult Children of Dysfunctional Families*. Downers Grove, Il.: InterVarsity Press, 1990.

Wright, H. Norman. *Making Peace With Your Past*. Grand Rapids, Mi.: Baker Books, Fleming H. Revell, 1985.

Books on Spiritual Formation

Allender, Dr. Dan B., and Dr. Tremper Longman III. *The Cry of the Soul: How Our Emotions Reveal Our Deepest Questions About God.* Colorado Springs, Co.: NavPress, 1994.

Allender, Dr. Dan B. *The Healing Path: How the Hurts in Your Past Can Lead You to a More Abundant Life.* Colorado Springs, Co.: Random House, Inc., Waterbrook Press, 1999.

Backus, William, and Marie Chapian. *Telling Yourself the Truth.* Minneapolis, Mn.: Bethany House Publishers, 1980.

Bickle, Mike. *Passion for Jesus: Perfecting Extravagant Love for God.* Lake Mary, Fl.: Creation House, 1993.

Blackaby, Henry T., and Claude V. King. *Experiencing God.* Nashville, Tn.: Broadman & Holman Publishers, 1994.

Collins, Dr. Gary. *The Soul Search: A Spiritual Journey to Authentic Intimacy With God.* Nashville, Tn.: Thomas Nelson Publishers, 1998.

Crabb, Dr. Larry. *Finding God.* Grand Rapids, Mi.: Zondervan Publishing House, 1993.

Crabb, Dr. Larry. *The Safest Place on Earth: Where People Connect and are Forever Changed.* Nashville, Tn.: Word Publishing, 1999.

de Sales, Francis. *Introduction to the Devout Life.* New York, N.Y.: Doubleday, Image Books, 1966.

Fenelon, Francois. *Talking With God.* Brewster, Ma.: Paraclete Press, 1997.

Foster, Richard, and James Bryan Smith, ed. *Devotional Classics: Selected Readings for Individuals & Groups.* San Francisco, Ca.: HarperCollins Publishers, HarperSanFrancisco, 1993.

Frangipane, Francis. *The Three Battlegrounds.* Marion, Ia.: Advancing Church Publications, 1989.

Gabriel of St. Mary Magdalen, O.C.D., Fr. *Divine Intimacy: Meditations on the Interior Life for Every Day of the Liturgical Year.* Rockford, Il.: Tan Books and Publishers, Inc., 1996.

Gangel, Kenneth O. and James C. Wilhoit, ed. *The Christian Educator's Handbook on Spiritual Formation*. Grand Rapids, Mi.: Baker Books, 1994.

Groeschel, Benedict J., with Kevin Perrotta. *The Journey Toward God: In the Footsteps of the Great Spiritual Writers*. Ann Arbor, Mi.: Servant Publications, Charis Books, 2000.

Groeschel, Benedict J. *Spiritual Passages: The Psychology of Spiritual Development*. New York, N.Y.: The Crossroad Publishing Company, 1983.

Guyon, Madame Jeanne. *Experiencing the Depths of Jesus Christ*. Auburn, Me.: Christian Books Publishing House, 1975.

Guyon, Madame Jeanne. *Final Steps in Christian Maturity*. Auburn, Me.: Christian Books Publishing House, 1985.

Hall, Dudley. *Grace Works: Letting God Rescue You From Empty Religion*. Ann Arbor, Mi.: Servant Publications, Vine Books, 1992.

Huggett, Joyce. *The Joy of Listening to God: Hearing the Many Ways God Speaks to Us*. Downers Grove, Il.: InterVarsity Press, 1986.

Joyner, Rick. *There Were Two Trees in the Garden*. Charlotte, NC: MorningStar Publications, 1992.

Lawrence, Brother, and Frank Laubach. *Practicing His Presence*. Sargent, Ga.: The Seed Sowers, 1973.

Lord, Peter. *Hearing God*. Grand Rapids, Mi.: Baker Books, 1988.

Marshall, Tom. *Living in the Freedom of the Spirit*. Tonbridge, Kent, England: Sovereign World Ltd, 2001.

Miller, J. Keith. *The Secret Life of the Soul*. Nashville, Tn.: Broadman & Holman Publishers, 1997.

Packer, Dr. J.I. *Knowing God*. Downers Grove, Il.: InterVarsity Press, 1973.

Payne, Leanne. *Listening Prayer: Learning to Hear God's Voice and Keep a Prayer Journal*. Grand Rapids, Mi.: Baker Books, Hamewith Books, 1994.

Powell, S.J., John. *He Touched Me: My Pilgrimage of Prayer*. Allen, Tx.: DLM, Inc., Argus Communications, 1974.

Powell, S.J., John. *Why Am I Afraid to Love?* Allen, Tx.: DLM, Inc., Tabor Publishing, 1982.

St. John of the Cross. *Dark Night of the Soul.* Translated and edited by E. Allison Peers. New York: Doubleday, Image Books, 1990.

Tenney, Tommy. *The God Chasers: My Soul Follows Hard After Thee.* Shippensburg, Pa.: Destiny Image Publishers, Inc., 1998.

Tozer, A.W. *The Knowledge of the Holy.* San Francisco, Ca.: Harper & Row Publishers, 1961.

Tozer, A.W. *The Warfare of the Spirit: Developing Spiritual Maturity.* Camp Hill, Pa.: Christian Publications, 1993.

West, Christopher. *Good News About Sex & Marriage: Answers to Your Honest Questions About Catholic Teaching.* Ann Arbor, Mi.: Servant Publications, Charis Books, 2000.

Willard, Dallas. *The Spirit of the Disciplines: Understanding How God Changes Lives.* San Francisco, Ca.: HarperCollins Publishers, Harper SanFrancisco, 1988.

Wilson, Dr. Sandra D. *Into Abba's Arms: Finding the Acceptance You've Always Wanted.* Wheaton, Il.: Tyndale House Publishers, Inc., 1998.

Books on the Healing of Sexuality

Allender, Dr. Dan B. *The Wounded Heart: Hope for Adult Victims of Childhood Sexual Abuse.* Colorado Springs, Co.: NavPress, 1990.

Bergner, Mario. *Setting Love in Order: Hope and Healing for the Homosexual.* Grand Rapids, Mi.: Baker Books, Hamewith Books, 1995.

Comiskey, Andrew. *Pursuing Sexual Wholeness: How Jesus Heals the Homosexual.* Lake Mary, Fl.: Creation House, 1989.

Courtright, John, and Dr. Sid Rogers. *Your Wife was Sexually Abused.* Grand Rapids, Mi.: Zondervan Publishing House, 1994.

Crossland, Don. *A Journey Toward Wholeness: Discover the Healing Power of Christ's Authority Over Sin and Guilt.* N. Little Rock, Ar.: Journey Press, 1991.

Crossland, Don. *Refocusing Your Passions: A Christ-Centered Approach to Overcoming Addictive Behavior*. N. Little Rock, Ar.: Journey Press, 1994.

Crossland, Helen, with Judy Doyle. *From Pieces to Peace*. N. Little Rock, Ar.: Journey Press, 1998.

Foster, David Kyle. *Sexual Healing: God's Plan for the Sanctification of Broken Lives*. Jacksonville, Fl.: Mastering Life Ministries, 2001.

Frank, Don, and Jan Frank. *When Victims Marry: Building a Stronger Marriage by Breaking Destructive Cycles*. Nashville, Tn.: Thomas Nelson Publishers, 1990.

Hall, Laurie. *An Affair of the Mind: One Woman's Courageous Battle to Salvage Her Family from the Devastation of Pornography*. Wheaton, Il.: Tyndale House Publishers, 1996.

Heitritter, Lynn, and Jeanette Vought. *Helping Victims of Sexual Abuse: A Sensitive, Biblical Guide for Counselors, Victims and Families*. Minneapolis, Mn.: Bethany House Publishers, 1989.

MacNutt, Dr. Francis. *Homosexuality: Can It Be Healed?*. Jacksonville, Fl.: Christian Healing Ministries, 2001.

Payne, Leanne. *The Broken Image: Restoring Personal Wholeness Through Healing Prayer*. Grand Rapids, Mi.: Baker Books, Hamewith Books, 1981.

Payne, Leanne. *Crisis in Masculinity*. Grand Rapids, Mi.: Baker Books, Hamewith Books, 1985.

Satinover, Jeffrey. *Homosexuality and the Politics of Truth*. Grand Rapids, Mi.: Baker Books, Hamewith Books, 1996.

Schaumburg, Dr. Harry W. *False Intimacy: Understanding the Struggle of Sexual Addiction*. Colorado Springs, Co.: NavPress, 1997.

Willingham, Russell. *Breaking Free: Understanding Sexual Addiction & the Healing Power of Jesus*. Downers Grove, Il.: InterVarsity Press, 1999.

Worthen, Anita, and Bob Davies. *Someone I Love is Gay: How Family & Friends Can Respond*. Downers Grove, Il.: InterVarsity Press, 1996.

Books on Theology & Ecclesiology

Barna, George. *The Second Coming of the Church*. Nashville, Tn.: Word Publishing, 1998.

Blazer, Dan. *Freud vs. God: How Psychiatry Lost Its Soul & Christianity Lost Its Mind*. Downers Grove, Il.: InterVarsity Press, 1998.

Hahn, Scott. *A Father Who Keeps His Promises*. Ann Arbor, Mi.: Servant Publications, 1998.

Joyner, Rick. *There Were Two Trees in the Garden*. Charlotte, N.C.: MorningStar Publications, 1992.

McGrath, Alister E. *A Passion for Truth: The Intellectual Coherence of Evangelicalism*. Downers Grove, Il.: InterVarsity Press, 1996.

McGrath, Alister E. *Christian Theology: An Introduction*, 2nd ed. Oxford, U.K.: Blackwell Publishers, 1997.

McMinn, Mark R. *Psychology, Theology, and Spirituality in Christian Counseling*. Wheaton, Il.: Tyndale House Publishers, Inc., 1996.

Ratzinger, Joseph Cardinal. "Letter to the Bishops of the Catholic Church on the Pastoral Care of Homosexual Persons." The Vatican: Congregation for the Doctrine of the Faith, 1986. Photocopied.

Ratzinger, Joseph Cardinal , ed. *Catechism of the Catholic Church*, 2nd ed. The Vatican: Libreria Editrice Vaticana, 1997.

Schaeffer, Francis A. *True Spirituality*. Wheaton, Il.: Tyndale House Publishers, 1971.

Stott, John R.W. *The Cross of Christ*. Downers Grove, Il.: InterVarsity Press, 1986.

David Kyle Foster

is also the author of:

*Sexual Healing: God's Plan for the
Sanctification of Broken Lives*

To obtain this book and
various other books, tapes and videos produced by
this ministry, visit our resource shop on the web at:

www.MasteringLife.org

or contact us at:

MASTERING LIFE MINISTRIES
P.O. Box 351149
Jacksonville, Fl. 32235

To contact Dr. Foster's office to arrange
for him to speak at your church or
conference, call 904-220-7474.

Transformed into His Image

Hidden Steps on the Journey to Christlikeness

For Those Who Want to Press on Toward the
Mark of the High Calling in Christ Jesus

Other Effective Tools Available by Mastering Life Ministries

- *Resource Catalog*
  Filled with books, tapes, videos and other items

- *Sexual Healing Video Course* (15 tapes)
  17 hours of teaching based on David's book, *Sexual Healing*

- *Cassette Teaching Tapes*
  From David's seminars, lectures, and radio program

- *Internet Web Site*
  http://www.MasteringLife.org

- *Seminars*
  To equip the saints for ministry to those who are bound and broken in their emotions, their sexuality, and other aspects of their Christian walk

MASTERING LIFE MINISTRIES is a Christian organization whose mission is to equip the saints for the ministry of the church through seminars, lectures, courses, radio, television and other forms of media.

We specialize in areas of modern life where people have been trapped by life-dominating issues that tap into the emotional fabric of life—issues such as sexual sin and brokenness, anger management, performance-orientation and intimacy with God.

We attempt to show that through intimacy with God the Father, the traumas of life, the allures of the world, and the deviances of the heart can all be overcome in the light of the glorious truth about our God and His Son, Jesus Christ.